S0-ANW-661

THE
BIBLE
IN THE
PARK

Series on Law, Politics, and Society
Christopher P. Banks, Editor

THE
BiblE
IN THE
ParK

Religious Expression, Public Forums,
and Federal District Courts

JOHN C. BLAKEMAN

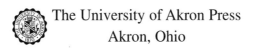

The University of Akron Press
Akron, Ohio

Manufactured in the United States of America
First edition 2005

09 08 07 06 05 5 4 3 2 1

Library of Congress Cataloging-in-Publication Data

Blakeman, John C., 1966–
    The Bible in the park : religious expression, public forums, and federal district
courts / John C. Blakeman.— 1st ed.
        p. cm. — (Series on law, politics, and society)
    Includes bibliographical references.
    ISBN 1-931968-13-6 (cloth : alk. paper)
    1. Freedom of speech—United States. 2. Freedom of religion—United States.
3. Public spaces—Law and legislation—United States. I. Title. II. Series.

    KF4772.B58 2004
    342.7308'52—dc22   2004021385

The paper used in this publication meets the minimum requirements of American
National Standard for Information Sciences—Permanence of Paper for Printed Library
Materials, ANSI Z39.48—1984. ∞

CONTENTS

LIST OF FIGURES

LIST OF TABLES

Preface

The past two decades have seen a significant amount of excellent scholarship on the links between religion and politics. Studies of religion and politics span diverse social science approaches and methods, and indeed are often interdisciplinary in nature, with roots not only in political science, but also economics, sociology, and the law. We now have clearer pictures of the relationships between, for instance, religious belief (and the intensity of that belief) and voting behavior, religiously based interest groups and public policy, and indeed the relationship between religious doctrine and litigation concerning religious liberty under the First Amendment. That religious values and beliefs affect local, state, and national politics is not exactly unique to our political system, but outside observers of American politics are often struck at how a progressive, advanced, liberal democracy such as ours can still allow religious conviction to influence our basic public policy debates and choices. To be sure, scholars of religion and politics have rigorously shown how and why religion affects our polity, and many have recently argued that the divide between religion and politics, between the sacred and the public, is diminishing.

This book adds to the literature on law, religion, and politics in the United States by focusing on federal district courts, which are oft-overlooked political institutions that truly play an important role in mediating conflicts between religion and politics. District courts are the trial courts in the national judicial system, and as such are "front-line" policymaking institutions charged with adjudicating a wide range of legal disputes, especially those concerning federal and constitutional law. As courts of first resort, district courts weigh evidence, apply the law, and render decisions that most likely will not be appealed through the appellate hierarchy. That process of weighing evidence and applying the law is, for social scientists, a policymaking process in which the outcome—the court's decision—is influenced by many different things.

Here, the links between courts, religion, and politics are explored in the context of one specific type of litigation: public forum disputes that concern religious speech. Public forums are publicly owned spaces that are often open to expressive activity and to which access is regulated by local, state, and federal governments. Public forum law is grounded in the First Amendment's Free Speech and Assembly Clauses, and was created by the Supreme Court to reflect that public properties serve as gathering places for speech-related activities. Public forum law is complex and changing, and importantly covers a wide variety of public spaces, from local public schools to government buildings and parks. Judges are often charged with applying public forum law to a myriad of places in order to determine if those properties are open to individuals or groups that wish to express a message.

Since the early 1970s litigants have linked public forum law to the expression of religious messages, and have turned to federal district courts to resolve tricky disputes over when and under what circumstances the government can limit access to a public space to someone wishing to proclaim a religious message to the public. Public forums are not only open to speech and expression; they are often places where the public tends to congregate. What better place, then, for a speaker wishing to get his or her religious message to as many people as possible?

This study of federal district courts and religious speech was prompted by a larger study of district courts and religious liberty that I am coauthoring and which is still very much under way. While collecting data on all religious liberty cases in federal district courts for the past forty years, I noticed a trend of cases, beginning in the early 1970s and not abating yet, that concerns religiously motivated speech in public places. More specifically, the trend of cases concerns plaintiffs who wish to publicly express their religious message, and government refusals to allow it. In a sense, then, this book on district courts and religious speech started as, and is intended to be part of, a larger project concerning district courts and religious liberty broadly construed.

With this book on district courts and religious speech, I am interested in basic case outcomes, and my research is driven in part by the following questions. When, for example, do courts allow religious speech into public forums? Do courts prefer some types of religious expression, such as the distribution of religious literature, to others? Do courts prefer some types of religious messages, such as proselytical, evangelical Christian speech, to others? Do interest groups or the types of litigants appearing in lawsuits influence district court policymaking? I am also interested in what social scientists term litigant symmetries. For example, who sues? Who defends? Which levels of government are most implicated in public forum and religious speech disputes? Do most litigants represent one specific religious faith, or do a diversity of faiths and religious traditions seek access to public forums?

In resolving religious speech disputes, I argue that district courts engage in a dual policymaking role. First, under public forum doctrine courts must determine if the actual, geographical location of the public place in question is open to expressive activity or not. Courts apply a sliding scale of public forum categories in order to determine how the forum has been regulated in the past, and whether and under what conditions the government may control access to the forum in the present. Second, courts must focus specifically on the issue of religious speech in public places. Religious speech is protected under the Free Speech Clause—or as the Supreme Court tells us, religious speech should be as protected under the First Amendment as other types of private expression—but do district courts always place religious speech in a preferred position, as a type of speech that should almost always garner First Amendment protection?

The dual policymaking role means that district courts determine the contours of public forums, as well as their content. That is, by ruling whether a publicly owned space is open to expression and under what circumstances, district courts define the outlines of geographic locations available for free speech and expression. Coupled with the decision on whether the forum is open, courts also determine its appropriate content. By resolving whether religious speech is allowed in, or granted access to, a specific space, courts in effect define those messages that are allowable in a public area, and those that can be excluded.

Adjudicating religious speech and public forum disputes helps district courts frame a larger debate in the American polity that concerns the extent to which religious expression is welcome in the public square. Since the mid-1980s, some scholars have argued that our public square is "naked," and devoid of any religious content. The "public square" is more of a metaphor than a precise location, and is used to represent that our discourse on public issues is increasingly secular and no longer infused with normative claims grounded in religious faith and tradition. To be sure, it is hard to empirically verify the secularization of political debate, just as it is difficult to measure the relative absence of religious claims from the public square. Yet, giving the public square debate an institutional grounding—here, in federal district courts—can further clarify the extent to which public discourse is hostile to religious expression. Chapter 1 discusses recent scholarship that gives the naked public square debate an institutional context, and I rely on that scholarship in part for my analysis of district courts. Courts and litigation serve to give the metaphorical public square an empirical foundation, albeit in a limited manner. Yet, placing the public square debate within discrete institutions, such as courts, allows small but relevant pieces of the puzzle to emerge that help construct a larger understanding of the whole.

THE SCOPE OF THE STUDY

Analysis of federal district court litigation and policymaking is based on a dataset of all federal court cases in which religious speech concerns were linked with public forum jurisprudence. Thus, all cases in which a litigant sought to place, or exclude, a religious message from a public area are studied. The final case population has 175 cases for analysis and covers the time frame from January 1974 to May 2001.[1] The dataset thus offers an exhaustive look at how this type of religious speech litigation develops, patterns of litigation that occur overtime, and how the cases are resolved by district courts. In general, most of the district court cases concern a plaintiff's attempt to place his or her specific religious speech in a public place. There are a small number of cases (n=17, or 9 percent of the case population) included for analysis in which a plaintiff seeks to enjoin, or prohibit, religious speech and expression in a public forum. Although these cases concern a slightly different type of dynamic, in substance they concern the same issue—religious speech in public forums—as the majority of the cases.

Importantly, the public forum/religious speech cases involve a twofold method of adjudication. As one district judge puts it, "forum classification and denial of access are distinct issues," meaning that judges must first classify the contested space under public forum jurisprudence, and then determine whether regulations on religiously motivated speech are constitutionally acceptable.[2] For each case, then, the trial court's decision was further split into two categories to allow analysis on two different issues. First, each decision is analyzed according to whether it is a "pro-forum" decision, defined according to whether the trial judge determined that a public forum existed or not. Second, each decision is analyzed according to its support for religious speech; thus, if the decision ruled in favor of a litigant's demand that religious speech should be protected, the case is considered "pro-religious message." Splitting the case outcome into two discrete parts reflects the dual nature of public forum and religious speech cases, and allows for a more detailed look at the types of issues and outcomes in the district courts.

Another mode of analysis concerns the litigants themselves, the plaintiffs and defendants, who frame the dispute before the trial judge. It is the litigants, through the adversarial process, who are primarily responsible to initiating and arguing legal disputes at the trial level. Thus, important questions of inquiry focus on "conflict over the ways in which citizens [as litigants] use the courts, the expectations that are developed, and the demands and ways in which courts respond to these demands."[3] Defining the parameters of litigation in district courts by focusing on who sues whom, and why—questions of institutional participation—along with trial court outcomes, facilitates the study of how legal doctrine develops. Since federal district courts are, in a sense, hostage to the types of litigants and disputes that come to them, it makes sense to understand how they work by focusing on how disputes are framed, and by whom. As Joel Grossman, Herbert Kritzer, and others point out, "because courts depend so heavily on the actions of others to shape their dockets, an understanding of the shaping of the docket is especially important to any full understanding of the role of courts."[4] Thus, a good starting point to understanding the role of courts—whether system wide, or within a specific doctrinal area, as here—is to study the "mores, values, and modes of participation" at the trial level.[5]

Studying the motivations of litigants is important in the context of cases involving religiously motivated conduct and expression. Richard Morgan noted three decades ago that "the reasons why groups struggle—the tensions which animate 'issues'—must not be lost sight of in the haste to discuss the tactics of group action."[6] Morgan's point is simply that the underlying value structure and belief system of a religious group is one variable, among many, that helps explain the motivations and goals of those groups, especially in the context of interest group politics.[7] Doctrinal religious belief is a variable with significant explanatory value in nonlegal contexts, and as scholars of the judicial process point out, the same approach applies to litigation as well.[8] Gregg Ivers, for instance, demonstrates the diverse litigation tactics and arguments that specific faith-based groups, such as the Baptist Joint Committee, or the American Jewish Congress, raise at the Supreme Court, and how those religious dynamics have helped reshape religious liberty jurisprudence.[9] Frank Way and Barbara Burt similarly demonstrate the importance of religious doctrine as one variable affecting judicial outcomes in their study of how marginal religious groups use courts and litigation to help establish their legitimacy in mainstream society.[10] Significantly, too, the whole point of cases concerning religious expression and the public forum is for litigants to seek constitutional protections for *religiously motivated speech*. Litigants in this study are typed according to the specific religious motivation underlying their expression, and are also typed according to the specific expression at issue, for instance whether it is preaching (pure speech), leafleting/tracting, soliciting, holding a worship service, or the like.

The following chapters explore the role of federal district courts in defining mini public squares and the content of those squares in the context of litigation concerning religious motivated expression. Chapter 1 provides a brief introduction to the ongoing debate on religious expression in public spaces—the so-called Naked Public Square argument inaugurated by Richard Neuhaus in the 1980s. I discuss the theoretical arguments over religious speech in public in order to situate courts and the First Amendment within a broader context.

Chapter 2 focuses on Supreme Court doctrine concerning religious speech and the public forum, and argues that the Court's policymaking is notably inconsistent. The justices often disagree over public forum doctrine under the First Amendment, and this disagreement is assessed in chapter 2 in terms of the policymaking impact it has on lower district courts. Not only is the Court's jurisprudence on *defining* the public forum inconsistent, but also its policies on the *content* of forums are likewise confusing. When the Court attends to the *content* of public forums, in order to determine when and under what circumstances religious speech can be regulated, it again is often unable to define clear-cut policies that can be applied by lower courts. Governments are often wary of allowing religious speech into public places due to the potential problems associated with government endorsement of religious messages and conduct. Thus, when faced with content-related questions, courts are often confronted with the argument that the Establishment Clause prohibits religious speech in certain public spaces, and in a sense controls the content of that space. The Supreme Court's treatment of the Establishment Clause and the threat of government endorsement of religion in public forums leaves much to be desired because of the justices' inability to agree on whether the clause is implicated at all in public forum disputes involving private religious expression. Importantly, chapter 2 shows how the high court's policymaking offers little guidance to lower federal district courts, which essentially allows lower courts, as trial courts, to make policy independently of upper court guidelines and precedent.

Chapter 3 shifts the focus back to the district courts, and empirically analyzes the patterns of litigation. The types of litigants are examined first, with attention given to the types of plaintiffs and defendants, the role of interest groups, and the levels and types of government entities involved (such as local, state, and federal agencies). In addition to the types of litigation, patterns of litigation over time are discussed. For instance, the fact that ISKCON (International Society for Krishna Consciousness) pioneered religious speech and public forum litigation in the 1970s, but disappeared from litigation trends after 1980, is addressed, among others, in order to understand how and why litigation patterns evolve and change over time.

Chapters 4 and 5 take a detailed look at the dual policymaking process in which district courts engage when adjudicating religious speech and public forum cases. Recall that courts must first determine whether a public space falls under public forum analysis, and in the process create a mini public square. Next, the courts focus on the content of the square, and determine whether the government can regulate it. Thus, two distinct, yet related, questions guide the analysis here. First, focusing on the actual forums created by courts—the types and locations of forums—helps to explain the overall policymaking role that courts serve. Second, focusing on the content of the forums in question—the types of speech and expression—allows again for a much more detailed look at district court policymaking.

Chapter 4 takes a nuanced and focused look at the public spaces and forums where plaintiffs seek to place their religious messages. The Supreme Court notes the importance of the geographical location and context of public forums in the development of the law: "the nature of a place, the pattern of its normal activities, dictate the kinds of regulations of time, place, and manner that are reasonable."[11] Thus, focusing on the types of forums litigated at the district level defines the parameters of litigation more broadly, and also facilitates analysis of the contexts in which the law is developing and evolving.

Chapter 5, in contrast, looks at the content of the forums adjudicated by detailing the kinds of religious messages litigated and the types of conduct at issue. Ultimately, the chapter argues that among the types of messages litigated, Christian speech far outnumbers all other kinds of speech involved, such as Jewish, Muslim, or other religious speech. As well, the Christian speech at issue involves many different types of conduct, such as prayer, evangelism, and worship-based activities, whereas the conduct of other faith-based litigants clusters around either the distribution of literature, or the display of religious symbols. Thus, the chapter argues that even though many different types of expressive conduct are involved in litigation, most of those types are associated and linked with one specific type of religious message.

Chapter 6 places district court policymaking within the ongoing, broad-based debates over the role of religious messages and religious speech in public places and argues that litigation at the district court level is dominated by one specific type of speech—Christian speech—which means that public forum jurisprudence is developing within the context of one specific message, perhaps to the detriment of other types of religious messages and speech. That is, since one specific religious message, albeit spoken by different and distinct types of speakers, tends to be the focus of court policymaking, the law on religious speech is developing and evolving in a lopsided, uneven manner. Chapter 6 also addresses an ongoing discussion between courts, Congress, and interest groups concerning religious expression in public schools, and assesses district court policymaking in the context of a "constitutional dialogue" over the extent to which public schools must allow student religious expression.

A few words are in order about what this project does not concern. First, it is a study of federal district court policymaking, and as such pays credence to appellate courts—regional federal circuit courts or the United States Supreme Court—only to illustrate the outcome of a particular case under discussion. Therefore, this study is not concerned with flows of litigation that follow a case through from its inception to its final end. Many scholars have fruitfully studied litigation from starting to ending points in order to understand how claims develop and change, and as many illustrate elsewhere, district court/appellate court interaction is important since the regional circuit in which a district court is located can affect its policymaking role.[12] The focus of this study, however, is not on the relationship between districts and circuits, but instead studies and details how and why district courts make policy in religious speech and public forum disputes.

Second, this study does not formally model, per se, the policy-making role of district courts. Advanced statistical techniques are used elsewhere on the database generated for this study, and to be sure yield some very interesting results.[13] For this work, though, statistical analysis of the database is intentionally kept basic so as to keep the work as accessible to as many readers as possible. It is hoped that it will appeal not only to scholars of federal district courts, but also to students of religion and politics, law and society, and constitutional law, among others. Keeping the statistical analysis available to many different types of readers schooled in diverse disciplines makes the work broadly applicable beyond just the political science study of district courts.

Acknowledgments

I have incurred many intellectual debts throughout this project, so I thank the following for their help and support along the way. Thanks especially to my wife Kathryn and all the extended family: Margaret and Angus, my mother Janet, Rachel, Jeff (and Ryan), and David and Judith. Thanks also to Henry J. Abraham and David M. O'Brien at the University of Virginia; Chris Banks at the University of Akron; Barbara Perry, Jeff Key, and Steve Bragaw at Sweet Briar College; Don Jackson and Mary Volcansek at Texas Christian University; Ben Vetter at the University of Chicago Law School; Lu Leake at Wake Forest University; and Jim Curry, Derek Davis, and many others at Baylor University. Two anonymous readers for the University of Akron Press provided very helpful comments in their review of the manuscript, and the editing, production, and marketing staff at the Press proved indispensable in turning the manuscript into a book. I also thank the Political Science faculties at the following universities for their insightful and helpful comments: University of Northern Iowa, University of South Florida (especially Steve Tauber and Thomas Smith), Linfield College, Concord College, Wright State University, Cal State University Chico, and the University of Wisconsin-Stevens Point. I received many helpful comments from panelists at the American Political Science Association and Southwest Political Science Association annual meetings in 2002 and 2003, as well as many insightful and helpful comments from the American Constitution Society at the University of Chicago Law School.

Parts of chapter 3 were previously published in the *Journal of Church and State*. Many thanks to the *Journal* for granting permission to reproduce parts of my essay in this book. The citation is: "Federal District Courts, Religious Speech, and the Public Forum: An Analysis of Litigation Patterns and Outcomes," *Journal of Church and State* 44 (Winter 2002): 93–113.

CHAPTER 1

Courts, Religious Speech, and the Naked Public Square

LIKE MANY UPPER MIDWESTERN TOWNS in the United States, Marshfield, Wisconsin, is tidy, neatly planned out, and safe. Seventy percent of the city's residents reported their ancestry in the 2000 census as German, Polish, or Norwegian, and Marshfield is still possessed of the cultural influences of the immigrants who sought to remake central Wisconsin after their homes and villages in Europe. From the food, to surnames, to Polish and German masses said in Catholic churches, Marshfield identifies in many ways with its diverse heritage.

Part of that heritage is the public display of religious messages and icons. Around Marshfield, many a central Wisconsin highway is adorned with small Christian chapels or statues of Mary and other saints that are reminiscent of wayside religious icons scattered throughout Europe to provide weary travelers with rest and respite, and perhaps spiritual strength to continue a difficult journey. To be sure, religious symbols for travelers are a declining tradition in Europe, just as in the United States. The advent of automobile travel and good highways perhaps makes religious symbols less important, and indeed less noticeable. Yet, Marshfield is one of those places where the public display of religious icons endures, grounded as it is in the predominantly Catholic makeup of the area. Wood County, Wisconsin—in which Marshfield is located—is overwhelmingly Catholic. Of 75,500 residents in Wood County, 57,472 report adherence to a specific religious faith; of those adherents, 30,265 (53 percent) are Catholic.[1]

Marshfield, like many towns, has a forty-five-year-old wayside religious display that of late has stirred controversy. In 1959, a local Knights of Columbus group donated a religious statue to the city for public display. The white marble statue of Jesus is fifteen feet high, and depicts Christ with outstretched arms standing atop a large globe. The globe rests on a base that contains a readily visible inscription: "Christ Guide Us on Our Way." The statue is located on public property, and faces the busy highway that enters Marshfield from the south. In 1964, a member of the Knights of Columbus, Henry Praschak, donated his time and supplies to build a comfort station at the statue, complete with picnic tables, signs, and outdoor grills. In response, the city agreed to build and maintain a public park surrounding the comfort station, which it subsequently named the Praschak Wayside Park.

In 1998, Marshfield businessman Clarence Reinders and the Wisconsin-based Freedom From Religion Foundation sued the city in the federal district court for the Western District of Wisconsin, claiming that the city's maintenance of the park with the religious statue violated the Establishment Clause of the First Amendment. The city was, in effect, sponsoring and endorsing one specific religious message. Soon after the lawsuit was filed, Marshfield erected a disclaimer sign that stated, "the location of this statue . . . does not reflect an endorsement of a religious sect or belief by the city of Marshfield."[2] The city subsequently sold the statue and .15 acres of city land surrounding it to the newly formed Henry Praschak Fund for $21,560, or $3.30 per square foot, which was the highest price per square foot the city had ever received for public land. All state requirements for the municipal sale of pub-

lic land were met, and the city even severed the electrical con-
nection to the park. The sale was based on a restrictive covenant
that deeded the property to the Praschak Fund for public use.
By selling the statue and surrounding property, the city priva-
tized the park, thus making the religious speech within it the
product of private individual expression. Marshfield was no longer
the "speaker" expounding the religious message of "Christ Guide
Us on Our Way." The new speaker was the Henry Praschak Fund,
a private organization that retains all the rights and privileges con-
ferred by the Free Speech Clause of the First Amendment. In response to the now private nature of the religious expression at
issue, the federal district court dismissed the lawsuit. Reinders and
the Freedom From Religion Foundation appealed that dismissal to
the Seventh Circuit Court of Appeals, and argued that the private
park is not differentiated in a meaningful way from surrounding
public property, thus the Establishment Clause is still violated.
The Seventh Circuit agreed in part, and noted that the wayside
park, prior to its sale, was a traditional public forum owned and operated by the government, and historically and customarily open
to individual speech and expression. The sale of the forum meant
that the property was no longer controlled by the city, and its traditional openness to speech and expression was now foreclosed.
Moreover, any speech associated with the property is now the private choice of the property's owner. Thus, the statue in the park is
now the Praschak Fund's private religious expression, and not that
of the city of Marshfield. To address the Establishment Clause
issue, the court inquired into how a reasonable person would view
the statue and private park, and whether that person—the typical
passerby—would view the statue of Jesus as a government-sponsored
religious message. The court's answer was straightforward.

Since its creation in 1964, the park has expressed only one
message, which is the religious message conveyed by the

statue. The park was created to display the statue, and the City presents no evidence that other groups have ever used the park to present alternative messages. *For this reason, a reasonable observer familiar with the history of the park would have no reason to be aware of non-sectarian reasons for the government's endorsement of religion. The current physical state of the park also leads a reasonable person to conclude that the statue is part of the public park and that the government, rather than a private entity, endorses religion. As we have noted, the [Praschak] Fund land is visually indistinguishable from City land.*[3]

Although the Praschak Fund now owned the statue and park, the court concluded that the historical and spatial links between the park and the city still led passerby to conclude that the message was the city's, and not the fund's. The case was remanded to the district court, which was invited to "explore, in concert with the parties," remedies to Marshfield's endorsement of a religious message in violation of the Establishment Clause. To separate the city and private property, the circuit judges suggested the creation of a "defining structure, such as a permanent gated fence or wall . . . accompanied by a clearly visible disclaimer, on City property," so that a reasonable person would not "confuse speech made on fund property with expressive endorsement made by the City."[4] The district court's order, entered on May 9, 2000, mandated that Marshfield shall build a four-foot-high wrought-iron gated fence on its property to create a perimeter around the fund's 15 acres and statue. In addition, a disclaimer is to be attached to the fence in two places, and in highly visible lettering the disclaimer will read: "Private Park. This property is not owned or maintained by the City of Marshfield, nor does the City endorse the religious expression therein." Marshfield duly complied with the order. Carl Reinders moved away from Marshfield soon after, and seemed somewhat pleased with the outcome of the case. Reinders noted that public buildings and parks belong "to all people—believers and unbelievers alike. I always recommended that they have a big, naked statue of Buddha in the park. You can't just exclude it to the Christians."[5]

THE PROBLEM OF THE PUBLIC SQUARE

In one respect the Marshfield case is unique. Rarely do cities privatize a public square in order to maintain the religious message in it. Yet, the case reflects a broader issue that concerns the extent to which religious speakers and messages can, and should be, allowed into the public square. Individuals and groups often seek out publicly owned places in which to express religious ideas through evangelism, preaching, worship and prayer services, solicitation of other people, and similar expressive conduct. The First Amendment Free Speech Clause protects religious speech, and the United States Supreme Court reminds us time and again that expressive conduct so often linked with a religious message is as protected under the First Amendment as other types of speech and expression. As Justice Antonin Scalia recently put it in *Capital Square Review & Advisory Board v. Pinette*, "private religious speech, far from being a First Amendment orphan, is as fully protected under the Free Speech Clause as secular private expression. Indeed . . . a Free Speech Clause without religion would be *Hamlet* without the prince. Accordingly, we have not excluded from free speech protections religious proselytizing, or even acts of worship."[6]

From government buildings to airports, public places serve as suitable locations for religious expression since religious speakers can repeatedly interact with and speak to large numbers of other people. They can, literally, reach the masses with their religious message. Yet, the presence of religious speech in public places is controversial. There are deeper tensions caused by its presence in public spaces, tensions that resonate with ongoing debates over the extent to which the public square should accommodate religious speech and expression. For some, religious speech and expression contribute positively to our increasingly pluralistic and secular conversations on social and political issues. For instance, the display of the Ten Commandments by a private speaker in a public park or courthouse plaza or even government building continually reminds us of our Judeo-Christian heritage and the religious foundations of our modern society. Similarly, the display of crèches and menorahs on public property during the appropriate holiday seasons helps defeat the increasing secularization of fundamentally religious holidays, and again tells us of the religious underpinnings and meanings of Christmas and Hannukah. And finally, religious groups that worship in public parks or buildings remind us that public property is open to the use of all, regardless of social, political, or religious affiliations.

For others, though, religious speech and expression in public places is worrisome. The public square should be secular, and religious speech should be prohibited as much as possible. Displaying the Ten Commandments in government owned and maintained spaces, such as courthouses and public schools, erodes the "wall of separation" between government and religion, and brings the government perilously close to endorsing religious beliefs in violation of the Establishment Clause of the First Amendment. Establishment violations are not the only concern either. Since religious expression is inherently nonpluralistic and grounded in theological claims, its presence in the public square excludes or offends those who disagree with it or do not belong to its base religious tradition. Religious speech is intrinsically morality based, and presupposes the truth of its foundational claims. Thus, it is exclusive and cannot be as easily rebutted by other claims in the public square, and displays of the Ten Commandments, nativity scenes, menorahs, or other religious symbols in publicly owned places excludes from the public forum those who do not agree, as do other types of expression such as preaching or the distribution of literature.

Some religious speakers are granted access to publicly owned spaces and allowed to express their message. Others are denied access, and it is often that denial that prompts litigation. Litigants seeking access to public spaces regularly invoke public forum law under the First Amendment, since public forum doctrine holds that government owned spaces should be open to the free exchange of ideas. Supreme Court Justice Anthony Kennedy put it best in his concurring opinion in *International Society for Krishna Consciousness v. Lee*, where he wrote that

> The liberties protected by our doctrine derive from the Assembly, as well as the Speech and Press Clauses of the First Amendment, and are essential to a functioning democracy. Public places are of necessity the locus for discussion of public issues, as well as protest against arbitrary government action. At the heart of our jurisprudence lies the principle that in a free nation citizens must have the right to gather and speak with other persons in public places. The recognition that certain government-owned property is a public forum provides open notice to citizens that their freedoms may be exercised there without fear of a censorial government, adding tangible reinforcement to the idea that we are a free people.[7]

Religious speech, as with most other types of private speech, is entitled to protection and access to government-owned properties, or so-called public forums.

Many religious speech claims tend to make their way into the federal court system and thereby allow federal courts to frame the ongoing debate over the proper (and constitutional) role of religious speech in public places. The continuing attention given to religious speech claims by the Supreme Court shows the presence of such disputes in the federal system, and indeed the high court's consideration of such cases mirrors the regular filing of religious speech litigation in lower federal courts. Importantly, lower federal courts often influence and determine when, where, and how religious speech occurs in public squares. District courts are the starting point for litigation in the federal system, and as the initial policymakers in a chain of litigation they have a significant role in setting the parameters of legal policy. Through adjudication of disputes, district courts mold and influence how the law develops as an initial step, prior to any appellate and Supreme Court review.

When district courts adjudicate religious speech and public forum claims, they help frame the ongoing debate over the proper role of religion in the public square in two important ways. First, by applying First Amendment public forum law (detailed below) to real, geographically definable places, district courts in effect *create* public squares open to speech and expression. Thus, when a court determines that a government building, public park, or other publicly owned place is a public forum, that court effectively opens that location to speech and other expressive activity. Second, linked with the public forum analysis is the court's policymaking about the forum's *content*, and whether the religious speech being litigated can be granted access to it. By defining public forums open to the exchange of ideas, and then determining the content of those forums or spaces, courts mold and shape the debate over religious speech and expression.

The following cases illustrate the pressures that district courts encounter when deciding cases concerning the constitutionality of religious speech in public places. As one district judge puts it, such disputes "explore the tension between religious practice and public space."[8] How district judges initially resolve those tensions helps determine which kinds of religious speech and messages are welcome in the public square, and indeed where those public squares are actually located. As well, how courts address enduring issues over religious speech in the public square adds an important dimension to our understanding of the broader links between religion, law, and politics.

SISTER MARY REILLY'S GUITAR

In the early 1970s, Sister Mary Reilly and several other nuns sought to protest the State of Rhode Island's policies limiting welfare benefits. In the context of a national energy crisis and rising energy costs, the nuns argued that scaling back benefits egregiously harmed the poor. For them, the issue was defined in stark moral terms. As a means of lobbying the Rhode Island legislature they decided to hold several worship services in the State Capitol Rotunda to publicize the plight of the poor. Since the rotunda was historically a place where groups and individuals gathered to hold short meetings and discussions on topical issues, Sister Reilly and her colleagues considered it a very appropriate place to hold short, nonobtrusive worship services. And so they did, starting on Ash Wednesday in 1974, and every subsequent Wednesday during Lent. The first meeting had a small number of people and two guitars for music. Subsequent meetings ranged from sixty to seventy-five participants, some of whom were Rhode Island legislators.

The group was asked to cease its meetings because they were too noisy and disrupted public business in the statehouse. In fact, the governor of Rhode Island, Philip Noel, personally ordered their expulsion and denied them further access to the public space. There were no written rules or guidelines affecting public gatherings in the rotunda, and in practice the governor's unfettered discretion could determine who had access to this traditional gathering place, and who did not.

Sister Mary Reilly sued after her expulsion.[9] She argued that the rotunda historically and traditionally served as a place where people and groups gather for political debate and other types of communicative activity, and public forum law under the First Amendment to the Constitution governed access to it. Indeed, the First Amendment protected her conduct in more than one way. First, public forum doctrine, a derivative of the Free Speech Clause of the First Amendment, stipulated that the legislative rotunda was a traditional gathering place for speech and expressive activities, thus she had a right to access it and use it for speech and other expressive purposes. Second, religious expression in the form of prayer, worship, or song is likewise protected under the Free Speech Clause, so not only did she have a constitutional right to speak in the public square, but the manner and content of her speech were protected as well.

The federal district court agreed, and ruled that Rhode Island violated Reilly's First Amendment free speech rights. Relying on public forum doctrine the district court noted that the legislative rotunda is a traditional public forum open to all individuals and groups for communicative activity. As the Supreme Court noted in an early public forum case *Hague v. CIO*, some public spaces "have immemorially been held in trust for the use of the public and, time out of mind, have been used for purposes of assembly, communicating thoughts between citizens, and discussing public questions."[10] The statehouse rotunda was just such a public space, and in fact the Rhode Island government had an open-door policy for its use. No government official or agency monitored its usage or noise levels and there were relatively few regulations affecting who used the rotunda, and for what expressive purposes. Thus, to deny Reilly's group access is the equivalent of censorship and is prohibited by the First Amendment.

The central essence of public forum doctrine focuses on whether a public space is open to debate on "public questions." The Court has defined several different types of public forums, discussed in detail below, in which the rights of the speaker are balanced to varying degrees with the need of the government to regulate a specific property that it owns. The different types of forums simply reflect that not all public property is amenable to speech and expressive conduct. Although the rotunda was historically and customarily open to speech-related activities, not all publicly owned places are, and spaces such as airports, train stations, and other government buildings may indeed be less open to speech due to their specific characteristics.

Sister Mary Reilly successfully linked public forum doctrine, and its attendant focus on actual, spatial dimensions and usages of a specific public space, with religious speech and communicative activity protected under the First Amendment. Importantly, Reilly's case in the early 1970s inaugurates a new litigation trend where litigants seek to place a religiously motivated message—whether prayer, evangelism, religious solicitation, or the like—into a public space. To do so, they often turn to public forum doctrine to first establish whether the space is indeed a public forum. If so, then their religiously motivated expression should be protected speech as well.

ISKCON CONTINUES THE TREND

The International Society for Krishna Consciousness (ISKCON) litigated several public forum and religious speech cases at the federal district court level throughout the 1970s, and had a pronounced effect on the development of legal doctrine and litigation strategies in this area of the law. In contrast to Sister Mary Reilly's single case, ISKCON developed a much more organized, coordinated effort to protect its religious expression in public spaces. One of the central tenets of ISKCON is *sankirtan*, a religious practice in which Krishnas must approach other people in public and solicit them for donations to the ISKCON movement. Krishnas regularly encountered official hostility to *sankirtan* especially when practiced in crowded public forums such as state fairs, airports, bus and train stations, and city parks and sidewalks. Government agencies charged with managing public spaces would either deny access to Krishna speakers altogether, or try to confine *sankirtan* to a fixed location such as a booth or other area. To counter government regulations of *sankirtan*, ISKCON initiated a litigation strategy in federal district courts using public forum doctrine to protect a basic expression of their religious belief. Not only was *sankirtan* a type of expressive activity conducted in public places, but it was also a religious exercise mandated by Krishna principles. Several types of public forums were involved. For instance, cases concerning whether Krishnas could be confined to booths at state fairs were litigated to mixed results,[11] as were attempts to protect ambulatory *sankirtan* in airports and other travel terminals.[12] For some district courts Krishnas often engaged in *sankirtan* in crowded, congested areas and government regulations simply served to maintain the orderly nature of the forums in question. Other district courts upheld *sankirtan* as a type of expression that could not generally be regulated or limited by the government.

ISKCON successfully placed a couple of cases on the Supreme Court's docket in order to resolve the conflicts lingering in the lower district and circuit courts over how and when *sankirtan* can be regulated. The Court was generally unsupportive of ISKCON's activities, however, and allowed regulations of *sankirtan* practices to stand.[13] The high court's decisions are discussed in more detail in chapter 2. Importantly, ISKCON's litigation strategy of linking public forum doctrine to religiously motivated expression placed the issue of religious speech in the public forum squarely on the agenda of federal courts.

A CHILD'S POSTER OF JESUS

Whereas Sister Reilly's litigation concerned a government building, and the Krishnas often litigated in the context of state fairgrounds, public parks, and travel terminals, more recent cases focus on public schools, and whether or not schools are public forums open to religious speech. A case in point is *C. H. v. Oliva, et al.*[14] Here, an elementary school child's poster of Jesus was placed on display in a school hallway, subsequently removed, and then placed in a less prominent location. The child was also denied permission to read a religious story from *The Beginner's Bible* to his class during a time reserved for such reading activities. The child's parents sued, claiming that their child's First Amendment rights to freedom of speech were violated. For them, the public school hallway and classroom are both public forums, and the school's power to regulate expression in them is strictly limited by the Constitution. Not only did the school censor the child's speech when it denied permission to read from the Bible in class; it also censored his speech when it moved his poster of Jesus to a less prominent position in the school hallway. The federal district court disagreed strongly, noting first that the classroom in question was not a public forum and pedagogical concerns allowed teachers and school administrators to inspect and reject a child's reading selection. As to the poster of Jesus, its relocation was again reasonably related to pedagogical concerns and thus was not a violation of the First Amendment.

Some scholars note that cases like *Oliva* demonstrate a new development in public forum speech disputes where litigants try to use the First Amendment to *place* religiously motivated expression back into the public schools, and for some observers of religion and politics this is a worrying trend. For example, Gilbert Holmes argues that linking free speech doctrine to "student-initiated religious expression" is an attempt to circumvent more restrictive Supreme Court precedents prohibiting school-sponsored prayer and Bible reading. As he puts it, litigating such disputes is a "stratagem for returning religion to public school."[15] Martha McCarthy similarly points out that "in the 1990s . . . by framing issues to focus on the speech aspect of devotional activities . . . [courts have] concluded that private (personal) religious and nonreligious expression should be treated the same under the Free Speech Clause."[16] Analysis of public forum cases involving religious speech demonstrates that lawsuits treating public schools as public forums open to religious expression increased in the 1980s and especially the 1990s. Yet, such litigation only accounts for approximately one-third of all such cases in federal district courts, thus the significance of schools as forums should not be overstated.[17] Nonetheless, it is an important trend in how the law is developing in the federal judicial system.

The *Oliva* case also demonstrates the increasing dominance of Christian evangelical messages in public forum and religious speech litigation with a concomitant decrease in litigation filed by Krishnas and other non-Christians. Although ISKCON did not pioneer the litigation strategy of linking religious speech to public forums, it did develop a coordinated litigation strategy that consistently placed such dispute on the dockets of federal district courts and the Supreme Court. Yet, in terms of the overall trend of litigation, ISKCON ceased to be a litigant by the mid-1980s. Reasons for this are discussed in a subsequent chapter, but to be sure, other groups and individuals began to dominate this area of the law, beginning in the early 1980s, and have not abated since.[18]

Sister Mary Reilly, ISKCON, and the child C. H. had different motivations for their litigation. Reilly sought to hold prayer services in a government building historically open to the public for group gatherings. ISKCON sought First Amendment protection for its ambulatory colporteuring, which was expressive conduct motivated by deeply held religious convictions. The child C. H. simply sought to read a Bible story to classmates, as well as display a poster representing Jesus in a public school hallway. Different issues were litigated, but the three cases all have something in common: they all sought to use First Amendment public forum doctrine to protect religiously motivated expression in publicly owned spaces. Importantly, too, they turned to federal district courts—the trial courts in the federal judicial hierarchy—to litigate their claims.

RELIGION IN THE PUBLIC SQUARE

Federal district court policymaking on religious speech in public forums is linked with a larger and deeper theoretical debate over the proper role of religious speech in the public square. Richard John Neuhaus highlighted the debate over religious speech in public places in the early 1980s when he argued that the public square is "naked," and essentially devoid of religious content. In his words, "the naked public square is the result of political doctrine and practice that would exclude religion and religiously grounded values from the conduct of public business."[19] The increasing secularization of American political debate (and other types of debate for that matter) has increasingly marginalized religion to the point that religious expression is no longer welcome in public deliberations. Moreover, religious expression and religious motivations in public debate are "increasingly surreptitious and suspect," and not to be countenanced by a modern liberal polity. "There are remnants [of religion] in public oaths, prayers in legislatures, and the like," as Neuhaus puts it, but "residual religion in public poses no threat."[20] Thus, the public square allows religious expression in lingering terms, such as in the benign form of persistent religious oaths that have no meaning. But religious expression that seeks to effect social and political change is perceived as increasingly dangerous to modern liberalism's emphasis on a secular, religiously neutral state. As Neuhaus further argues,

> The question of religion's access to the public square . . . is first of all a question of understanding the theory and practice of democratic governance. Citizens are the bearers of opinion, including opinion shaped by or espousing religious belief, and citizens have equal access to the public square. In this representative democracy, the state is forbidden to determine which convictions and moral judgments may be proposed for public deliberation . . . in a democracy that is free and robust, an opinion is no more disqualified for being "religious" than for being atheistic.[21]

Ultimately for Neuhaus, "the question . . . is not the access of religion to the public square. The question is the access, indeed the full and unencumbered participation . . . of citizens, who bring their opinions, sentiments, convictions, prejudices, visions, and communal traditions of moral discernment" to our public deliberations.[22] Thus, there is a larger normative dimension that extends beyond the role of courts and the law and focuses more prominently on themes of democracy and the nature of political debate.

Other prominent scholars of law and religion echo Neuhaus's concerns, although with some differences. Stephen L. Carter agrees with Neuhaus's conception of the public square devoid of religious expression to an extent, but he qualifies the argument in important ways. Whereas Neuhaus perceives that the public square is hostile to religion, Carter argues that the public square merely treats religion as a diversion. As he puts it, "the legal culture that guards the public square still seems most comfortable thinking of religion as a hobby, something done in privacy, something that mature, public-spirited adults do not use as the basis for politics."[23] Still, for Carter, religious expression is still part of the public square, sometimes in very prominent ways. Thus,

> When the guardians of the public square inveigh against religious dialogues, or when pundits worry about the influence of religion on politics, they are worrying, as it were, against history. The battle for the public square is already over. The rhetoric of religion is simply there . . . The important question is not whether religions can act as autonomous, politically involved intermediary institutions, or whether religious people should have access to the public square . . . The question crying out most vitally for resolution, given the presence of religions in the public square, is whether and how to regulate that presence.[24]

Here, Carter poses an intriguing normative question that has pronounced empirical overtones. How *should* religion be regulated in the public square? Necessarily, Carter links this normative question to an empirical focus on *whether* religion is regulated in the public square. Religious expression in the square is a fact, unlike Neuhaus's analysis that focuses on the nominal absence of religion from the square. And, for Carter, important questions concern how, when, and why religion in the square is limited.

To put Neuhaus and Carter in perspective, they would both value Sister Mary Reilly's prayer service in the Rhode Island statehouse rotunda as injecting an important normative and religious dimension to political debate, although the Rhode Island government's attempt to drive Reilly's expression out of the public place serves as an example of what they condemn, chiefly, government action that is hostile to religious expression. And in Reilly's case, it was left to a federal court to place her religious speech back into the public square. Krishnas perhaps pose a slightly different problem, since their religious speech in the public square serves not so much to effect social and political change as to support ISKCON's specific religious mission. The main Krishna expressive activity, *sankirtan*, serves to raise revenue and win converts, not necessarily to engage in social and political debate from a religious perspective. As for the child C. H., proponents of religious speech might be troubled by religion in public schools, but may also argue that children have free speech rights that are just as important as those of adults.

Others take issue with religious speech in the public square, however, and it is important to address their arguments here in order to place Neuhaus and Carter in a broader perspective. In general, those unsympathetic to religion in the public square locate their arguments around the imperatives of social and political discussions in a pluralistic polity. Since religious justifications and expressions are ultimately grounded in noncontestable claims of higher authority, the civility of public discourse is undermined simply because religious justifications are nonnegotiable.

Summing up diverse arguments as to why religion should be kept out of the public square, Jeff Spinner-Halev maintains that "civil and civic discussions" best proceed when religion is kept out of political debate. "People who act in the name of God tend to feel quite strongly about their beliefs. Rational debate and discussion followed by compromise are not necessarily possible." Spinner-Halev contends too that not only is religious discourse in the public square divisive; it may also generate even more religious expression: "some people see others inserting their religious views in politics, then they will respond in kind; with so many religions trying to insert their views into politics, discord will shortly follow."[25] Spinner-Halev ultimately argues that exclusion of the religious voice threatens democracy more so than protects it, since "excluded groups are more likely to become passionate . . . about their beliefs than included groups." Those whose religious messages are excluded may have even less incentive to compromise, and thus make their religious expression even louder and bolder. Robert Audi views pluralistic society and democracy in similar terms, yet with different results. For Audi, secular justifications in the public square are the goal of public debate, not the exception. Thus, when discussing public affairs, "it seems *generally* best to conduct discussion in secular terms." However, he recognizes that religious motivations will, and do, creep into public debate. Therefore, "if one does articulate religious reasons in a public debate, it should help to be able to express both commitment to the principle of secular rationale and reasons that accord with it. This would show a respect for a religiously neutral point of view that any rational citizen may share."[26] For Audi, secular justifications in the public square, especially for laws and policies that restrict human conduct, respect the religious pluralism underlying the public square, and the polity in general. Accordingly, "any educated religious person . . . who comes to the obligations of citizenship in a liberal democracy is already aware of plural bases, both religious and secular, of moral and sociopolitical obligation, and of the fallibility of even one's careful interpretations of those sources and obligations. The cultivation of civic virtue should reflect this sense of multiplicity and tension."[27] In Audi's terms, then, the imperatives of the public square grounded in a religiously pluralistic society are such that religious expressions and justifications are generally not to be a prominent part of debate in the square. To do so erodes the need for compromise and civility. When religious justifications are in the public square, they should be accompanied by secular rationales that will appeal to the broadest group of citizens as possible. The public square is not hostile to religion per se, in Audi's view. It is simply that the imperatives of the pluralistic public square determine that religion should serve only a minor role.

Patrick Glynn, in a somewhat different tack, argues that "politics is not a spiritual activity . . . because it involves the soul in strife." Thus, "a too direct coupling of religion and politics in the public square is usually pernicious, not only for politics but also for religion itself. The result is typically not the sanctification of politics but the politicization of religion."[28] In an argument with strong Madisonian overtones, Glynn's point is that religion stands to lose greatly from participating in the public square anyway. The more involved religion is in public and political discourse in the square, the more it becomes corrupted by secular politics. Therefore, the public square's hostility to religion is actually a good thing, as the integrity of religion is ultimately preserved.

Spinner-Halev places an extra gloss on the public square debate by pointing out that we should be talking about public *squares*, plural, instead of one, metaphorical public square. Communicative activity often takes place in smaller groups, or smaller publics. Thus, "the idea of a public square recalls the image of the New England town square. . . . today, however, there are many small public squares that tie particular communities together."[29] These smaller public squares might be organized along ethnic and religious lines, to be sure, as well as other distinguishing factors that group people together. As Spinner-Halev notes, though, these smaller publics do not exist in isolation from each other, but often interact with the "public square of mainstream society," which is basically "a rather loose national conversation that may be considered the larger public square."

Diana Eck echoes Spinner-Halev's point that smaller, local public squares comprise one larger, national public square. As she puts it, "the American public square is scarcely 'naked,' but filled with religious voices on all sides of the issues—from abortion to capital punishment. And it is not Christian, nor Judeo-Christian, nor

Judeo-Christian-Islamic, but increasingly multireligious. Diverse religious communities are visible . . . and diverse voices contribute to the public discussion."[30] Significantly, these religious voices choose diverse public forums for their expression, from zoning boards and city councils to public schools to government buildings.[31] The debate over religious expression in the public square should more properly be seen, then, as a debate over expression in public squares high in number yet spatially and geographically small and spread out.

One scholar who places an empirical stamp on small public squares is David Yamane, who argues that whether or not the public square is naked, "scholars must approach this issue as an empirical question to be answered through systematic research on the *actual* relationship between religion and politics in American society. Those who have done so in the past have found the situation to be far more complex than partisans on either side [of the debate] have suggested."[32] Yamane studies religious advocacy in state legislative hearings and focuses on how religious groups use religious and secular legitimations for policy positions. He concludes by noting that neither those who decry the absence of religion from the public square, nor those who wish to keep religion out of the public square, have it quite right: "religious groups do participate actively in the political system, though they do so very much on the political systems own terms."[33] Importantly, though, in Yamane's case the legislative process—here, state legislative hearings in Wisconsin—can serve as an important institutional expression of the public square. As well, giving the metaphoric public square an institutional framework, such as a legislative hearing, allows for the collection and analysis of empirical data concerning the relationship between religious expression and the public square in particular, and the connections between religion and politics in general.

Just as state legislative hearings are empirically grounded examples of religious discourse in a public square, so too can federal courts be seen as institutional expressions of the public square debate. As Spinner-Halev notes above, small public squares tie communities together into a larger, national public square.[34] His conception of smaller public squares open to speech neatly encompasses courts, especially district courts that adjudicate religious speech and public forum cases. Likewise for Eck, who also points out that courts are "important sites for the negotiation of religious difference" under the Constitution.[35] As district courts are one part of the federal judicial system, their policymaking in religious speech cases feeds into an appellate hierarchy that is more regional and national in scope. Courts serve to denominate smaller public squares that contribute to the larger national dialogue. This is especially so in the context of religious expression and public forum doctrine, where courts actually define a geographical space as a public forum, with its attendant First Amendment concerns, and then subsequently define the allowable content of that forum. Other empirical locations for the public square, such as state legislative hearings in Yamane's analysis, concern preexisting public squares that are simply put to use by religious groups seeking to add their religious discourse to a larger debate. Courts do something different: they create public squares open to speech and expressive activities, and they also police the content of those squares.

EXPLORING THE TENSIONS BETWEEN RELIGIOUS PRACTICE AND PUBLIC SPACES: PUBLIC FORUM DOCTRINE AND THE CONTOURS AND CONTENTS OF PUBLIC SQUARES

The case studies above point to a distinctive policymaking role for district courts, in that not only do they define the contours and locations of public squares open to speech, but they also determine the appropriate content of those squares. The dual policymaking role of courts in defining the contours and content of public squares is linked to the doctrinal imperatives of First Amendment public forum law. Under public forum law, as one district judge puts it, "forum classification and denial of access are distinct issues," meaning that judges must first classify the contested public space in question under public forum categories, and then determine whether regulations on religiously motivated speech are constitutionally acceptable.[36] Specifically for religious speech cases, as another puts it, judges must "explore the tension between religious practice and public space."[37]

"Exploring" that tension hinges upon public forum doctrine, as created and refined by the Supreme Court. Defining or categorizing the public forum is the first step, and here courts focus on the spatial dimensions of the public area in question, as well as its historical and customary usages. Justice Felix Frankfurter pointed out as much in his concurring opinion in Niemotko v. Maryland: "Where does the speaking which is regulated take place? Not only the general classifications—streets, parks, private buildings—are relevant. The location and size of a park; its customary use for the recreational, esthetic and contemplative needs of a community; the facilities, other than a park or street corner, readily available in a community for airing views, are all pertinent considerations."[38]

In a different case, Perry Education Association v. Perry Local Educators' Association, the Court neatly summarized its public forum doctrine and created a useful guide to public forum jurisprudence in general.[39] In Perry, the issue was whether an internal mail system in a public school is a public forum open to mailings by non-school affiliated groups. As the Court noted, there are three specific types of forums under the First Amendment: the traditional public forum, the designated or limited public forum, and the nonpublic forum. Traditional public forums are those that "by long tradition or by government fiat, have been devoted to assembly and debate." In traditional public forums, "the rights of the State to limit expressive activity are sharply circumscribed . . . for the State to enforce a content-based exclusion, it must show that its regulation is necessary to serve a compelling state interest and that it is narrowly drawn to achieve that end."[40]

The second type of forum, the designated or limited forum, is one that "the State has opened for use by the public as a place for expressive activity."[41] The state does not have to keep the designated forum open indefinitely, but as long as it is open the same limits on the state's power to regulate speech in the traditional public forum apply: "reasonable time, place, and manner regulations are permissible, and a content-based prohibition must be narrowly drawn to effectuate a compelling state interest."[42] A third category, the nonpublic forum, focuses on "public property which is not, by tradition or designation, a forum for public communication . . . In addition to time, place, and manner regulations, the State may reserve the forum for its intended purposes, communicative or otherwise, as long as the regulation on speech is reasonable."[43]

Courts use public forum categories to classify a public space based on its historical or customary usage and how the government uses and regulates it. The spatial and geographical characteristics of the property in question are also central to public forum policymaking. Justice Kennedy noted again in his concurring opinion in *ISKCON v. Lee* that "the inquiry must be an objective one, based on the actual, physical characteristics and uses of the property."[44] Thus, "the doctrine focuses on the physical characteristics of the property, because government ownership is the source of its purported authority to regulate speech. The right of speech protected by the doctrine [comes] . . . from the constitutional recognition that the government cannot impose silence on a free people."[45]

In categorizing a public space as a traditional or designated forum, or indeed not a forum at all, courts review the physical traits and usages of the property, and by so doing create and maintain spaces for public discourse and debate. It may be that an area in question has historically been open to public debate, and thus the public forum was created by historical usage over time. By adjudicating the forum as such, courts are placing the locale in question under the heightened protections of the First Amendment, with the result that courts resolve lingering questions about the status of the public area and how the government can regulate expressive conduct within it. Courts create, or at least validate, miniature public squares where the public can interact and engage in the free trade of ideas. To adjudicate a geographical site as a public forum "provides open notice," for Justice Kennedy, that the area in question is free from government censorship.

As already noted, public forum analysis is a two-step process. Courts must first classify the space in question under public forum analysis. Once the forum's status is defined, courts must then figure out whether the specific expression at issue is allowed in the forum. The second inquiry reflects the fact that litigants do not normally go to court over the forum question only, since there is no real reason to contest whether a space is or is not a forum without also wanting to place a specific type of expression or message into it. The status of a public space does not exist in a legal vacuum; it is always accompanied by a specific request for courts to protect a certain message and expressive conduct linked with that message.

In forum analysis, "the constitutional tilt is in favor of the speaker and not the regulator" and the law clearly works to the speaker's advantage in protecting access for most types of messages in the public square.[46] First Amendment law generally prohibits

the government from denying access to a public area because of
the content of a speaker's message. Reasonable time, place, and
manner regulations on the speaker are allowable, however, and
the government can control the timing of a message, the place
where it is communicated, and the manner in which it is communicated. Determining the content of a public space involves courts
in detailed questions about the usage of the space, for instance
whether the space has historically and traditionally been open to
expression, or whether there are relevant public safety concerns
that justify regulation of a message. The Supreme Court in
Grayned v. City of Rockford defined some of the considerations
that courts must take into account.

> Clearly, government has no power to restrict such activity
> because of its message. Our cases make equally clear, how-
> ever, that reasonable "time, place and manner" regulations
> may be necessary to further significant governmental inter-
> ests, and are permitted. For example, two parades cannot
> march on the same street simultaneously, and government
> may allow only one. A demonstration or parade on a large
> street during rush hour might put an intolerable burden on
> the essential flow of traffic, and for that reason could be pro-
> hibited. If overamplified loudspeakers assault the citizenry,
> government may turn them down. Subject to such reason-
> able regulation, however, peaceful demonstrations in public
> places are protected by the First Amendment. . . . The nature
> of a place, the pattern of its normal activities, dictate the
> kinds of regulations of time, place, and manner that are rea-
> sonable. Although a silent vigil may not unduly interfere
> with a public library, making a speech in the reading room al-
> most certainly would. That same speech should be perfectly
> appropriate in a park.[47]

The Court subsequently explained in *Grayned* that "the crucial question is whether the manner of expression is basically incompatible with the normal activity of a particular place at a particular time . . . in assessing the reasonableness of a regulation, we must weigh heavily the fact that communication is involved; [and] the regulation must be narrowly tailored to further the State's legitimate interest . . . Free expression must not, in the guise of regulation, be abridged or denied."[48] Importantly, the government can regulate the *process* of communication in the square through regulating the timing of expression, its location within the square, and the manner of expression or conduct.

Different issues arise if the government limits expression in the public square based on its substance, or content. Any content regulation must further a compelling state interest, and it must be "finely tailored to serve substantial state interests."[49] As the Court stipulated in *Police Department of City of Chicago v. Mosely*, a labor picketing case,

> Government may not grant the use of a forum to people whose views it finds acceptable, but deny use to those wishing to express less favored or more controversial views. And it may not select which issues are worth discussing or debating in public facilities. There is an "equality of status in the field of ideas," and government must afford all points of view an equal opportunity to be heard. Once a forum is opened up to assembly or speaking by some groups, government may not prohibit others from assembling or speaking on the basis of what they intend to say. Selective exclusions from a public forum may not be based on content alone, and may not be justified by reference to content alone.[50]

Government generally may not deny access to a public forum based on the content of the speech at issue, since to do so interferes with the equality of ideas that the public forum incorporates and encourages. Bans on speech due to its content are only justifiable by a substantial state interest in regulating that content. Moreover, the regulation must be minimally restrictive, in that it must limit only that speech proscribed by the state's substantial interest.

As *Perry* pointed out, the standards of adjudication that courts apply to the content of the square vary, according to the specific type of forum at issue. When a traditional public forum is created, any state regulation of the content of speech in the forum must be justified by a compelling government interest, and the regulation in question must be narrowly drawn to achieve the compelling interest. For a nontraditional forum, a so-called designated or limited forum that "the State has opened for use by the public as a place for expressive activity," all regulations on the forum's content must likewise meet the compelling interest test as long as the designated forum remains open by the government.[51] Although the government is not obligated to keep the forum open for an indefinite period, its ability to regulate expression while the limited forum is open is sharply circumscribed: "reasonable time, place, and manner regulations are permissible, and a content-based prohibition must be narrowly drawn to effectuate a compelling state interest."[52] Finally, when a court determines that a public space falls under nonpublic forum guidelines because it is not, "by tradition or designation, a forum for public communication," the state has a lower burden to meet with regulating speech. Government regulations must only be reasonable, and "not an effort to suppress expression merely because public officials oppose the speaker's view." This is so because "[t]he State, no less than a private owner of property, has power to preserve the property under its control for the use to which it is lawfully dedicated."[53]

THE POLICYMAKING ROLE OF
FEDERAL DISTRICT COURTS

Scholars generally agree that district court outcomes—policy—are the product not only of the law, per se, in the form of higher court precedent, constitutional provisions, and federal statutes, but also of environmental concerns, in the form of the surrounding political and social climate within which a court operates. The literature on federal district court policymaking is vast, thus only the prominent studies are discussed in order to give a good, general view of their policymaking roles.

In his monumental study of federal district judges and desegregation litigation in the wake of *Brown v. Board of Education*, Jack Peltason addresses trial court policymaking directly in a very controversial and emotionally charged area of constitutional law.[54] Peltason demonstrates that district court policymaking in desegregation cases was affected by the political social contexts surrounding specific local desegregation disputes. Thus, "what happens in [trial] courtrooms will determine whether the Supreme Court's 1954 decision [in *Brown*] is promise or reality . . . the litigation before these judges cannot be isolated from its political context."[55] And, for Peltason, "the Constitution may be what the Supreme Court says it is, but a Supreme Court opinion means, for the moment at least, what the district judge says it means."[56] The political and social context surrounding a federal district court so affect its policymaking that, to a degree, it means that district judges have significant discretion in interpreting and applying the Constitution, and high court precedent, to the facts in a specific trial.

Federal district courts exist within a straightforward judicial hierarchy. District courts are trial courts, and are supervised by appellate circuit courts, and ultimately the Supreme Court. The Supreme Court of course is the highest appellate court, national in scope, whereas circuit courts are regionally organized and are expected to take a more regional approach to appeals and the development of the law. As the trial courts in the hierarchy, district courts are expected to be the most local in orientation, representing to a certain extent the local morays and politics of their specific districts. For Robert Carp and C. K. Rowland, district courts are "organizational anomalies. They are national institutions operating in and constrained by state and local environments."[57] As federal institutions district courts represent the interests of the national government. Still, the hierarchical and geographical ordering of the federal judiciary means that district courts are also predominantly local in outlook, and are only concerned with litigation from their specific district.[58] Indeed, "as federal judicial officials in a local setting they are required to respond to cases and controversies in their jurisdictions and to resolve controversial disputes between local majoritarian values and national, constitutional values."[59]

Trial courts resolve individualized disputes by interpreting and applying the law and by so doing "allocate social values and privilege." As Carp and Rowland note in more detail,

> When judges hear cases of first impression, they establish precedent, and in a common-law system this is the essence of policy formation. When opinions are codified and published, they become the rules of the litigation process. When trial judges apply general statutes to individual cases, they implement legislative policies . . . Judges even make policy when they are serving as "fact finders." When, for example, a district judge supervising mass-tort litigation finds that the "facts" of exposure justify the certification of a plaintiff class, he simultaneously initiates a sequence of value reallocations and establishes evidentiary criteria for analogous future cases.[60]

In allocating values through trial decisions, district courts largely depend upon appellate court precedent to guide their interpretation and application of the law. To that end, as Bradley C. Canon and Charles A. Johnson point out, district courts belong to the interpreting population in the judicial hierarchy charged with applying high court policies at the trial level.[61] The interpreting population essentially tells other parties such as the litigants what higher court decisions mean. As Canon and Johnson note, "judges are at the heart of the interpreting population," and their interpretation is authoritative and binding on other members of the same group. Trial courts comprise the most predominant aspect of the interpreting population, and lend stability and identifiability to the interpreting population. There is thus a very important relationship between lower trial courts and appellate courts, especially when trial courts are called upon to interpret and apply higher court decisions.

Many scholars are quick to note, however, that some areas of the law are "relatively free of clear, precise appellate court and legislative guidelines; and as a consequence the opportunity for trial court jurists to write on a clean slate, that is, to make policy, is formidable."[62] There is a plain relationship between the clarity of appellate court policy decisions and trial court discretion. Thus, for Carp and Rowland, "the discretion exercised by trial judges is a function of the quantity and precision of messages communicated to them by the appellate courts and particularly by the Supreme Court."[63] Kevin Lyles echoes this argument, noting that "given the broad formulations and resulting ambiguity that characterize most higher court rulings, especially those of the Supreme Court, the more numerous district judges are given considerable leeway and opportunity to interpret and apply higher court decisions to many cases, most of which are disposed in these lower courts."[64] Although district courts cannot be understood outside of the context of the appellate hierarchy, in the sense that they interpret and

6

32 THE BIBLE IN THE PARK

apply higher court policies, there is within that legal context significant leeway to study the various factors influencing how trial courts respond to upper court commands.

INTERPRETING AND CREATING THE PUBLIC SQUARE: FEDERAL DISTRICT COURTS, RELIGIOUS EXPRESSION, AND THE PUBLIC FORUM

Scholars of law and religion incessantly focus on Supreme Court policymaking, especially on how the Court develops and refines legal doctrine concerning religious liberty. To be sure, the Court's role in setting national policy under the First Amendment is extremely important. Its decisions on religious liberty and free speech are almost always final, and often clarify disagreements among lower circuit courts, and even district courts, as to how the Constitution should be interpreted. As the above discussion of federal district courts indicates, however, there is also good reason to study the dynamics of trial court policymaking in the context of religious liberty and free speech. Moreover, as the gatekeepers in the federal judicial hierarchy—courts of first instance—district courts must make policy by interpreting and applying high court policies. In deciding cases of first instance, district courts set the parameters for future appellate review of trial court policymaking. They are "formulating policy to guide other judges and . . . potential litigants."[65]

In the context of religious expression and public forums, and the ability of courts in general to create new mini public squares for debate and control the content within those public squares, it makes sense to describe and explain how district courts make policy in this growing area of litigation. The Supreme Court has, of course, decided a handful of disputes concerning religious expression and public forums, but through an even larger number of cases district courts have consistently developed policy in the area.[66] One result is that district courts have created more mini public squares open to public discourse of all kinds. Here, studying district court policymaking allows for larger scale analysis of litigation trends to demonstrate how cases develop and policy outcomes are decided, in order to pinpoint and analyze large-scale historical trends in litigation. Only by studying courts more broadly over time can trends be observed, and only district courts provide enough case studies that illustrate closely how litigants use public forum law to protect religious speech in the public square. District courts provide enough case activity so that the cumulative policymaking is observed. As Lynn Mather puts it in her study of trial courts, "the accumulation of similar individual decisions defines policy just as much as one major decision."[67] Importantly, too, district courts as the interpreting population can exercise an important policymaking role in creating and policing the content of new public squares. Charged with applying appellate court policy at the trial level, as Canon and Johnson demonstrate above, district courts often have an important ability to mold and shape the development of the law at the outset, prior to any appellate review.

CHAPTER 2

Hamlet without the Prince:
Religious Speech and the Supreme Court

WHEN THE KU KLUX KLAN sought an official permit to place an unattended Christian cross in the plaza surrounding the Ohio statehouse, it met stiff resistance. The Capitol Square Review and Advisory Board determines who can access the plaza for expressive purposes, and it denied the KKK's request. For the board, granting access for the Klan's religious message—in the form of the unattended cross—would be construed as government endorsement of religion and thus an infringement of the Establishment Clause of the First Amendment. The typical passerby, as this argument goes, would view the cross and conclude that the Ohio government had either placed it in the plaza, or supported it being there, and thereby directly or indirectly supported its religious message. Ironically, the KKK had been granted access to the plaza to hold political rallies on several prior occasions, indicating that at least its *political* speech was protected in the public square. The review board seemed to discriminate against the KKK's Christian cross display too, as it had previously allowed the display of menorahs, Christmas trees, and other unattended displays.

The KKK sued in federal district court and won an injunction ordering the board to allow its cross into the public forum. The

Sixth Circuit affirmed the lower court's decision, and Ohio appealed to the Supreme Court for final review, contending that the cross display violates the Establishment Clause. The KKK ultimately won its case, and by a 7:2 vote the Court sustained the district court's original grant of access to the capitol plaza. Since the Ku Klux Klan was engaged in private religious expression, the majority reasoned that the board's denial of access to the public plaza was viewpoint discrimination, and the Klan's religious speech was limited solely because the board did not like the substance of its message.

Writing for the Court, Justice Scalia articulates a forceful statement of religious speech in the First Amendment.

> Our precedent establishes that private religious speech, far from being a First Amendment orphan, is as fully protected under the Free Speech Clause as secular private expression . . . Indeed, in Anglo-American history, at least, government suppression of speech has so commonly been directed precisely at religious speech that a Free Speech Clause without religion would be *Hamlet* without the prince.[1]

Protecting religious speech in theory is one thing. Actually determining *when* religious speech is allowable, and under *what* circumstances, are different concerns altogether. The other justices on the Court probably share Justice Scalia's view of religious speech as akin to private speech and therefore entitled to the full force of First Amendment protections. Yet, as the Court's policymaking makes very clear, there is often significant disagreement among the justices about when and under what circumstances religious speech is allowable in public squares and forums. Indeed, the Court has not maintained a consistent approach to religious speech claims, and its policymaking in this area of the law tends to be less predictable than Justice Scalia's strongly worded statement indicates. It is fair to say that the Court is often unable to articulate clear policy guidelines for lower federal courts, with consequent ramifications for lower trial court policymaking. Since the policy cues that the Court sends to lower federal district courts are not always clear, lower district courts engage in a much more prominent type of policymaking in which the surrounding political and social contexts of litigation become extremely influential. The less clear the guidelines from the Supreme Court, the easier it is for trial courts to make policy independent of high court precedent, and thus the greater the influence of the context surrounding district court litigation on case outcomes.

The following discussion of Supreme Court cases concerning religious expression and public forums reveals the main principles of public forum law and religious speech that lower district courts are expected to interpret and apply in litigation. The main points of disagreement within the Court are also highlighted to show how its policies are so often ambiguous. When the two-part process of policymaking in public forum cases is considered, the Court's inability to define clear guidelines for lower courts is all the more apparent. The Court's policies on the *contours* of public forums—how they are defined, their spatial and geographical dimensions, and so forth—are seemingly based on clear, workable principles established in prior decisions as demonstrated by the case *Perry Education Association v. Perry Local Educator's Association* in 1983.[2] *Perry* is considered by judges and legal scholars to be the summarizing precedent for public forum doctrine, a view supported by Justice Kennedy who notes that public forum doctrine "was not stated with much precision or elaboration . . . until our more recent decisions" in *Perry* and *Cornelius v. NAACP Legal Defense & Educational Fund.*[3] However, *Perry*'s run as a concise statement of public forum principles lasted less than a decade. In *ISKCON v. Lee*, a public forum case involving Hare Krishna solicitations at crowded airports, the Court was divided over the proper inquiry for defining public forums, indicating that its doctrine concerning the contours of forums is not well settled after all.[4]

Linked with the question of the spatial and physical dimensions of the forum is the issue of the forum's substance. When the Court attends to the content of public forums, in order to determine when and under what circumstances religious speech can be regulated, it again is often unable to define clear-cut policies that can be applied by lower courts. Governments are wary of allowing religious speech into public places due to the potential problems associated with government endorsement of religious messages and conduct. Thus, when faced with content-related questions, courts regularly confront the argument that the Establishment Clause prohibits religious speech in certain public spaces, and in a sense controls the content of that space. Whether the Establishment Clause and the threat of government endorsement of religion are a bar to religious speech in public forums has been roundly addressed by the Court in a very inconsistent manner.

FIRST, TO THE FORUM!

Hague v. CIO is considered the forerunner of public forum law, and sets the foundation for the Court's development of the law altogether. In *Hague*, several individuals and an unincorporated labor union were denied permission by city officials in Jersey City, New Jersey, to hold lawful meetings to discuss the National Labor Relations Act, and many were arrested for distributing material pertinent to their labor cause. The Court determined that the city ordinances and conduct in question violated the petitioners' First Amendment rights, and thus were void. For our purposes here, though, *Hague* is important as the genesis of public forum law. Justice Reed, highly critical of how the Jersey City officials interfered with the labor union's right to assemble and engage in expressive conduct, noted that certain public properties have "immemorially been held in trust for the use of the public" to address and debate political issues. Moreover, the First Amendment confers a broad right to access public spaces for speech-related activities, although Reed is quick to note that right is "not absolute, but relative, and must be exercised . . . in consonance with peace and good order."[5] In Justice Reed's terms, certain public spaces are held by the government as a public trust, and are historically and customarily devoted to the free exchange of ideas on public issues. Access to these public spaces could be regulated by the government as long as the purpose of the forum—political discussion—remained intact and the right to free speech was not abridged. Reed's "sweeping dictum" set the stage for the development of public forum law, and in *Perry* the Court articulated concisely what that law was. There were, of course, several public forum disputes between *Hague* in 1938 and *Perry* in 1983. However, *Perry* was the first case to synthesize existing law into a workable precedent, thus it represents the Court's consensus on the means of defining public forums in general.

Perry concerned a labor dispute in a public school, and whether a rival teachers' union could use an internal public school mail system, even though the school's collective bargaining agreement with another union prohibited it. The Court used *Perry* to clarify its public forum jurisprudence, and noted that the right to access public property for speech related activities depends on the *character* of that property.

In places which, by long tradition or by government fiat, have been devoted to assembly and debate, the rights of the State to limit expressive activity are sharply circumscribed. At one end of the spectrum are streets and parks, which have immemorially been held in trust for the use of the public and, time out of mind, have been used for purposes of assembly, communicating thoughts between citizens, and discussing public questions. In these quintessential public forums, the government may not prohibit all communicative activity. For the State to enforce a content-based exclusion, it must show that its regulation is necessary to serve a compelling state interest and that it is narrowly drawn to achieve that end. The State may also enforce regulations of the time, place, and manner of expression which are content-neutral, are narrowly tailored to serve a significant government interest, and leave open ample alternative channels of communication.

A second category consists of public property which the State has opened for use by the public as a place for expressive activity . . . Although a State is not required to indefinitely retain the open character of the facility, as long as it does so, it is bound by the same standards as apply in a traditional public forum. Reasonable time, place, and manner regulations are permissible, and a content-based prohibition must be narrowly drawn to effectuate a compelling state interest.

Public property which is not, by tradition or designation, a forum for public communication is governed by different standards. We have recognized that the "First Amendment does not guarantee access to property simply because it is owned or controlled by the government." In addition to time, place, and manner regulations, the State may reserve the forum for its intended purposes, communicative or otherwise, as long as the regulation on speech is reasonable and not an effort to suppress expression merely because public officials oppose the speaker's view.[6]

With *Perry*, the Court defined three types of forums: traditional forums historically open to the public, limited forums opened by the government for specific purposes, and nonforums, which are public property not generally open to speech activities. This concise statement of the law seems to indicate that public forum doctrine was well settled by 1983, and categorizing public spaces under forum analysis simply meant that judges assess the historical and customary usage of the property, its physical characteristics, and other objective issues, and thereby fit the property into one of the three categories.

However, *Perry's* consensus broke apart in *ISKCON v. Lee* in 1992.[7] *Lee* concerned whether Hare Krishnas could practice *sankirtan*—a religiously motivated form of ambulatory solicitation—at airports owned by the Port Authority of New York and New Jersey. JFK, La Guardia, and Newark airports, all owned and operated by the Port Authority, prohibited the repetitive solicitation of money or distribution of literature within their terminals. The Krishnas sued, contending that the terminals are public forums and thus open to their religiously motivated expressive conduct. As Chief Justice Rehnquist pointed out, one of the main questions in *Lee* concerns whether the public properties are forums open to expression. Both parties in the dispute agreed that forum analysis, defined by *Perry*, should govern the Court's decision. They disagreed on how *Perry's* framework should be applied. For the Court, Chief Justice Rehnquist determined that the terminals were not public forums open to expression: "the tradition of airport activity does not demonstrate that airports have historically been made available for speech activity. Nor can we say that these particular terminals, or airport terminals generally, have been intentionally opened by their operators to such activity. . . . In short, there can be no argument that society's time-tested judgment, expressed through acquiescence in a continuing practice, has resolved the issue in petitioner's favor."[8] Additionally, airport terminals are often owned by public authorities (unlike bus and train stations), and are usually managed to generate profits and revenues for their operating expenses. For instance, airports often lease out commercial space to restaurants, bars, and shops for revenue purposes. Thus, airports are commercial establishments for the "facilitation of passenger air travel, not the promotion of expression."[9] For the majority, the Port Authority's ban on solicitations and the distribution of literature was reasonable in light of its need to maintain the orderly flow of air travelers and others throughout crowded terminals, and to cut down on fraudulent solicitations that might be compounded by the "duress" that air travelers are often under.

The Court's final vote was 6:3. Justice Kennedy concurred that Krishna speech could be regulated as an allowable time, place, and manner type regulation of expressive activity, especially in the context of a crowded and congested airport. Kennedy disagreed, though, with the majority's application of public forum doctrine, and was joined by Justices Stevens, Souter, and Blackmun. Their main point of contention was that the majority viewed public forum doctrine too categorically and simplistically, and placed most of the airport spaces in question outside of public forum doctrine altogether, thereby closing them off to expressive activity. For Kennedy, the Court's analysis should be more discerning. For example, the secure areas of the airports can be considered nonpublic forums, but the areas where shops and other passenger conveniences are located should be public forums open to expressive activity. In addition, the majority on the Court ignore the fundamental tenet of public forum analysis that starts its inquiry from the speaker's point of view, not from the government's desire to limit expression. Since public forum scrutiny developed to define "an analysis protective of expression," the Court's reading and application of public forum doctrine in *Lee* is too narrow, and basically "grants the government authority to restrict speech by fiat."[10] As Kennedy finally put it, the Court changes the mode of forum analysis in *Lee* by basing public forum doctrine on either the *absence* of government regulation of speech in the case of traditional forums, or the government allowance of speech in the case of a designated forum. By so doing, the Court switches public forum inquiry from the standpoint of the speaker with its attention to the free speech rights of individuals to a focus grounded in the government's ownership and dominion over its own property (or the people's property).

The starting point for public forum analysis, for Justice Kennedy, is based on the First Amendment foundations of public forum doctrine that view public property in terms of its capacity for speech. The *Lee* majority neglected that main principle, however, and as a result allowed government more leeway to control the speech within its property, and thus the content of expression in public places. In his words, "The Court ignores the fact that the purpose of the public forum doctrine is to give effect to the broad command of the First Amendment to protect speech from governmental interference. The jurisprudence is rooted in historic practice, but it is not tied to a narrow textual command limiting the recognition of new forums." To be sure, Kennedy suggests that the Court is too narrow in its determination of what counts as a forum open to speech, and what does not. The Court should recognize "that open, public spaces and thoroughfares which are suitable for discourse may be public forums, whatever their historical pedigree and without concern for a precise classification of the property. . . . Our failure to recognize the possibility that new types of government property may be appropriate forums for speech will lead to a serious curtailment of our expressive activity."[11] For Kennedy, then, the majority takes too literally the forum typologies in *Perry* and other cases. The categorical approach used to classify public spaces into three distinct types—traditional forum, designated forum, and nonforum—is applied in too limiting a manner, and in the process the Court loses sight of the original purpose of public forum doctrine in protecting the rights of assembly, speech and press. Under Justice Kennedy's approach, the Court should especially broaden its doctrine on traditional public forums to include any open spaces and thoroughfares through which the public travels. Not to do so locks public forum doctrine into a very limited, narrow, and rigid view of public property and the public square in general.

Justice Kennedy's criticisms of the narrow application of public forum doctrine in *Lee* indicate a divisive split among the justices on how public forums should be defined. Thus, any consensus that existed with *Perry's* concise categorization of public spaces is jeopardized by this disagreement over how public forum categories expand and evolve to take account of new developments in the law or new places where litigants engage in religiously motivated speech and expression. Kennedy's opinion raises a significant question, then, in terms of the ability of current public forum categories, defined in *Perry*, to take account of new types of forums as they arise. To determine that all public properties and squares devoted to expressive activity fit within the categories of traditional, designated, or nonforums, belies the fact that litigants seek new outlets for their religious speech. Thus, public squares as forums evolve and change, and Kennedy perhaps shows the difficulty the Court faces in applying rigid categories to new types of spaces.[12]

WORSHIP OR ENDORSEMENT? RELIGIOUS SPEECH CONFLICTS WITH THE FIRST AMENDMENT

The Court's policymaking on whether public spaces meet the requirements of traditional, designated, or nonforum spaces is seemingly straightforward. Justice Kennedy's concurrence in *Lee*, joined by three other justices, indicates that the neat framework for categorizing forums posed by *Perry* is not so tidy after all. The same can be said for the Court's policies in defining the appropriate *content* of public spaces. It evidences no clearer policymaking role in the latter analysis than in the former. Indeed, the Court's content policymaking is fraught with strong disagreement among the justices over the proper and allowable limits on religious speech in the public square. Such disagreement was evident with the first cases concerning religious expression in public places, most of which centered on attempts by Jehovah's Witnesses to proselytize and solicit donations for their version of the Gospel. There are several cases concerning the attempts of the Witnesses to proselytize, solicit donations, and distribute religious literature in violation of state and local ordinances regulating such activities in general, and to be sure the Court initially viewed their conduct negatively and allowed local and state governments to regulate and punish it. However, the Court did change its mind early on, thus setting the stage for further development of the links between religious speech and public forum doctrine.

For instance, in *Jones v. Opelika* the Court sustained the convictions of several Witnesses who violated a municipal ordinance requiring payment of a licensing tax for all engaged in house to house canvassing to distribute and sell books.[13] The majority opinion, written by Justice Reed, indicates that the right to proselytize and evangelize is protected by the First Amendment, but not in absolute terms. "The proponents of ideas cannot determine entirely for themselves the time and place and manner for the diffusion of knowledge or for their evangelism, any more than the civil authorities may hamper or suppress the public dissemination of facts and principles by the people."[14] Moreover, the licensing tax was a valid exercise of local government power, and "when proponents of religious or social theories use the ordinary commercial methods of sales of articles to raise propaganda funds, it is a natural and proper exercise of the power of the state to charge reasonable fees for the privilege of canvassing."[15] Deference to state and local governments controlled the majority decision, and for the Court to interfere with the basic taxing and spending powers of local governments threatened the federal/state relationship in the Constitution itself. Even more, "it may well be that the wisdom of American communities will persuade them to permit the poor and weak to draw support from the petty sales of religious books without contributing anything for the privilege of using the streets and conveniences of the municipality. Such an exemption, however, would be a voluntary, not a constitutionally enforced, contribution." Thus, there would be no religious exemption from license taxes for those engaged in the distribution of religious literature unless the local majority specifically granted it.

Jones was a very divided opinion though. Four justices dissented on the grounds that the licensing tax interferes with the dissemination of ideas, especially religious ideas, and is unconstitutional as applied to the Jehovah's Witnesses. *Jones* was overturned less than a year later by *Murdock v. Pennsylvania* and *Jones v. Opelika II*. The dissent from *Jones I* basically became the majority opinion in *Murdock* and *Jones II*. That the Court vacillated over whether the conduct of the Witnesses was protected under the First Amendment is standard ground, and need not be discussed here.[16] The following cases concerning the Jehovah's Witnesses and their conflicts between their religious speech and state and local laws are included for discussion because they clearly demonstrate the tensions inherent in religious speech and public forum cases, and serve as an excellent backdrop for understanding the Court's development of the law.

One early example from 1938, *Schneider v. New Jersey*, concerned a Jehovah's Witness who was canvassing and proselytizing house to house in Irvington, New Jersey. She was convicted under a town ordinance for canvassing without a permit. The Court invalidated the ordinance under the First Amendment, and noted that "although a municipality may enact regulations in the interest of the public safety, health, welfare or convenience, these may not abridge the individual liberties secured by the Constitution to those who wish to speak, write, print or circulate information or opinion."[17] Since "pamphlets have proved most effective instruments in the dissemination of opinion," and "the most effective way of bringing them to the notice of individuals is their distribution at the homes of the people," the Court reasoned that Schneider's canvassing of private homes to distribute literature was protected under the First Amendment.[18]

The Court focused on the discretionary nature of the town's permit process. When an individual applied for a canvassing permit, the police retained almost complete discretion to grant or deny it. As the Court noted, such broad discretion to deny expressive conduct is a form of censorship, and thus violates the First Amendment since it grants "a discretion in the police to say some ideas may, while others may not, be carried to the homes of citizens."[19] In *Schneider*, and in similar cases, the Court concentrated on how and why officials controlled access to forums through licensing schemes, permitting requirements, or even the imposition of taxes. By concentrating on access permissions, the Court was less concerned with the tangible, spatial dimensions of the forum, and similarly less focused on its actual content. It was primarily concerned with who grants access to the forum, and on what grounds.

Other Jehovah's Witness cases illustrate how the Court linked religiously motivated expression with broader protections for free speech under the First Amendment, and further developed the circumstances under which religious speech is allowable in the public square. In *Lovell v. City of Griffin*, for example, Alma Lovell was convicted of violating a town ordinance that prohibited leafleting without a permit. Lovell refused to apply for a permit, since "she regarded herself as sent 'by Jehovah to do His work,' and that such an application would have been an act of disobedience to His commandment."[20] The Court struck the ordinance down as unconstitutional, noting that "the liberty of the press is not confined to newspapers and periodicals. It necessarily embraces pamphlets and leaflets."[21] Thus, *Lovell* establishes a right to distribute religious tracts under the Free Press Clause of the First Amendment.

To be sure, in certain cases the Court did limit the speech and conduct of Jehovah's Witnesses. In *Cox v. New Hampshire* the Court sustained the conviction of several Witnesses for holding a parade without a permit,[22] and in *Chaplinsky v. New Hampshire* the Court articulated its famous "fighting words" doctrine and again upheld a Jehovah's Witness's conviction for using offensive and derisive speech.[23] In *Prince v. Massachusetts* the Court refused to allow a child member of the Witnesses to distribute literature in contravention of child labor laws, indicating that even though adult Witnesses have a right to bring children up within the tenets of their faith, the children do not have the same rights as adults to preach and disseminate the gospel.[24] Yet, the main trend of the Witnesses cases ran in favor of protecting religious speech, a trend the Court made quite clear in subsequent cases.

Murdock v. Pennsylvania serves best to demonstrate how the Court began to view religious speech.[25] Here, the town of Jennette, Pennsylvania, imposed a flat license tax on people who sought to solicit money for goods or services. As the municipality saw it, the tax primarily regulated commercial conduct, and since the

Jehovah's Witnesses are often engaged in soliciting money for religious tracts, they too had to pay it. The Court disagreed, with Justice Douglas contending for the majority that distributing literature by hand is vital to how the Witnesses perceive their own religious obligations. As Douglas put it, the Witnesses "claim to follow the example of Paul, teaching 'publickly, and from house to house.' They take literally the mandate of the Scriptures, 'Go ye into all the world, and preach the gospel to every creature.' In doing so, they believe that they are obeying a commandment of God." Their "age-old" evangelism is, for Douglas, a form of expressive activity that "occupies the same high estate under the First Amendment as do worship in the churches and preaching from the pulpits. It has the same claim to protection as the more orthodox and conventional exercises of religion. It also has the same claim as the others to the guarantees of freedom of speech and freedom of the press."[26]

The Court in *Murdock* squarely announced that religiously motivated expression retains a higher protection under the First Amendment. Notably, that protection stems from the Free Speech and Press Clauses, as well as the Free Exercise Clause. Controversially, though, the majority effectively created a religious exemption from commercial licensing taxes, thus those engaged in religiously motivated conduct such as the solicitation of money for religious literature may be exempt from similar flat-tax laws that regulate commercial activity.

The Court adhered to Douglas's *Murdock* reasoning in *Niemotko v. Maryland*, which concerned whether Jehovah's Witnesses could hold a Bible study in a public park without a permit, even though there was no ordinance or regulation requiring a permit for usage of the park in any capacity. Permits had customarily been sought by those wanting to hold gatherings in the park, and were normally granted by municipal authorities. The Jehovah's Witnesses were an exception, though, and their request for a permit was denied. They opted to hold their Bible service in the park anyway. The Court overturned their subsequent conviction for disorderly conduct, stipulating that "the use of the park was denied because of the City Council's dislike for . . . the Witnesses or their views. The right to equal protection of the laws, in the exercise of those freedoms of speech and religion protected by the First and Fourteenth Amendments, has a firmer foundation than the whims or personal opinions of a local governing body."[27] Again, the Court's primary concern is how local authorities use discretion in granting or denying permits to public places. Here, a permit was denied the Witnesses simply because their message was disliked and unwanted. Justice Frankfurter noted "the State cannot, of course, forbid public proselyting or religious argument merely because public officials disapprove the speaker's views. It must act in patent good faith to maintain the public peace . . . or for equally indispensable ends of modern community life."[28]

The Court's jurisprudence, developed in the context of the Jehovah's Witness litigation, indicates a strong tendency on the part of the justices to view religiously motivated expression in line with private expression in general, and thus deserving of First Amendment protection. Public proselytizing, evangelism, preaching, worship services in public, and the distribution of religious tracts are all forms of expressive conduct under the First Amendment. Yet, there is a strand of dissent running through many of the Jehovah's Witnesses cases, most of which centers on deference to state and local officials in controlling access to public spaces.

A prime example to return to is *Murdock v. Pennsylvania*. In overturning the convictions of the Jehovah's Witnesses for soliciting without a permit, Justice Douglas argued that their conduct was protected under the Free Speech, Free Press, and Free Exercise Clauses and the fee-based permits—basically taxes—served to interfere with the exercise of those rights by being "taxes on knowledge."[29] For the *Murdock* majority, religiously motivated

expression is exempt from taxes on its distribution. Justices Reed
and Frankfurter, joined by Justice Jackson, strongly dissented from
Douglas's majority view. For Justice Reed, the issue is one of taxation, not First Amendment freedoms: "it will be observed that
there is no suggestion of freedom from taxation, and this statement is equally true of the other state constitutional provisions. It
may be concluded that neither in the state or the federal constitutions was general taxation of church or press interdicted."[30] Further, the Court granted a tax exemption to Jehovah's Witnesses for
proselytical purposes that had no grounding in its prior doctrine.
As Justice Reed explained, "is there anything in the decisions of
this Court which indicates that church or press is free from the financial burdens of government? We find nothing. Religious soci-
eties depend for their exemptions from taxation upon state
constitutions or general statutes, not upon the Federal Constitution."[31] The real issue for the Court, according to Reed, is the taxing authority of municipalities, and by implication states.
Religious expression was important, to be sure, but it had to be
balanced with the traditional regulatory functions of local governments. In his terms, the Court should be deferential to state and
local governments on this issue: "Whatever exemptions exist from
taxation arise from the prevailing law of the various states."[32]
Thus, the "withdrawal of the power of taxation over the distribution activities of those covered by the First Amendment fixes . . .
an unfortunate principle of tax exemption, capable of indefinite
extension."[33] As well, municipalities will be burdened by this new
tax exemption, as "the distributors of religious literature, possibly
of all informatory publications, become today privileged to carry
on their occupations without contributing their share to the support of the government which provides the opportunity for the exercise of their liberties."[34] By crafting an exemption to a license
fee, or tax, on the distribution of "informatory publications," the
Court interfered with the basic regulatory functions of states and

local governments. Since there was no specific grant of a tax exemption in the Constitution, the matter was best left to other sub-
divisions in our federal system.

Justice Frankfurter reiterated Justice Reed's argument of deference to local authorities in matters of taxation. For Frankfurter,
the Jehovah's Witnesses were literally availing themselves of a
government forum without paying for its upkeep. By not contributing to government coffers through the fee-based permit system, the Witnesses were placing an extra burden on the
government's financial ability to regulate and police the public
square. As he put it, local governments have an interest in maintaining the public peace, safety of the roadways, and public health.
These benefits of government cost money, however, and Frankfurter pointed out that the Jehovah's Witnesses receive these same
benefits as do other citizens. Indeed, "There is nothing in the
Constitution which exempts persons engaged in religious activities from sharing equally in the costs of benefits to all, including
themselves, provided by government."[35]

The Court's early review of religious expression and public
forum cases focused on the powers of local (or state) authorities in
controlling access to public forums, and it thus makes sense that
disagreements about the Court's developing jurisprudence that
protected religious expression centered on access-related issues
such as official discretion in granting permits, or fee-based permits
as a way to control and fund the forum. Justices Frankfurter and
Reed were not the only ones to dissent and defer to local and state
government decisions on forum access. Other examples come from
Justices Jackson and Roberts. Justice Jackson's dissenting opinion
in *Douglas v. City of Jeanette*, a companion case to *Murdock*, considered the activity of the Witnesses in going house to house to
proselytize as an especially aggressive type of religious expression
that often interferes with the homeowner's expectation of privacy.
He noted that most of the cases arise out of smaller communities

where people may simply be more polite and thus compelled to answer the door and engage strangers that seek their attention. For Jackson, then, the issue in *Murdock* and *Douglas* is the intensity with which the Witnesses pursue their religious expression and not the conflict between that expression and municipal regulations. In Jackson's view, the Jehovah's Witnesses are almost a nuisance: "For a stranger to corner a man in his home, summon him to the door, and put him in the position either of arguing his religion or of ordering one of unknown disposition to leave is a questionable use of religious freedom." As Jackson further explained, the Witnesses often place local authorities in a difficult position, "caught between the offended householders and the drive of the Witnesses," and to be sure the Court's jurisprudence made it difficult for local governments to maintain the public peace within their jurisdictions. In fact, for Jackson, by protecting the right of the Witnesses to proselytize the Court "tied the hands of all local authority, and made the aggressive methods of this group the law of the land."[36]

Murdock was followed by *Follett v. Town of McCormick*, a case in which the Court struck down a local ordinance taxing street vending as it applied to Jehovah's Witnesses.[37] As the majority noted, the tax on the evangelical activities of the Witnesses was no different from a tax on a preacher in a pulpit. The First Amendment would certainly not allow a tax on preaching, and neither does it allow a tax on the worship and proselytical activities of the Witnesses. Justice Roberts forcefully dissented from the six-justice opinion, though, and as with Justices Frankfurter and Jackson articulated a deference based argument. In his words,

Follett is not made to pay a tax for the exercise of that which the First Amendment has relieved from taxation. He is made to pay for that for which all others similarly situated must pay—an excise for the occupation of street vending. Follett asks exemption because street vending is, for him, also part of his religion. As a result, Follett will enjoy a subsidy for his religion. He will save the contribution for the cost of government which everyone else will have to pay.[38]

Justice Roberts read *Murdock* as applying to itinerant evangelists, whereas *Follett* concerned an evangelist who lives in the same locale in which he seeks to convert others. The license tax in *Murdock* fell heavily on those simply passing through a town with little interest in its upkeep, whereas *Follett* presented the issue of a citizen of town seeking as exemption from paying for the services that he consumes on a consistent basis. Roberts also raised a broader issue that extends beyond judicial deference to local governments on taxing issues by noting that the Court is basically granting religiously based exemptions from local regulatory laws on an ad hoc basis, and as an institution it simply is not equipped for the task. Thus, the Court runs the risk of stating that some religious activity is protected and exempted, but other activity is not: "Multiple activities by which citizens earn their bread may, with equal propriety, be denominated an exercise of religion, as may preaching or selling religious tracts. Certainly this court cannot say that one activity is the exercise of religion and the other is not. The materials for judicial distinction do not exist." The Court, for Roberts, is simply incapable of properly defining which religiously motivated activities are exempted from regulatory statutes, as in *Murdock* and *Follett*, and which are not. And to grant such exemptions to one faith essentially entitles its believers "to be free of contribution to the cost of government" even though others of different faiths still must shoulder the burden.[39]

In reviewing the free speech, press, and religious exercise claims of the Jehovah's Witnesses from the late 1930s to the early 1950s, the Court primarily focused on the use of official discretion in controlling access to public spaces where the Witnesses could engage in their evangelical and preaching activities. As Justice Vinson made clear in *Kunz v. New York*, the Court's main point of inquiry concerned "licensing systems which vest in an administrative official discretion to grant or withhold a permit upon broad criteria unrelated to proper regulation of public places."[40] Inconsistencies in the Court's approach to how and why officials controlled access to public spaces are quite evident, and indeed the Court did not resolve these inconsistencies within its doctrine, nor did it attempt to do so. However, when the Court chose to revisit issues arising out of cases concerning religious speech in public forums three decades after *Kunz* and *Niemotko*, both in 1951, the focus of its review no longer dealt with official discretion in granting access, but instead concerned the basic contours of public spaces, as forums, and their content.

It was not until *ISKCON v. Heffron* and *Widmar v. Vincent*, both in 1981, that the Court entertained other public forum cases concerning religious speech. To be sure, there were several public forum cases between 1950 and 1980, but all concerned either political speech or labor-related speech, such as in *Perry*. In revisiting the linkage between religious speech and public forums in *Heffron* and *Widmar* the Court indicated it would devote attention to such disputes, and indeed similar cases have consistently been on its docket since 1981. However, both cases also showed that disagreement among the justices shifted from the split over the appropriate amount of deference for local authorities in controlling access to public spaces to completely new disputes that concerned the content of speech and expression within specific forums. Generally speaking, the Court is most divided over the appropriate content for public forums, with much of that division centering on the precise nature of religious speech, for instance whether it merely seeks to inform, or actually seeks to convert others. As well, several justices focus on arguments about whether the government, by allowing religious speech in public spaces, runs the risk of endorsing that speech and thus violating the Establishment Clause in the First Amendment. In this respect, *Widmar* is instructive as it demonstrates the pressures and tensions that the current Court faces with religious speech and public forum disputes. In *Widmar v. Vincent,* a public university, the University of Missouri at Kansas City, made its facilities available to registered student groups for meetings and other types of gatherings. The university prohibited the use of its buildings and grounds for the purposes of religious worship or training, thus religiously oriented student groups were often denied access to meeting rooms and other areas generally available to secular student organizations. One evangelical Christian group, Cornerstone, was denied access to university facilities to hold its meetings for over four years, and ultimately sued the university in order to use its facilities like any secular student group could. By a vote of 8:1 the Supreme Court struck down the university's blanket ban on worship-related activities as an unconstitutional content limit on speech. As Justice Powell writes for the Court,

> The University's institutional mission, which it describes as providing a "secular education" to its students . . . does not exempt its actions from constitutional scrutiny. With respect to persons entitled to be there, our cases leave no doubt that the First Amendment rights of speech and association extend to the campuses of state universities. . . . Here, UMKC has discriminated against student groups and speakers based on their desire to use a generally open forum to engage in religious worship and discussion. These are forms of speech and association protected by the First Amendment.[41]

The university defended its policy by arguing that avoiding an Establishment Clause violation, or endorsement of religion, was compelling enough to justify the ban on religious speech. The Court disagreed, however, and found no violation of the clause under the controlling precedent *Lemon v. Kurtzman*. The Court and the university focused mainly on the "primary effect" prong of the *Lemon* test, with the Court noting that "we are not oblivious to the range of an open forum's likely effects. It is possible—perhaps even foreseeable—that religious groups will benefit from access to university facilities. But this Court has explained that a religious organization's enjoyment of merely 'incidental' benefits does not violate the prohibition against the 'primary advancement' of religion."[42] For the Court, then, opening university facilities to religious groups would not advance religion in any major sense even though religious groups such as Cornerstone would place religious messages in the government-maintained public square. Its decision in *Widmar*, as the Court also noted, should be viewed narrowly. Thus, the university still has considerable leeway in creating reasonable time, place, and manner restrictions on the content of its forums, and the Court does not question "the right of the University to make academic judgments as to how best to allocate scarce resources" or determine "who may teach, what may be taught, how it shall be taught, and who may be admitted to study."[43] Deference to the university's academic mission does not preclude judicial inquiry into how and why it limits access to its facilities. For the Court, "having created a forum generally open to student groups, the university seeks to enforce a content-based exclusion of religious speech. Its exclusionary policy violates the fundamental principle that a state regulation of speech should be content-neutral" and not based on the underlying content, or substance, of the speech and expression at issue.

The Court revisited the issue of public forums in the context of public education in *Board of Education v. Mergens*, and this time the justices were more divided over the conflict between religious speech and the Establishment Clause's prohibition against endorsement of religion. *Widmar* concerned a public university, where presumably the students were better educated, more mature, and thus capable of distinguishing between religious group usage of public facilities and the government's endorsement of that group's message. That is, university students would not infer from a religious group's use of the public square that the government actually endorsed or supported its message. *Mergens* is different since it concerns a public high school's denial of access to its facilities to a student-run Christian group engaging in Bible study and other worship activities.[44] Whether high school students could differentiate religious group usage from government endorsement was a fundamental disagreement among lower courts, and something the Supreme Court had to address.

The school allowed "curriculum related" student groups to use its facilities, but denied access to religious groups in general. Members of the Christian group sued, contending that since the school opened a "limited public forum," it could not deny access based on the content of the group's speech. Moreover, the new Equal Access Act, passed by Congress in 1984, granted a statutory right of access to public schools for religious groups, provided certain guidelines are met.[45] A very divided Court decided the case on statutory grounds and affirmed the right of the religious student group to use school facilities that were generally open and available, as part of a larger policy, to other student groups. The school raised an Establishment Clause defense to the statute, however, and argued that by allowing religious group access, the school will "effectively incorporate religious activities into the school's official program, endorse participation in the religious club, and provide the club with an official platform to proselytize other students."[46] Four of the justices addressed the Establishment Clause defense, with Justice O'Connor contending

> There is a crucial difference between government speech en-
> dorsing religion, which the Establishment Clause forbids,
> and private speech endorsing religion, which the Free Speech
> and Free Exercise Clauses protect. We think that secondary
> school students are mature enough and are likely to under-
> stand that a school does not endorse or support student
> speech that it merely permits on a nondiscriminatory
> basis. . . . The proposition that schools do not endorse every-
> thing they fail to censor is not complicated.[47]

Importantly, Justice O'Connor highlights the value of private religious expression in the context of secondary schools, and further
points out that just because a school allows student-initiated religious expression (at the appropriate times and places, to be sure),
it does not mean or imply that the school in any way endorses the
message. Thus, Justice O'Connor significantly severs a school's
grant of access to religious expression from that school's endorsement of the religious message.

That only a plurality of justices agreed with Justice O'Connor's
analysis of the Establishment Clause issue demonstrates the degree
of disagreement within the Court. Justice Kennedy, for one, argues
that the Court applies the wrong Establishment Clause test. The
Court should use an establishment standard based on whether the
law is neutral and noncoercive. Since the Equal Access Act does
not grant "direct benefits to religion," and does not coerce "any
student to participate in a religious activity," it is neutral under Establishment Clause doctrine. In Kennedy's view, the Court relies
on the endorsement test for deciding the issue, and applies the
wrong standard. Justice Marshall, like Justice Kennedy, concurs,
but writes separately to point out that the school in *Mergens* must
take affirmative steps to avoid Establishment Clause problems associated with religious speech in public high schools. For Marshall, the Court should inquire into the "nature and function" of

student clubs at Westside, and must ensure that the school's policy is not one that endorses the religious message of those clubs. "Although a school may permissibly encourage its students to become well-rounded as student-athletes, student-musicians, and student-tutors," as Marshall points out, "the Constitution forbids schools to encourage students to become well-rounded as student-worshippers."[48]

Although willing to sustain the application of the Equal Access Act to the facts in *Mergens*, Justice Marshall indicates some troubling aspects of the law as written. By simply allowing religious student groups access to secondary school facilities generally open to other student groups, the statute ignores that schools may operate different types of forums. As Marshall points out, the high school in *Mergens* does not allow student groups that represent "controversial viewpoints" to use its facilities, and the groups that do meet at school are, in a sense, viewpoint free. Thus, the religious group seeking access is different than the other groups in kind and degree. For Marshall, then,

> If the religion club is the sole advocacy-oriented group in the forum, or one of a very limited number, and the school continues to promote its student-club program as instrumental to citizenship, then the school's failure to disassociate itself from the religious activity will reasonably be understood as an endorsement of that activity. That political and other advocacy-oriented groups are permitted to participate in a forum that, through school support and encouragement, is devoted to fostering a student's civic identity does not ameliorate the appearance of school endorsement unless the invitation is accepted and the forum is transformed into a forum like that in *Widmar*.[49]

Justice Marshall thus raises a very significant point that conflicts with the plurality's vision of public forums. The Mergens forum is different from that in Widmar, as it is more limited in the types of messages present. The university forum in Widmar was relatively "wide-open," and receptive to many different kinds of viewpoints. Mergens, in contrast, had a limited number of participating groups, with no controversial viewpoints present at all.

The Court again revisited the issue of schools, forums, and religious speech in Rosenberger v. University of Virginia, which concerned whether a public university could deny funds, garnered from a mandatory student-fee based system, to a student-run religious publication. Under established policy, the University of Virginia allowed some monies to be redirected by a Student Activities Board to student publications. However, university policy also prohibited funding for any student publication that "primarily promotes or manifests a particular belief in or about a deity or an ultimate reality." Understandably, the policy's purpose was to prevent Establishment Clause violations in the form of Virginia's direct or indirect endorsement of religion. Wide Awake Productions, a student-run evangelical Christian publication, sought funding, was denied, and then sued the university under the Free Speech Clause. A divided Court struck down the university's prohibition against religious speech, with Justice Kennedy first noting that the student-fee system was a "forum more in a metaphysical than in a spatial or geographic sense."[50] But, public forum principles apply all the same, and the University of Virginia had to demonstrate a compelling interest in denying Wide Awake's speech. A five-justice majority for the Court ruled against the university's Establishment Clause defense. Writing for the majority, Justice Kennedy argues that to avoid the Establishment Clause problem, public officials affiliated with the university had to "scan and interpret student publications to discern their underlying philosophical assumptions respecting religious theory and belief." By so doing, the university committed viewpoint discrimination and thus violated the Free Speech Clause. As Kennedy explains, "There is no Establishment Clause violation in the University's honoring its duties under the Free Speech Clause."[51]

Rosenberger is notable for the range of disagreement among the justices, particularly on the issue of religious expression and the Establishment Clause. Justice Souter's dissent, for instance, argues that the Establishment Clause should be construed to sustain the University of Virginia's denial of funding for the evangelical Christian magazine. For Souter, the Court must focus on the substance of the magazine's message, and not just its place within the larger context of student-run newspapers and publications. The magazine is overtly evangelistic, as Souter points out: "this writing is not merely descriptive examination of religious doctrine or even of ideal Christian practice in confronting life's social and personal problems. Nor is it merely the expression of editorial opinion that incidentally coincides with Christian ethics and reflects a Christian view of human obligation. It is straightforward exhortation to enter into a relationship with God as revealed in Jesus Christ."[52] The magazine, then, is "nothing other than the preaching of the word, which (along with the sacraments) is what most branches of Christianity offer those called to the religious life." Such conduct—the preaching of the gospel, or word—is "categorically" prohibited by the Establishment Clause, and the Court's validation of monies for Wide Awake Publications essentially allows, in Souter's terms, a "direct state funding" of evangelical activities.

Souter's dissent contrasts sharply with the majority's approach to the dispute. First, for the majority, the primary issue was whether the University of Virginia created a public forum open to all viewpoints. The Court ruled that subsidies for student publications did indeed create a forum—a "metaphysical" instead of spatial forum—and access to it could not be limited based on the viewpoint of a specific speaker or message. The university refused access to the forum for religious publications, and in so doing discriminated against speakers because of their specific views. The majority mainly focused on the *contours* of the forum, and simply determined that once the forum was created, all messages were allowed. Souter's focus on the real substance of Wide Awake's publication, though, indicates significant disagreement within the Court. For Souter, what mattered most was the *content* of Wide Awake's speech. Since the magazine's content was strongly evangelistic and proselytical, to allow it access to the forum would effectively force the University of Virginia, as a public agency, to subsidize and endorse a religious message.

The Court addressed similar Establishment Clause barriers to religious speech in the same term in *Capitol Square Review & Advisory Board v. Pinette*, discussed above. In a 7:2 vote, the Court determined that denial of the permit to erect the cross infringed the free speech rights of the Ku Klux Klan. Writing for the seven-justice majority, Justice Scalia hones in on the context of religious expression in the public square, and points out that the right to access public property for expressive purposes is not guaranteed, but "depends upon whether the property has by law or tradition been given the status of a public forum." If it is considered a public forum by the government, the power to limit the speech within it "is sharply circumscribed: it may impose reasonable, content-neutral time, place and manner restrictions (a ban on all unattended displays, which did not exist here, might be one such), but it may regulate expressive content only if such a restriction is necessary, and narrowly drawn, to serve a compelling state interest." Since the Capitol Square was found to be a traditional public forum by the lower district and circuit courts, the high court considered that the compelling interest test applied. As Scalia further points out, the "essence" of the case is the KKK's contention that its speech was excluded "precisely because its content was religious," and the square was closed to that religious speech in order to avoid an official endorsement of Christianity, by the state of Ohio, in violation of the Establishment Clause.[53]

Addressing the Establishment Clause argument, Justice Scalia stipulates that "There is no doubt that compliance with the Establishment Clause is a state interest sufficiently compelling to justify content-based restrictions on speech. Whether that interest is implicated here, however, is a different question."[54] Indeed, the review board did not have a compelling interest at all, and the state was not in danger of endorsing the Klan's religious expression. Additionally, "the State did not sponsor respondents' expression, the expression was made on government property that had been opened to the public for speech, and permission was requested through the same application process and on the same terms required of other private groups."[55] Justice Scalia concludes by defining a bright-line rule notable for its clarity that "religious expression cannot violate the Establishment Clause where it (1) is purely private and (2) occurs in a traditional or designated public forum, publicly announced and open to all on equal terms. Those conditions are satisfied here, and therefore the State may not bar respondents' cross from Capitol Square."[56]

Pinette's approach to the conflict between religious speech and the Establishment Clause hinges upon whether the religious speech is privately motivated and placed in a traditional or designated forum generally open to all types of speech. To be sure, making the distinction between private and government-sponsored religious speech helps define the boundary between religious speech and the Establishment Clause, but it is reasonable to speculate that when public forum disputes involve religious speech, that speech is always privately motivated. Thus, Justice Scalia's distinction between private and government speech may not be so helpful in the context of the public forum, and in a very real sense may be an artificial distinction that certainly reflects the realities of religious speech in public places, but in no way deals with the various tensions that such speech creates.

More recent cases build upon this idea of privately motivated religious speech, though, indicating that Justice Scalia's approach is catching some support. The dispute in *Good News Club v. Milford Central School District*, for instance, centers on an elementary school's denial of access to its facilities for a Christian evangelical club geared toward elementary age students. The school's policy prohibited access to individuals and groups seeking to use school facilities for religious worship, and in this case, the school determined that the club's purpose was mainly worship. The school allowed groups to use its facilities for discussion of secular matters from a religious perspective, however. The Good News Club sued under the Free Speech Clause of the First Amendment.

Writing for a six-justice majority, Justice Thomas argued that the school denied the club access based on its religious message and therefore violated the First Amendment's implicit command against viewpoint discrimination. "Speech discussing otherwise permissible subjects cannot be excluded from a limited public forum on the ground that the subject is discussed from a religious viewpoint."[57] Again, as with *Rosenberger*, the majority noted the importance of the *contours* of the forum, and how the school regulated access to it. The simple argument made by the majority is that once the school opens its facilities for the public, it creates a designated public forum open to discussion in general, and cannot deny access to it based on the specific message or viewpoint of a speaker. What matters, then, is that the school created a forum, as in *Rosenberger*, and thus had to abide by the contours and parameters it created for its use.

Yet for Justice Souter, the issue is not the creation of the forum, but the content of the speech and expression seeking access. In a different twist on the Establishment Clause as a bar to religious speech, Souter focuses on the *motivation* of religious speech at issue, and concludes that in this dispute the club's speech was clearly evangelistic. Good News sought to use the public school "for an evangelical service of worship calling children to commit themselves in an act of Christian conversion." Thus, for Souter, the majority's "bland and general characterization" of the club's speech as the "teaching of morals and character, from a religious standpoint," was erroneous.[58] Focusing on the content of the expression in the forum, or why groups and individuals wish to use the forum, is a valid point of review for Justice Souter. Approving access for the Good News Club without addressing the evangelistic motivations for their speech is the equivalent of opening a public forum, and public school, for worship-based activities.

Justice Stevens likewise dissents, and points out that religious speech must be treated categorically. As he puts it,

> Speech for "religious purposes" may reasonably be understood to encompass three different categories. First, there is religious speech that is simply speech about a particular topic from a religious point of view. . . . Second, there is religious speech that amounts to worship, or its equivalent. . . . Third, there is an intermediate category that is aimed principally at proselytizing or inculcating belief in a particular religious faith.[59]

Stevens argues that if schools open their facilities as public forums, they cannot discriminate on the basis of viewpoint. But, schools can rightly distinguish between expression and speech in the forum that has the goal of informing others, and speech and expression that serve to recruit others to a political cause. Schools cannot regulate the former, but they can regulate the latter, since speech geared toward recruiting others to a political cause will have a divisive effect on students and others. Thus, "school officials may reasonably believe that evangelical meetings designed to convert children to a particular religious faith pose the same risk [of divisiveness]. . . . a school [can] allow discussion of topics such as moral development from a religious (or nonreligious) perspective without thereby opening its forum to religious proselytizing or worship."[60]

Good News indicates the range of disagreement among the current justices, and also shows the point to which policy has evolved on religious speech in public places. As the case makes clear, a majority of the Court is willing to allow private religious expression into forums that are generally open to other types of speech, without due concern for Establishment Clause violations. Religious speech in general is no different from other types of private expression: "What matters for purposes of the Free Speech Clause is that we can see no logical difference in kind between the invocation of Christianity by the Club and the invocation of teamwork, loyalty, or patriotism by other associations to provide a foundation for their lessons."[61] Also important is that at least five justices do not view the Establishment Clause as a bar to religious speech. Yet, Justice Souter calls for a deeper inquiry into the motivation of religious speech in order to determine if it is informative religious speech or proselytical and evangelistic. Religious speech that seeks merely to inform debate and prompt discussion on topical issues is allowable, since it engages in a larger conversation in which many varied viewpoints on the same issue are present. When religious speech serves to convert others, though, it departs from general discursive purposes and becomes the equivalent of a worship service geared toward winning converts. Such religious expression, in Souter's terms, brings the Establishment Clause into play, and governments run the risk of endorsing religious messages that are inherently worship based. Agreeing with Souter, Justice Stevens posits that the Court should create categories of religious speech to reflect its purposes, or perhaps more prominently the purposes of the speaker. Thus, religious speech that seeks to inform must be treated differently than religious speech that seeks to convert, and from speech that is primarily worship-based. Stevens's categorical approach to religious speech has (of yet) no takers, but it indicates the shifting dynamics of the Court's policymaking in disputes involving religious expression in general.

CONCLUSION

The very substance of religious speech and expression creates content problems, due perhaps to the pluralistic nature of the public square. Richard John Neuhaus argues that "citizens are the bearers of opinion, including opinion shaped by . . . religious belief, and citizens should have equal access to the public square."[62] The public square, writ large, is pluralistic, and open to all opinion bearers, even those of a religious persuasion. Importantly for Neuhaus, excluding the religious voice from the square not only makes the square less pluralistic, but also keeps out a valuable counterweight to the secular propensities of discourse and political debate. The pluralistic nature of the public square, and indeed the inherent pluralism of the Supreme Court's public forum doctrine, state in theory that all views are welcome. But religious speech is problematic, as the Court's own jurisprudence makes clear.

"It is true," as Steven Gey posits, "that by permitting religious groups to conduct overtly religious activity on public property the Court created a situation that will often be perceived by the public as an impermissible linkage between church and state."[63] Moreover, for Gey, in the pluralistic public forum open (theoretically) to all opinions and discourse, religious speech is different, due to attendant Establishment Clause issues. Thus, "there is evident tension in the Court's public access cases between the desire to allow religious speakers to partake of public benefits (that is, access public facilities), and an equally strong urge to preserve the separation of government and religion."[64]

In early access cases concerning the Jehovah's Witnesses, the Court's primary focus on official discretion in granting or denying access to forums often mitigated any Establishment Clause concerns. Indeed, the Court early on never addressed whether the Establishment Clause barred religious speech until *Widmar* raised the issue in the 1980s in the context of public education at the university level. To be sure, Establishment Clause concerns are absent when nonreligious speech seeks access to the public square, thus religious speech is different and distinctive and brings with it a conflict with another constitutional provision.

Arguably, the Court has reached a consensus that the Establishment Clause does not bar religious expression from public forums. But, the recent dissenting opinions by Justices Souter and Stevens in *Good News* indicate that perhaps the issue is not settled after all. Souter's distinction between religious speech that seeks to participate in a broader debate to inform others of a specific religion's approach to topical issues, and religious speech that outright seeks to convert others, casts doubt on the argument by Justices Scalia and Thomas, and others, that private religious expression is no different from private expression in general. In Souter's terms, to allow in public places religious expression that seeks to convert others truly risks government endorsement of that specific religion, since public spaces would be used to facilitate a religion's drive for new members. Since evangelistic activities are inherently a form of religious exercise, their inclusion in public forums is problematic from the Establishment Clause perspective.

The Court, it is fair to say, will not resolve the tensions in its jurisprudence any time soon. As the Jehovah's Witnesses cases demonstrate, divided Courts continually build upon doctrine decided by narrow margins. Since the Court ultimately shifted the

terms of its review of religious speech and public forum cases—
from review of local discretion in granting or denying access to the
actual content of the square itself—the doctrinal confusion in the
Witnesses disputes ceases to be important. The same can be pre-
dicted for the current Court's forays into the circumstances under
which religious speech belongs in the public square, and when it
can be kept out. Generally speaking, the Court's recent cases
demonstrate that it will rarely sustain attempts to keep religious
speech out of the square, and in a real sense Justice Scalia's argument that religious speech is the same as any other type of speech,
and thus protected by the Constitution, basically compares with
the Court's policies. Yet, the disagreements among the justices indicate that the law is indeed unsettled and unpredictable. One can
expect, then, attendant consequences of that imprecise law in
lower trial courts.

CHAPTER 3

Standing in the Temple and Teaching the People: Litigants, Courts, and the Public Square

PUBLIC FORUMS ATTRACT SPEAKERS WHO wish to publicly communicate a specific message. Whether that message is political, social, artistic, or religious, there is some underlying reason why the speaker thinks it belongs in a public space. Understanding district court policymaking in religious speech and public forum cases depends, then, to a large extent on the messages and motivations of the speakers seeking access to public spaces for their messages. Litigants invoke the power of courts to protect their rights, and courts respond accordingly. Thus, to fully comprehend the role of district courts in adjudicating religious speech and public forums disputes, it is necessary to discuss why and under what circumstances speakers seek access to the public square for their messages.

For example, Krishnas of the International Society for Krishna Consciousness (ISKCON) base their presence in the public square around *sankirtan*, a mandatory religious ritual in which devotees greet members of the public and solicit them for donations to support the Hare Krishna movement.[1] Whereas the Krishnas engage in a type of expression that depends on face-to-face encounters with other people, other speakers choose different means to get their religious views across to the public. The Jewish group Chabad-Lubavitch, for instance, puts menorahs in public places to remind Jews of their obligations to Torah law. Likewise, a myriad of Christian speakers, from individuals motivated by basic evangelical tendencies to more organized groups such as the Promise Keepers, similarly seek access to the public square to communicate evangelical, proselytical messages aimed at motivating existing evangelical Christians while also trying to convert those of other faiths. Indeed, Christian litigants sometimes seek access to the public square in order to circumvent more restrictive court decisions under the Establishment Clause that tend to raise barriers to religious expression in the form of public prayer, for instance. "Rather than expending their energy and resources defending themselves against charges of establishment," as Philip Kenneson puts it, "they have gone on the offensive, arguing for their right to free religious expression."[2]

Litigation trends and pressures affect federal district court policy-making in public forum cases, and demonstrate how the law is used to gain and protect access to the public square. Two fundamental questions are in order. First, who litigates? Second, why litigate? The first question centers on the status of the plaintiffs: are they individuals seeking to protect rights of access to public spaces for their specific religious message, or are they more often interest groups seeking to establish broader public policy through the federal court system? The type of defendant is important too. Since almost all constitutional complaints are directed at government institutions, certain questions are central to understanding how governments defend their management of public forums. Thus, which levels and types of governments are often swept up in public square access disputes?

Importantly, studying the symmetries of litigation yields two broad trends. First, over one-half of the litigants seeking access to a public forum are individuals who simply wish to engage in some kind of religious speech or expression. Other litigants are interest groups, other religious organizations, and churches and congregations. Thus, individual "rights seekers" file most of the claims, and very few individual cases are linked with interest groups that might provide counsel or other types of assistance. The second broad trend focuses on the fact that most of the forums at issue are owned and managed by local government agencies such as schools boards, port authorities, or even public libraries. The predominance of local government forums fits into Richard Spinner-Halev's discussion of religious speech in the public square, presented in chapter 1, that views most public spaces as "mini public forums" that are not national stages for speech and expression at all. That almost 75 percent of defendants in religious speech cases are local governments tends to prove his argument, and it also means that local political processes and regulatory agencies are the most involved and affected by how religious speech and public forum law develops.

Aside from who wants into the forum, and who denies access, the motivations of the litigants also shed light on the kinds of issues that district courts must address. Focusing on the specific messages that litigants seek to place into the public square and their primary type of expression again highlights the tensions and pressures to which district courts respond when deciding religious speech cases. Christian litigants present by far the most dominant type of religious speech involved in these disputes, with Krishna and Jewish speech coming in a far second and third. Additionally, Christian speakers use a variety of different types of expression, from pure speech through preaching to the holding of worship services in public places. Other faiths tend to cluster their messages around very specific types of expression. For instance, almost all of the Krishna cases concern *sankirtan* solicitation and almost all of the Jewish speech cases focus on the display of menorahs on public property. As noted below, one interesting comparison can be made between religious speech disputes and religious liberty disputes in general, in that religious speech cases involve only a very small group of specific faiths, whereas religious liberty litigation broadly construed involves many more different faiths and issues.

All of these points, and others, are addressed below. Focusing on these questions places federal district court policymaking in religious public square cases in bold relief and defines the pressures and trends to which courts respond when developing the law. Trial courts necessarily rely on litigants to bring cases to them. Thus, as Joel Grossman and others point out, "because courts depend so heavily on the actions of others to shape their dockets, an understanding of the shaping of the docket is especially important to any full understanding of the role of courts."[3] Part of that "docket shaping" process is explained by looking at the "mores, values, and modes of participation" in litigation in order to deduce patterns that mold and shape how trial courts can respond to certain types of disputes. The mores and values of litigants drive lawsuits and help explain why they turn to the courts to protect their rights. As well, the modes of litigation concern how courts and judicial power are invoked, and to what ends, and help assess what it is that litigants want trial courts to do for them.

Broadly speaking, litigants use courts to protect their rights and interests, and in so doing, as Frank Zemans proposes, "employ the power of the state and so become state actors themselves."[4] Zemans points out too that litigation is primarily an entrepreneurial activity, as litigants choose to use courts to protect their interests. After weighing the costs and benefits of litigation, and the rights and interests to be protected, litigants opt to become "active agents in the growth of the law," and invoke court and state power accordingly to achieve their legal objectives. Litigation is thus a type of political participation, in that litigants use state power to further their own objectives such as gaining access for their religious message in a public place.

District court cases certainly do not comprise all of the disputes over religious speech in the public square. Although there are no clear statistics on legal and nonlegal disputes over religious speech, it is fair to say that many disagreements are resolved through negotiation and compromise shy of litigation. Perhaps many unresolved disagreements simply disappear. Litigants who sue to gain access do so as entrepreneurial actors and consumers of court services who presumably are aware of the costs and benefits associated with using courts to try to get into a public place. For those seeking access to the public square for their religious message, turning to courts may be a last resort.

There are plenty of examples where individuals or groups have sought access to public places for religious purposes and have resolved the dispute without going to court. In July 1999, for example, a local church in Hopkinton, Massachusetts, threatened to sue a local public school district after it refused to allow the church to hold a worship service in its high school auditorium. The school committee overseeing the school system determined that taxpayer dollars should not be used to defend its policy denying access to religious groups, and simply allowed the church access to avoid a protracted legal conflict.[5] Similarly, a coalition of Islamic groups sought to drive a religious message *out* of the public square when it asked the United States Supreme Court to sandblast an image of Muhammad from a frieze in the Court's main chamber. Citing a federal law barring the alteration of walls and other parts of the Supreme Court building, Chief Justice Rehnquist denied their request, since to remove the image of Islam's holiest prophet would violate the law governing the Court's physical spaces. For reasons that are not clear, the group coalition did not litigate.[6] In a 2002 dispute in the northern Texas town of Waxahachie, a student was expelled for wearing a pentacle necklace representative of her

Wiccan religion. The Waxahachie school district expelled her twice, but the district superintendent reinstated her to her high school class after the ACLU proffered counsel to the family and threatened to sue. As the superintendent put it, "while the Wiccan faith may not be the majority religion in our community, our board policies protect all faiths," recognizing that the pentacle necklace not only represented the student's exercise of her religion, but also involved freedom of expression under the Free Speech Clause of the First Amendment.[7] Not every dispute concerning religious speech in public places ends in litigation, and numerous examples abound where disputes are resolved easily and even perhaps amicably. It may well be that courts are truly a last resort for most disputes concerning religious expression in the public square.

Lawsuits occur when litigants are willing to invoke the power of courts, with attendant risks, costs, and benefits, to protect a specific right or interest concerning religious expression in a public square. The ensuing intractable conflict between the speaker seeking access, and the government regulating the forum, may only be resolved by a court of law. Thus, lawsuits represent instances in which the government managers of public squares refuse to accommodate religious speakers, and prior attempts by both parties to reach an agreement have not worked. The result is the invocation of judicial power by religious speakers, and the full-forced government response to deny them.

GETTING INTO THE PUBLIC SQUARE: TYPES OF PLAINTIFFS

Litigant symmetries are a basic indicator of the pressures affecting trial court policymaking. The question "who sues whom?" is best understood by first focusing attention on the status of the litigants, both plaintiff and defendant, to determine "who litigates—which persons, organizations, and interests" use the courts to establish policy outcomes.[8] The picture that emerges is one in which individual plaintiffs are the primary consumers of court services who seek to place their religious messages in the public square. Indeed, as figure 3.1 demonstrates, individual plaintiffs comprise 57 percent of all cases brought into district courts, with group plaintiffs (interest groups and religious groups) constituting 32 percent of the disputes. The federal government accounts for 2 percent of the cases, which consist of federal government prosecutions of individuals or groups that violated government bans on expressive conduct in federally owned areas. One such example of this type of dispute is *U.S. v. Silberman*, where a Krishna was prosecuted, and ultimately acquitted, for practicing *sankirtan* at the Castillo de San Marcos in Saint Augustine, Florida. The district judge concluded that the Krishna was engaged in religious expression, and was thus not covered by applicable federal administrative regulation governing the property at issue.[9] Federal government plaintiffs are rare, though, and do not constitute a significant part of litigants bringing religious speech claims into the district court system.

That over half of all litigants are individuals points to a litigation trend in district courts that is episodic at best, in the sense that court cases are not used to mount sustained, coordinated efforts to change public policy. Currently, some scholars of law and religion argue that many Christian litigants coordinate lawsuits to place their religious speech back into public forums such as public schools, government buildings, and public parks, in order to circumvent Supreme Court decisions that restrict such activities as prayer or Bible readings in public schools. The evidence, however, does not support that claim at all. Most individual litigants are "lone rights bearers"[10] who pursue their own individualistic claims about *their* specific religious message in a particular local forum.

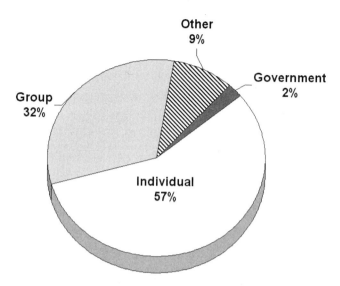

FIGURE 3.1

Types of Plaintiffs in Religious Speech and Public Forum Cases. Federal District Courts, 1974–2001.

Controlling for individual plaintiff cases in which an organized interest group provides counsel, and thus perhaps links that specific case to a larger litigation strategy, individual cases are still episodic and uncoordinated. Eighty-one percent of all individual plaintiff cases proceed without any input from an organized interest group counsel such as the liberal-leaning American Civil Liberties Union (ACLU) or the conservative-evangelical American Center for Law and Justice (ACLU), indicating further that individual plaintiffs act on their own initiative to place their specific religious message in a local forum, and generally do not act as part of a larger, coordinated litigation strategy. *Francis v. District of Columbia Armory Board* serves to illustrate the "lone rights bearer" argument. Here, the plaintiff sought to hang the sign "JN 3:16" at RFK Stadium, managed by the Armory Board, during a Washington Redskins football game. The plaintiff alleged that stadium staff continually obstructed his sign. The district judge "assumed arguendo" that RFK stadium was a public forum open to expression, and subsequently dismissed the claim because the plaintiff "seeks an uncompromising right to display his sign in a specific location without any restriction." Reasonable time, place, and manner restrictions on signage in RFK stadium are allowable, and the lawsuit was accordingly dismissed.[11] Francis's complaint and lawsuit were not part of a larger litigation strategy to display John 3:16 signs in public spaces; he simply sued to protect his specific message in a specific public context.

Individual plaintiffs are not the only story, however, since interest groups or religious groups are plaintiffs in approximately one-third of the cases. There are, of course, many ways groups can participate in the judicial process. Groups can directly sponsor litigation starting at the trial court level by seeking out test cases; doing so allows a group to "establish the factual context, the issue configuration, and . . . the initial court environment that it believes will best allow it to pursue its goals through the judiciary."[12] Sponsoring test cases is vastly different than participating in appellate court decisionmaking, especially at the Supreme Court, as an amicus curiae, or "friend of the court." As an amicus, a group participates in a case not as an immediate party such as the plaintiff or defendant (petitioner or respondent at the Supreme Court), but as a party with an outside interest in the resolution of the case. Amicus participation usually entails submitting a brief to an appellate court detailing a specific legal argument in a case.

In terms of group plaintiffs, the International Society for Krishna Consciousness stands out for its persistence and organization in seeking access to various types of public places. ISKCON litigated several early public forum cases in the 1970s and early 1980s and to a large degree inaugurated the modern litigation strategy of linking public forum doctrine and religious speech. At issue in all of the disputes was the ISKCON practice of *sankirtan*, which obliges Krishna followers to approach people in public places and proselytize and, perhaps more importantly, solicit donations.[13] Thus, ISKCON sought to inject its *sankirtan* practices into public squares such as state fairs, regional and international airports, the Visitor's Gate at the United Nations, and municipalities at large.[14] ISKCON's coordinated litigation strategy was moderately successful at the federal district level, but growing conflict among circuit courts reviewing lower trial decisions led to the Supreme Court's involvement in 1981. In *Heffron v. International Society for Krishna Consciousness*, the Court determined that confining *sankirtan* to a specific location, such as a booth on the grounds of a state fair, is an allowable "time, place, and manner" restriction justified by the state's compelling interest in protecting the orderly flow of patrons on the fair premises.[15]

Another group often litigating religious expression claims is the Jewish Chabad-Lubavitch group, with branches located in several states. The Chabad-Lubavitch, "by far the most missionary of Jewish groups,"[16] often seek to erect menorahs in public squares, especially when those public areas allow the display of Christian religious symbols.[17] Although not maintaining as prominent a presence in district courts as ISKCON, the Chabad-Lubavitch nonetheless pursued organized, coordinated strategies to place their religious expression in the public square.

Less than 10 percent of plaintiffs are typed as "other" since they do not neatly fit with the individual, group, or government categories. Most "other" litigants are local churches, usually evangelical Christian, that have no denominational affiliation, and thus few, if any, links to a larger, national organization. They are not organized groups similar to ISKCON since they generally have no larger organizational structure, for instance a national organizing body that coordinates church policies, ministerial activities, or how the church operates. Nor are these litigants individuals similar to Mr. Francis who sought to display "John 3:16" at a city stadium during a professional football game. The nondenominational churches most often involved in this category are usually acting for their own self-interest, for instance to gain access to the public square for their own worship services, and are not part of a larger litigation strategy to protect religious speech in general. In *Wallace and North Gate Community Church v. Washoe County School District*, for example, a local, nondenominational Christian church sought the *permanent* use of a local public high school auditorium for its Sunday services. The church had no facility for its own use, and had no future plans to build a facility either. For the district court, temporary access to the school's facilities was one thing; permanent access for the church every Sunday was a different issue altogether, and for the school to allow access under those circumstances would have the effect of advancing religion in violation of the Establishment Clause.[18]

REGULATING THE PUBLIC SQUARE: TYPES OF DEFENDANTS

Turning to who defends against religious speech claims—or more concisely, which level of the government—it is very significant that three-fourths of the defendants in these disputes are local government entities, as figure 3.2 makes very clear. Local governments defend 75 percent of all such cases in federal district courts, with state governments next at 17 percent, and the federal government last at 5 percent. The high number of local government defendants points again toward the idiosyncratic and episodic nature of religious speech litigation in that most disputes tend to concern very localistic disagreements about forums owned and managed by local governments. Thus, local governments bear the brunt of defending their regulations on public forum speech in

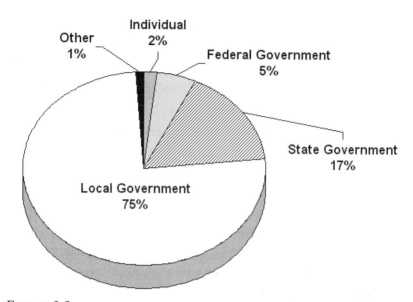

FIGURE 3.2

Types of Defendants in Religious Speech and Public Forum Disputes. Federal District Courts, 1974–2001.

places such as public parks and other spaces[19] or travel terminals owned and operated by government agencies.[20] Local public schools fall in this category too, and as discussed later, over one-third of forums litigated concern public school facilities, demonstrating the significant role local school boards and districts play in defending their regulations against religious speech in their facilities.

State and federal government agencies also defend public forum regulations, but only sporadically. Many of the state government cases concern ISKCON's early attempts to practice *sankirtan*, without interference, at state fairs.[21] Similarly, other litigants have sued in order to evangelize in state parks at times normally prohibited by government agencies,[22] or in one instance to place the moniker "GODZGUD" in the metaphysical public forum created

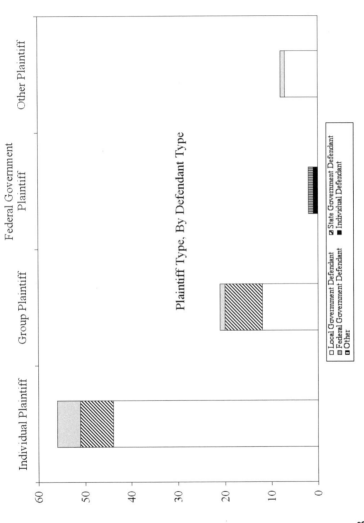

FIGURE 3.3

Litigant Symmetries in Religious Speech and Public Forum Disputes. Federal District Courts, 1974–2001.

by state automobile vanity license plates.[23] For the federal government, which rarely must defend public forum regulations in the context of religious speech, such cases include ISKCON's challenge of National Park regulations prohibiting solicitations, and therefore *sankirtan*, on the National Mall in Washington, D.C. Federal and state defendants tend to be the exception and not the rule.[24]

The contingent nature of this litigation is made even clearer by looking at litigation symmetries, or who sues whom. To that end, figure 3.3 demonstrates that most cases concern individual plaintiffs suing local governments, which of course stands to reason given the high percentage of cases for both types of litigants. With so many local government defendants in the litigation pool, the role of "lower courts, local battles, and discussions of issues" becomes all too important in analyzing the role of district courts in granting access to the public square for religious speech. Indeed, problems with the metaphorical public square quickly become evident, since the emphasis on local government lawsuits makes the importance of public forums as mini public squares even more pressing. Recall Richard Spinner-Halev's argument from chapter 1, as he indicates that "the idea of a public square recalls the image of the New England town square. . . . today, however, there are many small public squares that tie particular communities together."[25] As Spinner-Halev notes, these smaller publics do not exist in isolation from each other, but often interact with the "public square of mainstream society," which is basically "a rather loose national conversation that may be considered the larger public square."

The importance of local governments, and *local public forums*, in shaping the developing law on religious expression in public squares supports Spinner-Halev's point. Local government-owned forums offer a plethora of diverse types of public properties, forums, squares, and spaces that may or may not be open to expressive activity. Viewing litigation trends as comprised of disputes over mini public squares indicates the contingent, unorganized nature in which religious speech and public forum law may be developing.

The prominence of local government defendants has another meaning as well. Richard Morgan notes that local governments form a significant arena of conflict between religious groups and government over religious liberty issues. As he puts it, "here are waged those intimate little community wars over religious practices in particular schools . . . disputes over religious services and artifacts in public parks . . . state legislatures, mayors, school boards and municipal councils are the foci of struggle."[26] Indeed, research on the impact of the Supreme Court's religious liberty decisions focuses on how local and state government seek to *circumvent* rulings that limit government sponsorship of religious activities, such as school prayer.[27] That religious liberty disputes often have a disproportionate impact on state and local governments is not in doubt. For Ted Jelen,

> state and local governments have many opportunities to make policies that indirectly invoke the constitutional provisions on religion. To the extent that subnational governments are responsive for "visible" public opinion, they have strong incentives to pass measures that are generally accommodationist on issues involving religious establishment. . . . state and local policymaking in most areas of the United States is likely to take on a Christian preferentialist cast.[28]

For Jelen, and others, American public opinion usually leans toward accommodating religious exercises in public places, and local governments are institutionally suited to act upon those political leanings: "if subnational governments are in fact responsive to public opinion, and if the publicly visible aspect of public opinion is likely to be strongly accommodationist, it follows that local officials . . . will pass and enforce measures that may violate the establishment or Free Exercise Clauses."[29] Local governments are often caught up in religious liberty disputes because they blur the boundary lines between church and state by promoting religious activities such as prayer or by regulating others through Sabbath day (Sunday closing) restrictions. In public forum litigation local governments are implicated because they seek to regulate, if not ban, religious expression from the public square altogether. Thus, local government conduct does not neatly fit into that observed in the context of religious liberty disputes in general, where local governments tend to be more supportive of religiously motivated conduct.

A few cases do fit Jelen's model of local governments generally supportive of accommodating religious speech in public places, however. Some lawsuits seek to exclude religious speech from the public square, indicating that the government first allowed that speech in the public place to begin with. Of the seventeen cases (9 percent of the total) that seek to limit religious speech in the public square, sixteen center on locally "owned and operated" forums. Only one case concerns a forum maintained by a state government. Whether the local governments in question responded to public opinion and intentionally sought to accommodate religious speech specifically, or only sought to give it equal access, is not known. However, the thrust of these cases indicates that local governments allowed religious speech in a locally maintained public forum, and by so doing opened themselves to lawsuits to take it out of the forum. As well, most focus on potential Establishment Clause violations in which plaintiffs allege that local governments effectively endorse religion by allowing religious speech in public spaces.

Local governments maintain three-fourths of the public forums involved in lawsuits, thus indicating that most religious speech and public forum disputes revolve around speakers seeking to use small public squares for their speech. There is something to the fact that most public squares litigated are controlled by local political processes, such as town councils overseeing city parks or school boards operating public schools, and are thus affected by the vagaries of local politics and public opinion. To be sure, for every dispute that ends up in the federal district court system, there are probably countless disagreements between religious speakers and local governments over access to public properties that are either resolved amicably or dropped altogether. Indeed, one scholar of religious liberty and the Constitution argues that religious liberty decisions in general should be based on the "overall decency and religiously-accommodating instincts of local political institutions across the country."[30] The symmetries of litigation in religious speech disputes indicates that local governments are primarily charged with balancing the constitutional rights of religious speakers with the purposes, usages, and regulations of publicly owned spaces open to expressive conduct.

THE VALUES OF PARTICIPATION: FROM "AMBULATORY COLPORTEURING" TO CHRISTIAN EVANGELISM

Richard Morgan notes, "The reasons why [religious] groups struggle—the tensions which animate 'issues'—must not be lost sight of in the haste to discuss the tactics of group action." Further, "without some understanding of group motivations much about any political conflict will remain opaque . . . if one wishes to understand why a conflict arises . . . it is not enough to ask what groups do . . . It is also necessary to explore the fears and needs which shape group goals."[31] For Morgan, and others, the underlying value structure and belief system of a religious group helps explain the motivations and goals of those groups, especially in the context of interest group politics.[32] Importantly, Morgan's point extends beyond religious groups, as groups, and covers individuals and other types of litigants who are motivated by religion. Just as groups pursue political and legal gain, and are motivated by something very specific to them, so do individuals pursue political and legal gains based on very similar motivations. Those who study public opinion and political behavior indicate also the political salience of religion in understanding political attitudes and behavior, and especially note that identification with a specific religion is still the most common and intense form of group identification in the United States.[33] Doctrinal religious belief is a variable with significant explanatory value in nonlegal contexts, and as scholars of the judicial process point out, the same approach applies to litigation as well.[34] Gregg Ivers, for instance, demonstrates the diverse litigation tactics and arguments that specific faith-based groups, such as the Baptist Joint Committee, or the American Jewish Congress, raise at the Supreme Court, and how those religious dynamics help reshape religious liberty jurisprudence.[35] Frank Way and Barbara Burt similarly demonstrate the importance of religious doctrine as one variable affecting judicial outcomes in their study of how marginal religious groups use courts and litigation to help establish their legitimacy in mainstream society.[36] Since what is at issue in religious speech cases is a specific *religious message*, it makes sense to understand litigation in terms of the faith-based message being litigated.

Figure 3.4 provides a time reference for how public forum/religious speech litigation proceeds at the district court level. Litigants are typed according to the specific religious basis for the speech in question. As is evident, it is primarily Christian-based litigants who seek to place their speech in a public forum. Clearly, almost three-quarters (72.5 percent, n=124) of all the cases in federal district courts concerned Christian speech in some form. Most of them concerned litigants suing to place Christian expression into a public forum, although 12 percent of the Christian speech cases concerned litigants seeking to enjoin such speech from a public forum. ISKCON ranks a far second, with only 12 percent of the cases initiated, with Jewish and Muslim litigants bringing 7.4 percent and 2.3 percent of the cases, respectively. In terms of the "mores, modes, and values" of litigation, using religion as one variable of analysis at least helps identify, in broad terms, the message that litigants seek to drive into a public forum.[37]

To be sure the preponderance of Christian-based speech should not be viewed as one religion, denomination, or faith placing one specific message in the public square, or indeed monopolizing the public square. There are many different motivations for Christian speech in the square, as discussed below, and indeed such speech, when linked to specific types of expressive activity such as preaching, holding worship services, or distributing literature, tends to be very diverse and motivated by many different reasons. But in terms of all of the *types* of faith-based messages seeking access to public places, Christian speech maintains the most significant and consistent presence in litigation.

Faith-based messages are linked to many different types of conduct and expressive activity. The specific types of expressive conduct are derived from the cases themselves, and thus represent the actual issues litigated. The Krishnas offer an interesting example. ISKCON filed twenty-one cases (12 percent) in federal district courts to protect its religious speech. The Krishnas' primary form of expressive activity concerns *sankirtan*, its particular form of ambulatory solicitation, although one case does focus on ISKCON's attempt to hold a religious worship service in a public place. Almost all of the Krishna cases revolve around one specific type of expressive activity, demonstrating its very focused attempts to protect *sankirtan* in public squares. Such concise, focused activity easily supports ISKCON's attempts to create test cases and devise an

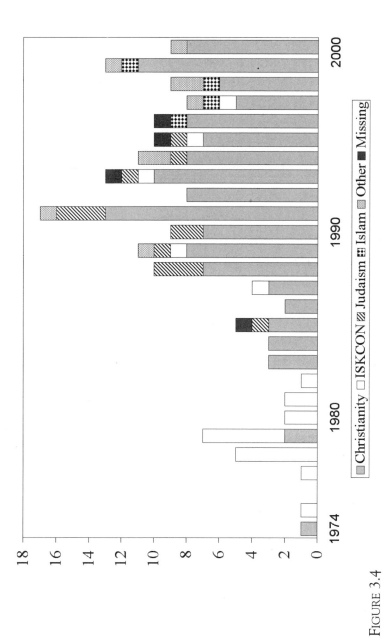

FIGURE 3.4

Litigants in Religious Speech and Public Forum Disputes, by Type of Religious Message. Federal District Courts, 1974–2000.

overarching litigation strategy applicable to district courts in diverse locales. Indeed, that the Krishnas only litigated one specific type of conduct indicates the organized nature of their litigation, as well as the focused religious activity that they practice in public.

Jewish litigants likewise engage in a narrow range of expressive activity. With only thirteen (8 percent) cases litigated in district courts, Jewish litigants simply do not maintain a prominent presence in public forum disputes. Over two-thirds of their cases deal with attempts by the Chabad-Lubavitch movement to place menorahs in public places, often to complement existing Christian displays of nativity scenes or crèches during the Christmas season.[38] In a real sense, the Lubavitch seek equal access to public forums for their specific religious message, contextualized by a religious display. Two cases concern attempts by litigants to get injunctions *against* a Lubavitch-sponsored menorah in a public place, and although concern a slightly different litigation dynamic—driving religious expression *out* of the public square—nonetheless the cases are similar in substance to Lubavitch attempts to place their religious message in the public square. Only two cases concern expressive conduct *other* than the display of a menorah, and instead deal with the distribution of literature in travel terminals generally open to the public.[39]

Muslim litigants curiously do not litigate many religious speech and public forum cases at all, as they comprise only 2.3 percent of all cases filed in federal district courts. Muslims litigate many claims concerning the free exercise of religion in prisons, many of which concern the attempts of local, state, and federal prison administrators to limit the liberties of Muslim prisoners, especially those affiliated with the Nation of Islam movement, in order to prevent prison violence.[40] But in terms of seeking to place specifically Muslim messages in the public square, there are very few cases at all. One example concerns placing a Muslim symbol—the crescent and star—in a public space. Thus, in *Medi and Khanhan*

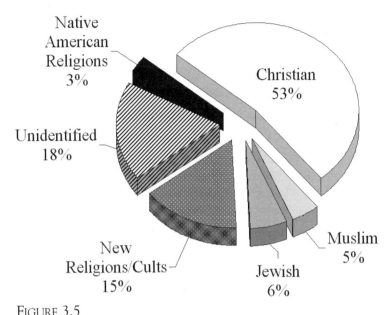

FIGURE 3.5

Percentage of All Religious Liberty Court Cases, by Religious Affiliation, 1981–1996.

Source: John Wybraniec and Roger Finke, "Religious Regulation and the Courts: The Judiciary's Changing Role in Protecting Minority Religions from Majoritarian Rule," *Journal for the Scientific Study of Religion* 40, no. 3 (2001).

The "Christian" litigant category is comprised of the following categories from the Wybraniec and Finke study: Protestant sects, Baptist (sectarian and mainline), Catholic (including orders), Mainline Protestant, Christian (general).

v. United States Postal Service, the secretary general of the National Council on Islamic Affairs sued to place a crescent and star in the Manhattan General Post Office where a Christmas tree and menorah were already on display during the holiday season. The district court determined that the post office was essentially a commercial enterprise, and therefore not a public forum; thus, the government had wide latitude in regulating speech on post office

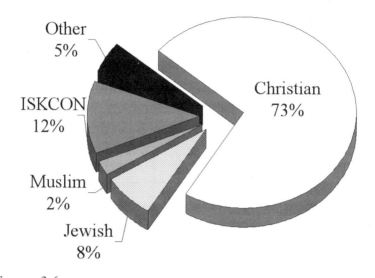

FIGURE 3.6

Litigants in Religious Speech and Public Forum Disputes, by Religious Affiliation. Federal District Courts, 1974–2001.

property, and its refusal to display the Islamic symbols did not violate the First Amendment.[41]

Christian-motivated speech far and away dominates district court litigation. Two prior studies of free exercise and Establishment Clause lawsuits help put the dominance of Christian litigants in perspective. In their study of free exercise claims in state and federal courts, Frank Way and Barbara Burt demonstrate the pluralistic nature of religious liberty litigation in American courts, and their analysis of the religious faiths and denominations that litigate indicates that Christian-based groups bring approximately 40 percent of cases within the larger case population of religious liberty disputes under the First Amendment.[42] Similarly, in a more recent study, John Wybraniec and Roger Finke show that Christian litigants file approximately 53 percent of all religious liberty lawsuits.[43] With 73 percent of all religious speech claims in federal district courts, Christian-based litigants pose an interesting contrast to the overall trend in religious liberty cases concerning the free exercise and Establishment Clauses. Religious speech disputes may be considered one subset of religious liberty disputes in general, and interestingly the data suggest that Christian groups cluster their litigation around speech-oriented activities, whereas other non-Christian groups tend to raise different, nonspeech issues in religious liberty cases. Nonetheless, that Christian-based speech so dominates district court litigation indicates that the way in which district courts contribute to the public forum debate, and serve as mini public squares that form part of a larger national public square, may be skewed toward one specific type of religious speech. The comparison also indicates that religious liberty disputes concerning the free exercise of religion, or government support for religious speech under the Establishment Clause, are much more heterogeneous. That is, a greater variety of religious groups, interests, and faiths is evidenced in religious liberty litigation in general, whereas cases over religious speech involve only four main types of religions: Christian, Jewish, Krishna Consciousness, and Muslim. And, so few cases are brought by Muslim speakers that in reality district courts focus their policymaking on three main types of religious messages. There are no Native Americans litigating religious speech and public forum claims, for instance, nor is there an assortment of "new religions or cults" other than the International Society for Krishna Consciousness. As compared with religious speech litigation in general, it is intriguing that the numbers and types of "voices" and faiths involved in lawsuits cluster around a few faiths, and thus in comparison with religious liberty cases in general present a narrow band of participation by mainly Christian, Krishna, and Jewish speakers. Moreover, within that narrow band of voices seeking access to the public square, Christian speech dominates district court policymaking. The Wybraniec and Finke study included federal and state trial and appellate courts, thus the picture that emerges with religious speech cases based only on federal district courts may be somewhat incomplete. But, there is very little evidence to suggest that state trial courts would hear *different* types of religious speech claims than federal district courts.

One final point concerns the "other" types of faiths or religions that seek access to the public square. These litigants in the main defy categorization under one of the other religious categories. *One World Family Now v. City of Miami Beach* offers a good example of the "other" type of religious message. In this case, solicitors sought to distribute T-shirts in the Art Deco area of Miami Beach, Florida, to teach the public about "issues such as global warming, toxic waste, vegetarianism and animal protection, and spiritual ecology."[44] The district court sustained Miami's regulations prohibiting sales from a fixed location, as the Family Members wished to do. The importance of the case for this analysis, though, is simply to show how the OWFN's "religious" message for the public square was very amorphous, and not easily typed relative to other messages from Christian, Jewish, or Krishna speakers.

FAITHS IN THE PUBLIC SQUARE

Where is all this religious speech going, and what form does it take? Which public forums or squares tend to attract religious speech? How is that speech linked to specific types of expressive conduct? Tables 3.1 and 3.2 link specific religious messages to detailed types of conduct and locations of forums, and indicate that certain types of religious speech are very much associated with certain types of activities. As well, the type of activity will often determine the public places in which religious speech is placed. For instance, Krishnas (ISKCON) almost exclusively sue over *sankirtan* practices, and by so doing implicate certain types of public

	CHRISTIANITY	JUDAISM	ISLAM	ISKCON	OTHER	TOTAL
Preaching or Evangelism	8 (100%)					8 (100%)
Solicitation for Donations	4 (16.7%)			20 (83.3%)		24 (100%)
Access for Student Religious Club in Public School	13 (100%)					13 (100%)
Distribution of Literature	19 (79.2%)	2 (8.3%)			3 (12.5%)	24 (100%)
Give a Prayer in Public Space or Meeting	3 (100%)					3 (100%)
Enjoin Some Kind of Religious Expression	15 (88.2%)	2 (11.8%)				17 (100%)
Erect Religious Display	17 (60.7%)	9 (32.1%)	2 (7.1%)			28 (100%)
Hold Worship Service/Religious Meeting	31 (83.8%)		2 (5.4%)	1 (2.7%)	3 (8.1%)	37 (100%)
Other	14 (82.4%)				3 (17.6%)	17 (100%)
Total	**124 (72.5%)**	**13 (7.6%)**	**4 (2.3%)**	**21 (12.3%)**	**9 (5.3%)**	**171* (100%)**

TABLE 3.1

Faith of Litigants by Type of Activity Litigated. Federal District Courts, 1974–2001.

*Four cases are excluded from the total of 175 cases due to missing variables.

Table 3.2

		SCHOOL	TRAVEL TERMINAL	GOVERNMENT BUILDING	PUBLIC PARK	OTHER	TOTAL
CHRISTIANITY	Count	64	3	11	32	14	124
	% Within Faith	51.6%	2.4%	8.9%	25.8%	11.3%	100.0%
	% Within Forum	98.5%	23.1%	68.8%	50.8%	100.0%	72.5%
JUDAISM	Count		3	3	7		13
	% Within Faith		23.1%	23.1%	53.8%		100.0%
	% Within Forum		23.1%	18.8%	11.1%		7.6%
ISLAM	Count	1		1	2		4
	% Within Faith	25.0%		25.0%	50.0%		100.0%
	% Within Forum	1.5%		6.3%	3.2%		2.3%
ISKCON	Count		6	1	14		21
	% Within Faith		28.6%	4.8%	66.7%		100.0%
	% Within Forum		46.2%	6.3%	22.2%		12.3%
OTHER	Count		1		8		9
	% Within Faith		11.1%		88.9%		100.0%
	% Within Forum		7.7%		12.7%		5.3%
TOTAL	Count	65	13	16	63	14	171*
	% of Total	38.0%	7.6%	9.4%	36.8%	8.2%	100.0%

Faith of Litigants by Location of Forum. Federal District Courts, 1974–2001.

*Four cases are excluded from the total of 175 cases due to missing variables.

forums. Since *sankirtan* is ambulatory, and theoretically must reach as many people as possible, Krishnas must do it in public places that are physically and spatially open enough to allow the practice, and that also experience high pedestrian traffic. Practicing *sankirtan* in rural county courthouses, or public schools, for instance, would not be preferable to *sankirtan* at county and/or state fairs that tend to attract significantly more people. Whereas Krishnas engage in a very mobile, flowing type of religious speech, cases raised by Jewish speakers search for more symbolic means to place their message in the public domain, such as through the display of a menorah. Unlike Krishna, Jewish, and Muslim speakers, Christian speakers represent a real diversity in activities by which they express their message, and forums in which they express their message. Each group is explored in more detail in turn.

The Rise and Fall of Hare Rama

The attempts by Hare Krishnas to practice *sankirtan* in public places offers an interesting look at the rise and decline of organized litigation centering on one specific religious message. Indeed, the Krishnas of ISKCON offer the only real example of sustained, coordinated lawsuits to place and maintain their message in the public square. Their litigation strategy took shape in the 1970s and early 1980s, but by 1984 ceased to exist, and ISKCON cases only sporadically appeared in district courts thereafter.

The reasons for ISKCON's rise and fall are twofold. One, the Supreme Court's *Heffron* decision in 1981 maintained that although *sankirtan* is protected religious expression under the First Amendment, it can be regulated under reasonable time, place, and manner restrictions in order, for instance, to preserve the orderly flow of pedestrian traffic at state fairs and other places where the public congregates. Thus, the Court's somewhat restrictive opinion quelled many of ISKCON's complaints. As well, ISKCON es-

sentially fragmented as a religious organization, and suffered not
only a loss in membership throughout the 1980s, but also a real
loss in income from a decline in revenue-generating *sankirtan*.

ISKCON began raising religious speech and public forum
claims in district courts in 1976 with *ISKCON v. Engelhardt*,
which concerned the right of Krishnas to engage in *sankirtan* at
the Kansas City International Airport.[45] Cases concerning *sankirtan* at state fairs in Ohio, Indiana, Texas, and Wisconsin followed,
as did disputes concerning the ability of Krishnas to engage in
sankirtan at the Kennedy Center for the Performing Arts, the Visitor's Gate at the United Nations in New York City, and Dallas–
Fort Worth International Airport.[46] Without doubt, the Krishnas
were casting their net widely in terms of the *locations* of public
spaces in which they sought to place their religious message, although their message for each place remained constant.

Recall that district courts must first determine if a public space
in question falls under forum analysis, and then determine
whether a specific religious message in that forum is allowable.
Krishna litigants prevailed on the forum question 90 percent
(n=19) of the time, which is actually the highest success rate of all
faith-based litigants. That district courts are in such agreement
over the Krishnas' public spaces shows that the Krishnas' forums
of choice allowed them to broadcast their message to a high number of people. That is, ISKCON sought very open, very public
spaces that easily accommodate not only large numbers of people,
but also their type of ambulatory expression. Instead of posting a
symbolic sign representing their religion, they actively solicit as
many people as possible. Since *sankirtan* is geared to raise money
for the larger ISKCON movement, it is probably the case that
higher numbers of solicitations lead to higher financial returns.
Thus, *sankirtan* dictates that Krishnas must solicit in forums
through which high numbers of people will pass. However, district
courts only protected *sankirtan* 62 percent (n=13) of the time, and

many concluded that government agencies charged with maintaining public forums could regulate *sankirtan*. Again, though, ISKCON received the most protection for its specific religious message out of all of the faith-based litigants in the study.

Yet, ISKCON's litigation strategy basically collapsed. The Supreme Court's *Heffron* decision in 1981 made clear that reasonable time, place, and manner restrictions on *sankirtan* at state fairs are constitutionally allowable, and thus made the law governing religious expression and solicitations more clear, at least as far as it affected the Krishnas. With a subsequent case in 1992, *ISKCON v. Lee*, the high court concluded that airport terminals operated by public authorities are not public forums at all, and thus any regulations limiting expressive conduct within them need only be reasonable. The Court made it quite easy for local governments to regulate speech and expressive conduct in travel terminals after the *Lee* decision, thereby limiting the Krishnas' ability to engage in *sankirtan* within them.

The collapse of ISKCON's litigation efforts is also rooted in elements intrinsic to the religious movement itself. As E. Burke Rochford points out, ISKCON's spiritual and cultural roots are based in India, thus Krishnas are considered religious "outsiders," in that their faith is not seen as conforming to Western religious and cultural values. To combat its "outsider" status, ISKCON insulated its members from outside influence through communal living and education, and imposed rigid group boundaries.[47] During ISKCON's formative stages in the United States, most of its adherents were single and relatively few were married, with even fewer families in the movement. By the 1990s, though, ISKCON became "a householder's movement in North America" as the number of married devotees and families dramatically increased. As Rochford shows, the increase in families in ISKCON basically caused its communal structure to collapse as more of its devotees sought to live, work, and raise families outside of the communal structure. The Krishna movement, as a result, saw a significant decrease in revenues from the practice of *sankirtan*. With more Krishnas owning homes, raising families, and working outside of the Krishna movement itself, there were simply far fewer followers engaged in the revenue-driven practice of *sankirtan*. For Rochford, "up until the early to mid 1980s, ISKCON's communities were supported financially by . . . *sankirtan*, whereby religious texts . . . were distributed in public places for donations."[48] By 1980 *sankirtan* revenues had declined by 75 percent, and ISKCON was no longer able to maintain its communal lifestyle and its own educational system. Increasing schisms within the movement shadowed the dramatic decline in revenue. ISKCON's founding "guru" died in 1977; by the mid-1980s, the ISKCON movement in North America was prone to factionalism, which only exacerbated the movement's worsening financial situation.[49]

ISKCON's primary, indeed almost exclusive, religious message for the public square is *sankirtan*. Because *sankirtan* has a dual purpose—it exists not only to spread Krishna doctrine and attract new devotees, but also to raise revenue—the ability of Krishnas to get their message in the public square was as much affected by district courts, and the Supreme Court, as it was by its own internal turmoil and disintegration. When the North American Krishna movement began to fragment during the 1980s, its ability to keep placing its message in the public square was hindered. As well, the decline in *sankirtan* among its followers caused a loss in revenue that only dampened further its ability to get its message to the public.

Happy Hannukah! (But Watch Out for Those Babylonians and Romans . . .)

Suzanna Sherry argues that "what sorts of political outcomes might we expect if we allow religious appeals to influence public policy? The answer may be summarized in two words: Jews lose. Christianity and Christian beliefs are so pervasive in our society that it is virtually impossible for most religiously-inspired political disputes to take place on neutral ground."[50] Sherry's point is simply that public religion in the United States—which would also include public religious expression—is almost always Christian based, to the detriment of religious minorities. Certainly Jews have not been silent in the face of Christian-dominated public religion. In terms of constitutional litigation, as Gregg Ivers notes, Jewish litigants (chiefly organized interest groups) have been very active in litigating cases at the Supreme Court level. Discussing the American Jewish Committee and others, Ivers points out that "through their participation both as direct sponsors and as amici curiae . . . these organizations exerted a considerable influence on the development of the First Amendment church-state law."[51] Organized Jewish groups primarily pursued a strict separationist line between church and state, which often made them very unpopular litigants, in the sense that they were perceived as interfering with the establishment Christian civil religion in America. Ivers, though, seems to cast doubt on Sherry's point that public religion in the United States is inevitably Christian, since that explanation does not truly account for the active role Jewish litigants played in forging contemporary church-state jurisprudence.

Turning to attempts to place Jewish messages in the public square, a similar kind of activism is seen, although of a different stripe. Jewish interest groups historically emphasize the need to preserve the high barrier between church and state, and generally speaking do not support the public display of Jewish messages and symbols in public places. However, an activist Jewish group, the Lubavitcher Hasidim, or Chabad-Lubavitch, disagrees with this view of the public square, and actively seeks to place religious messages and symbols in public forums and spaces.

Jews account for just less than 8 percent of all religious speech

and public forum cases, and almost all of that speech is from the
Chabad-Lubavitch, a messianic Jewish movement that seeks to return Jews to observance of Jewish laws to hasten the return of the
Messiah.[52] The Chabad-Lubavitch movement initiated a "massive
outreach program to the rest of Jewry. They deemed it essential
that Judaism and Jewish symbols be visible in the public square."[53]
The Lubavitch attempts to place menorahs in public places pose a
real contrast to how Jewish interest groups typically view issues of
church and state. Barbara Redman argues that "Jews in the United
States traditionally have been against government association
with any religious activity, because the particular religion so associated with is almost certain to be Christianity." Jews, then, are
often opposed to the public display of religious symbols not only
because such symbols are frequently Christian, but also because
they consider that their rights, as Jews, are best protected by a
strong separationist approach to government and religion that
seeks to build, and maintain, barriers separating religion from government, and vice versa. The Chabad-Lubavitch represent a much
more "missionary" strand of American Judaism, and their efforts to
return Jews to religious observance "strongly resemble those of
Christian evangelical groups . . . with the difference that Lubavitch activity is directed primarily toward less religiously obser-
vant Jews."[54] Displaying menorahs on public property is part of the
Lubavitch strategy to target Jews in general for messianic purposes.

Although only a limited number of Lubavitch cases exist, a
clear pattern of litigation concerning religious symbols emerges.
Generally, the Lubavitch only seek to place menorahs in public
squares where a Christian nativity scene already exists or has existed traditionally in the past. When required, the Lubavitch at-
tach disclaimers to indicate there is no government sponsorship of
the religious expression.[55] In addition, only two types of forums are
chosen for this type of expression: one, government buildings,
such as in the lobby of a city-county government building; and

two, publicly owned parks. Thus, the Chabad-Lubavitch movement limits its expression to a narrow band of public places and
does not target other public forums such as schools. Nor does it
necessarily seek out forums that have a large number of public visitors like, a state fair or recreational park. Moreover, the Lubavitch
litigation is geographically dispersed, and comes out of Des Moines
(Iowa), Burlington (Vermont), Chicago, Grand Rapids (Michigan), Atlanta, Indianapolis, and White Plains (New York). There
is no national strategy to place menorahs in public squares, and indeed it seems that the cases that do arise in district courts come
out of municipalities that contain vibrant and growing Lubavitch
communities. In this sense, Jewish speech litigation is very much
a product of specific Jewish communities that exist within a larger
city or other area.

The Lubavitch displays of Jewish symbols in the public square,
and their willingness to litigate their right to do so, reflects a type
of proselytism distinct from that found in Christian doctrine. As
Michael Broyde notes, in the Jewish tradition "proselytizing to the
world is not a priority. Calling Jews to heightened observance of
Jewish law is a priority; indeed, this is not viewed as a form of proselytizing at all. Jews are obligated to obey Jewish law, and anything
one can do to facilitate such observance is a good thing."[56] The
Jewish display of symbols is thus geared toward reminding other
Jews of their obligations to obey Jewish law and in this sense has a
limited scope and meaning. Displaying a menorah does not serve
to solicit converts or contributions to specific sects of Judaism. It
simply serves to remind those of like-minded faith of their religious obligations.

Beyond Menorahs: Demarcating the Eruv

An interesting departure from menorah display cases concerns
whether an orthodox Jewish group can use municipal utility poles
to delimit a religious area to assist the Sabbath observances of

Orthodox Jews. The case, *Tenafly Eruv Association v. The Borough of Tenafly*, is not in the case population of this study due to its recent vintage, but it should be discussed here because it may signal a real departure from the kinds of public forum disputes concerning Jewish speech. At issue is a local Jewish association's wish to place plastic strips, known as *lechis*, on Tenafly, New Jersey municipal utility poles in order to demarcate a ceremonial religious area called an *eruv*. The *eruv* is an "unbroken physical delineation of an area . . . and creates a legal fiction [under Jewish law] which converts a public domain into a private domain, solely for purposes of lifting, carrying, or pushing on the Sabbath."[57] By converting a public domain into a symbolic private domain, the *eruv* thus permits Orthodox Jews to engage in certain types of conduct outside of their own homes that would normally be prohibited on their Sabbath. The Borough of Tenafly refused permission to place the markers on municipal poles, and in response the Tenafly Eruv Association sued, countering that public utility poles constitute a public forum. For the association, the placement of *lechis* on those poles is a type of expression protected under the First Amendment public forum doctrine. The borough's argument prevailed, and although the district court agreed with the association that *lechis* are a type of symbolic expression, they still cannot be placed on utility poles to demarcate the *eruv*. "Rights-of-way and utility poles are certainly not traditional forums to which the public has had open access for discourse," as the court pointed out, thus the borough's refusal to allow *lechis* to be placed on its utility poles was not a denial of free expression to the Tenafly Eruv Association.[58]

Interestingly, the borough allowed churches to place directional signs on utility poles. The court pointed out, though, "the signs are not intended to express a religious viewpoint, or any other viewpoint for that matter. The evidence demonstrates that the Borough permits their continued maintenance on public property because they serve the utilitarian function of providing traffic directions." As the court concluded, "the church directional signs are of a different character than the *lechis*, and that simply because the Borough opened its right-of-way to one does not mean that it necessarily had to open its right-of-way to the other."[59] Whether other *lechi-eruv* cases arise in district courts remains to be seen. Yet, such disputes present different issues for resolution than those normally associated with disputes involving public forums and Jewish expression.

Muslim Speech and the Million Man March

Muslim expression consists of only 2 percent of the religious speech cases filed in district courts, and thus comprises an almost insignificant part of the larger body of case law. Nonetheless, the rarity of Muslim litigation is revealing—for that very fact. Scholars of religious groups in the United States disagree about the total number of Muslims in the United States. Fowler, Hertzke, and Olson peg the number at six million; Moore indicates that there are perhaps four million Muslims.[60] Regardless of the exact number of American Muslims, scholars agree that Islam in the United States is growing, both in terms of the numbers of converts and adherents, and the numbers of new mosques being built. Moreover, "the American Muslim community . . . has become politically active, and is presently engaged in the process of articulating a collective agenda that reflects Islamic moral principles. Generally, Muslim political activity has been bipartisan, but socially conservative."[61]

Of the four Muslim speech cases, three concern the refusal of local authorities in Denver, Colorado, and New York City to grant permits to the Nation of Islam to hold Million Man March rallies. In all three cases, district courts ordered local governments to grant the appropriate permits for the rallies, since the Nation of Islam sought to use public places for its own message. Only one case concerns an attempt to place an Islamic symbol in a public area. As discussed above, the *Mehdi and Khanhan* case, initiated by the secretary general of the National Council on Islamic Affairs, concerned whether the Manhattan General Post Office was a public forum in which religious symbols could be displayed. A Christmas tree and menorah were already on display in the post office's public lobby, thus Mehdi sought to place a Muslim crescent and star in the same vicinity. The district court refused to force the post office to allow it, though, and determined that post offices in general are not public forums, but instead are commercial enterprises in which government regulations on speech need only be reasonable.

The growing presence of Islam in the United States, and its increasing political activity, make the real absence of Muslim speakers from religious speech litigation very interesting indeed. There simply is not enough research on Muslim interest groups to definitively state why they are so absent from this area of constitutional litigation. To be sure, Muslim plaintiffs raise many First and Eighth Amendment claims in the context of prison confinement and treatment of Muslim inmates, as Moore notes, although there is no precise figure as to the percentage of prison cases filed by Muslim inmates versus non-Muslim inmates.[62] In their larger analysis of religious liberty litigation, Wybraniec and Finke indicate that Muslims litigate 4.5 percent of all religious liberty claims raised in federal and state courts, indicating a moderate presence of Muslim litigants overall. To speculate why there are so few Muslim litigants in religious speech cases, it may be simply a matter of fact that Muslims do not need to place their speech in the public square. Unlike the Chabad movement who feel a messianic call to return Jews back to observance of Torah law, or Krishnas who use *sankirtan* to win converts and raise money, there seems to be no equivalent motivation concerning Muslim religious speech.

Clamoring Loudest for the Right to Be Heard or Winning Equal Access for Christians

As noted above, Philip Kenneson argues that religious liberty disputes that end up in court are going through a subtle shift: "many members of the protestant majority . . . alter their tactics when it comes to church-state issues. Rather than expending their energy and resources defending themselves against charges of establishment, they have gone on the offensive, arguing for their right to free religious expression. What courts seem poised to do is to uphold these freedoms as long as there is equal treatment of religions."[63] As Kenneson also points out, though, this growing emphasis on religious expression leads to an "uneasy nervousness" on the part of religious minorities that a religious majority wants to use freedom of expression as a way to have the government indirectly endorse their religious message. The result is that religious speech under the First Amendment is used by the Protestant majority to reaffirm its privileged status, and to remind religious minorities that they are indeed "marginal."

Certainly, others would vehemently disagree with Kenneson's view. Evangelical Christians often perceive religious speech in the public square in terms of *freedom of speech*, and a host of relatively new public interest law firms, from the American Center for Law and Justice (ACLJ) affiliated with the Christian Broadcasting Network, to the Rutherford Institute and the Christian Legal Society, are more than willing to articulate this free speech argument in courtrooms.[64] As one American Civil Liberties Union lawyer commented on the ACLJ, it has been "successful in [its] crusade to say that religious speech is just another form of speech."[65] Thus the counterargument to Kenneson: freedom of expression means religious expression too, and if mainly Protestant speakers avail themselves of that liberty, then so be it. It is a right available to all.

Steve Brown details well the shift to the Free Speech Clause by Christian Right advocacy groups, which by the 1980s responded to Supreme Court cases that seemed supportive of religious speech in public spaces. After experiencing frustration with the Supreme Court's refusal to change Free Exercise and Establishment Clause jurisprudence to reflect Christian Right concerns, many advocacy groups turned to other parts of the First Amendment and recast their attempts to place religion back into public life in terms of freedom of expression.[66] Brown not only explains the recasting of religious liberty claims as free expression claims, but also addresses an underlying rationale as to why evangelicals focused on the issue of free speech. "Underlying the courtroom efforts of New Christian right public interest law firms is their conviction that they are divinely commissioned to use the judicial process to keep the public square open to that message. Religious liberty thus becomes more than a legal right; it becomes a gospel tool."[67] Thus, evangelicals engaged in litigation tactics that perhaps were geared toward success in federal courts, and merged those tactics with a substantive doctrine undergirding evangelical Christianity in general: the imperative of spreading the gospel in public.

The litigants seeking to place Christian messages in public squares certainly tend toward a predominantly evangelical Protestant message. Rarely, though, do Christian speakers indicate that a specific denominational message, such as Baptist, Methodist, Episcopalian, or Catholic, underlies their speech. It may well be that since the issue in these cases is *speech as speech*, and not religious liberty under the Free Exercise or Establishment Clauses, the denominational affiliation of the speaker matters significantly less. Unlike with Krishna and Jewish cases, disputes involving Christian speech invoke all kinds of expressive activity. Thus, it is useful to analyze and categorize their speech in terms of the specific conduct to which it is linked.

Holding Worship Services or Religious Meetings

Sister Mary Reilly's case, discussed in chapter 1, in which she sought access to the Rhode Island Capitol Rotunda, concerned her desire to hold a public worship service to protect impending welfare policy changes. To be sure, her worship and prayer service contained elements of a political protest, but arguably her main message was religious in nature. Reilly's dispute is not representative of this type of case, however. Local, nondenominational churches or church associations instigate most public forum disputes concerning access for worship services. For instance, in *Clergy and Laity Concerned v. Chicago Board of Education*, a local alliance of Chicago clergy sought access to Chicago public schools to provide information on alternatives to military service; the board refused access, but a district court disagreed, holding that since the board allowed military recruiters on its campuses, it had to allow the clergy alliance on campus too.[68] In other cases, local nondenominational churches have sought access to public schools to hold a Campus Crusade for Christ magic show,[69] hold regular Sunday services,[70] conduct religiously themed summer camps on public school properties,[71] or rent a school auditorium to show a religious movie.[72]

Of course, local, nondenominational churches are often mission or start-up churches, spun off from other congregations or instituted by groups of people simply interested in forming their own congregation. And what these usually smaller churches do not have, compared to established, "mainline" Protestant churches, are facilities. Thus, it makes sense that most claims for access to public forums in order to hold a worship service stem from congregations that do not have adequate facilities for their own members, or do not have proper facilities to produce and sponsor certain types of religious programs open to the public at large. District courts are generally sympathetic to such claims, and often decide that government refusals of access for worship services do violate First Amendment public forum doctrine. Almost 65 percent of the cases that concern a church or religious group seeking access to a forum for worship services or other types of religious activities are resolved in favor of the church. As well, churches most often seek access to public schools, and approximately 65 percent of the disputes involve public school facilities such as high school auditoriums, junior high classrooms, and the like. About 20 percent concern access to public parks and similar open properties, and the remainder of cases concern access to government buildings, travel terminals, or other types of public spaces. Using public forum arguments, churches are moderately successful at getting district courts to grant and protect their access to public spaces, and they frequently target public schools as forums for their worship-based activities. It is important to note, though, that these worship-based activities are not conducted during regular school hours. Churches simply seek the use of school facilities to hold their own worship and religious services.

There are limits to access, however, as district courts have made quite clear. For instance, a church seeking *permanent* access to a public forum—a public school auditorium—in order to hold services every Sunday was denied access by the local district court. As the court noted, the church had no sanctuary of its own, and no plans to build one, thus it sought to use a publicly owned forum, maintained by public monies, as its own sanctuary in perpetuity.[73] Such access amounted to permanent government support for one religion in violation of the Establishment Clause.

The Supreme Court addressed this debate in *Lamb's Chapel v. Center Moriches Union Free School District*, where it focused on the constitutionality of allowing churches to use public school facilities, after hours, for their own religious activities. In this case, the evangelical and nondenominational Lamb's Chapel sought access to a public school auditorium to show a film series by Dr. James Dobson on the importance of Christian family values. The school district denied access, arguing that to allow the church to use its facilities to show religiously themed movies would violate the Establishment Clause. The Court unanimously disagreed. Applying public forum precedent from the *Perry* and *Widmar* decisions, the Court reasoned that "there would have been no realistic danger that the community would think that the District was endorsing religion or any particular creed, and any benefit to religion or to the Church would have been no more than incidental."[74]

Prior to *Lamb's Chapel* in 1993, district courts supported the right of churches to access public forums to hold worship services 71 percent of the time, thus churches were very successful in using public forum doctrine to gain admission to the public squares in the form of public schools. There are twenty-one such cases prior to *Lamb's Chapel* in 1993, and sixteen cases afterward. Intriguingly, district courts after 1993 only granted access to churches in 56.3 percent of the cases. The impact of *Lamb's Chapel* on district courts, churches seeking access, and local forums is perhaps questionable then, in the sense that courts seem less inclined to grant and protect a church's admission to a public space after the high court clarified the law in favor of churches and their right to congregate in public forums for expressive purposes.

Some of the cases that followed *Lamb's Chapel* concern churches and religious groups that sought to hold worship services in public schools. In general, they argued that since the schools in question allowed nonreligious community groups such as the Boy Scouts or Rotarians to use their facilities, they must also grant equal access to religious organizations. Federal courts often focused on the *type* of access generally allowed by schools, for instance whether outside groups held informational meetings, programs, and the like open to the public. In general, courts denied entry to churches when it was clear—at least in the judicial record—that nonreligious groups received minimal access to school facilities, or received access to programs open to all members of the commu-

nity. Thus, churches that are denied access by federal courts are
frequently asking for a type of forum use, for instance to hold a
worship service mainly for its own congregants instead of sponsoring a community-wide event, which is usually not granted to nonreligious groups.

Interestingly, one case in which access was denied to a local
congregation is *Good News Club v. Milford Central School District*.[75]
Here, a local evangelical minister and his church sought access to
elementary school facilities to hold religious meetings for students
after school hours. Although the district court initially granted a
preliminary injunction granting the group entry to the forum, it
vacated the injunction at a later point, reasoning that New York
State law prohibited access to religious denominations to hold religious worship services, thus the school acted under state law and
did not violate the First Amendment rights of the congregation.
As the club's minister, Reverend Steve Fournier, argued, the issue
concerned free speech: "we should have the same rights as any
other group, and we shouldn't be excluded simply because we
speak of God during the course of our club. It's a matter of wanting to use space in a building."[76] The dispute is very similar to
Lamb's Chapel in that a nonschool affiliated group seeks to use
school facilities for a religious activity, and in this case a local religious group headed by adults wishes to use school facilities after
hours to conduct evangelical meetings for students. In this sense,
Good News falls between a local congregation seeking access for a
religious service, and a student group seeking access to hold student meetings. Nonetheless, the group in question was organized
and headed by a local minister, and importantly was not organized
by the students themselves. The meetings have more of the flavor
of a worship service, then, primarily due to the minister's organization and guidance.

On appeal, the Supreme Court decided the case in favor of the
outside group seeking access, although the main issue had shifted

by the time the case came up to the Court. The Court did not focus on when and why congregations can gain access, and unlike the district court did not perceive the *Good News Club* as a religious denomination but instead viewed it as a religious student-group seeking access to elementary schools. As Justice Thomas explains for the majority,

> Applying *Lamb's Chapel*, we find it quite clear that Milford engaged in viewpoint discrimination when it excluded the Club from the after-school forum.... Like the church in Lamb's Chapel, the Club seeks to address a subject otherwise permitted under the rule, the teaching of morals and character, from a religious standpoint.[77]

The Court's *Good News* decision demonstrates the confusion that lower district courts face in religious speech disputes concerning churches, religious groups, and local schools. The high court's decision notably indicates, albeit indirectly, that perhaps there is no real distinction between organized congregations that seek access to public school facilities, and other groups that do not rank as congregations but likewise seek after-hours access. Importantly, too, the Court's decision shows that public forum law is perhaps not settled as it pertains to churches and groups seeking to hold worship services and religious meetings in public spaces.

These types of disputes can also be placed in a broader social and historical context. That local, nondenominational churches litigate public forum disputes primarily to gain access for their own worship services, or in *Good News* access to hold a worship service for students, reflects a much broader trend toward the growth of evangelical congregations from the 1970s onward. As "mainline" Protestant churches saw their membership rolls and congregation numbers decline, smaller, more evangelical churches stepped into the breach.[78] As Robert Booth Fowler and others put it, the mainline Protestant churches (Episcopalians, Methodists, Presbyterians, United Church of Christ, Evangelical Lutheran congregations, and Congregationalists) may have declined, but they still "possess a wealth of inherited capital in the form of buildings, institutions, and endowments."[79] Thus, it makes sense that established churches would not need to use public forum doctrine to gain access to public facilities to hold worship services and the like, and the main consumers of the law here will be those congregations in search of space for their own services.

Moreover, the *Good News* case is the direct result of a national organized effort to evangelize to young children, and thus does not fit the local, nondenominational church as litigant mold. Good News Clubs were created by the national Child Evangelism Fellowship, and local clubs are sponsored and supported by local congregations and CEF affiliates. As the director of a local CEF chapter puts it, "when children are old enough to realize they're sinners, they are old enough to recognize Jesus as their savior."[80] Moreover, evangelizing children reaches the rest of the family and especially the child's parents.[81] The Good News Clubs present slightly different issues in that overtly evangelical groups not necessarily organized as religious churches or congregations seek access to public schools based on the same grounds justifying church access. Churches can use school facilities that are normally open to nonreligious community groups, and *Good News* establishes that more loosely organized fellowship groups can likewise get the same rights of access.

Preaching and Evangelism

Slightly different from disputes involving local churches or other religious groups seeking access to the public square are cases concerning access for individuals to engage in religious activities such as preaching and evangelism. To be sure, Good News Clubs and similar groups are evangelical and seek to spread the gospel, but they often do so through group meetings and religious services. Here, individuals are directly engaged in face-to-face encounters with others, much like the Krishnas, and are not participating in student meetings or religious services held in enclosed spaces. These types of cases often concern one individual or group that seeks to use a public space in order to win converts. Churches and groups that seek public forums for their worship services are also interested in evangelizing, to be sure, but in a less overt way. Churches seek access for a defined congregation; for individual preachers and proselytizers, there is no defined congregation except for the public that happens to pass through the forum while these expressive activities go on.

An example is *Gilles v. Torgersen*, in which the plaintiff sought access to the Virginia Tech University drill field in order to preach to the masses of students passing by. Since the drill field was reserved for the exclusive use of student-sponsored events, the university allowed him use of its amphitheater instead. The district court determined that the drill field was indeed a public forum, but that the university's regulations for it were reasonable.[82] The speaker, Gilles, sought to preach to students and others passing through the public forum, thus he was not seeking access to hold a specific worship service for an identifiable congregation or group.

There are very few cases involving preaching and evangelism in public places and all of them are filed by individual plaintiffs. The litigation dynamic that emerges, then, simply concerns individuals who seek to proselytize in the public square. All the cases concern a type of individual-based activity, similar to Mr. Gilles preaching on the Virginia Tech campus, that focus on the speaker's desire to engage in a kind of religious outreach. The speaker may wish to warn the world and decadent college students of the sinful errors of their ways (Gilles), or may simply concern an elementary school child's request to show a video of her singing a proselytical song.[83] Of the small number of cases, district courts allow the individual preacher or evangelist to speak in a forum 37.5 percent of the time, indicating that for various reasons this type of activity is generally not protected in the public square. However, the small number of cases does not allow for easy generalization, and it may be that individual preachers are frequently allowed into government-maintained public forums without resort to lawsuits, and that litigation is the exception and not the rule.

Soliciting Donations, Distributing Literature, and Public Prayers

These three types of activities are of course closely linked to preaching and evangelism in public. It may well be that there is no real distinction between evangelism, broadly construed, and the more limited type of expression of distributing religious literature or soliciting donations. Thus, it can be argued that distributing literature and other things are subsumed under the broad rubric of evangelism. District courts, however, tend to focus specifically on the type of expression and conduct involved in religious speech disputes, thus these categories of conduct—soliciting, distributing materials, and praying in public—are often distinguished by courts and treated as specific types of expressive conduct under the law.

In terms of solicitations for money, presumably to fund further religious missions and activities, very few Christian-based speakers tend to litigate such claims. The Holy Spirit Association for the Unification of World Christianity litigated two cases, and in both cases district courts affirmed their First Amendment rights to engage in religious solicitations.[84] Courts also protected the right of members of an evangelical Christian church to solicit at a street intersection where commercial vendors (flowers, newspapers) were allowed to ply their trade, and also protected the rights of church members to solicit for alms in Los Angeles parks and other public places.[85]

In these cases distributing literature is different than soliciting donations since the distributor is not asking for monetary support for a specific religious cause. Litigants seeking to distribute religious materials are often part of a larger organization such as the Gideons who hand out the New Testament, or other groups that distribute religious literature published by national organizations. Thus, plaintiffs who wish to distribute literature in the public square do so as part of a larger national or international movement or publication. One example here is *Bacon v. Bradley-Bourbonnais High School District No. 307*, in which members of the Gideons sought to give the New Testament to public high school students. They confined their conduct to the public sidewalk in front of the school, and not on school grounds itself. The district court noted that the sidewalk was a public forum open to unrestricted use, and also pointed out that the school board's claim that the Gideons created hazards for pedestrians by clogging up the sidewalk was unsupported by evidence. Thus, the Gideons' distribution of the New Testament was protected by public forum doctrine.[86] Importantly, though, when the Gideons distribute New Testaments on school grounds, or in school facilities, the public forum calculus tends to change.

For example, in *Schanou v. Lancaster City School District*, a district court sustained a school district's policy that *allowed* the Gideons to hand out Bibles to students on school grounds and in public school hallways by using such catchy slogans as "the Bible is red and meant to be read."[87] The district judge determined that the school was a public forum, the school's policy allowing the Gideons access passed constitutional muster under the *Lemon* test from *Lemon v. Kurtzman*, and the school did not establish or endorse religion by allowing the distribution of religious literature on its property.[88] However, the district court's opinion was vacated and remanded by the Eighth Circuit due to standing concerns, not because the school's policy violated the Establishment Clause. As the Eighth Circuit noted, "absent specific facts demonstrating the continuing or threatened direct effect of the allegedly unconstitutional policy on his child or himself, the mere fact that Schanou's son was once a student in a school district which allows yearly bible distribution to fifth grade students after school does not confer standing."[89] In a similar case, the Gideons were allowed to distribute Bibles in a public school during school hours as long as the Bibles were placed on a table for the students to voluntarily pick up, and a sign on the table prominently disavowed the school board's or administration's sponsorship.[90]

Other cases concern individual students who wish to distribute the national, evangelical publication "Issues and Answers" to fellow students in public schools. In contrast to the Gideon cases, which concern nonschool affiliated persons, these "Issues and Answers" disputes almost always concern students enrolled in their own specific schools. For instance, in *Thompson v. Waynesboro Area School District*, a district court determined that distributing a religious magazine within school facilities did not amount to a "meeting," and thus did not fall under a school district's policy allowing access to community groups for meetings and other types of gathering. The court also noted that the Equal Access Act does not apply to the distribution of religious literature, and the school's policy did not violate that federal statute.[91] In contrast, another district court did allow students to distribute the magazine on a sidewalk in front of a school prior to the start of the school day.[92] Interestingly, one court distinguished between the "personal" distribution of "Issues and Answers" to a student's friends, and the more general distribution of the magazine campus-wide to the student body. The court determined that a school's policy prohibiting general distribution of "leaflets" and similar materials in school hallways was a reasonable time, place, and manner regulation on the circulation of religious materials.[93]

Of the literature distribution cases, 68 percent (n=13) concern public schools, almost all of which are secondary junior high or high schools, and in 70 percent of those cases district courts rule in favor of the religious speaker and determine that public forum doctrine does protect a right to distribute religious literature. Very few cases involve other forums such as travel terminals or public parks, and with these public places courts are evenly split about protecting the distribution of religious materials since half the cases protect the plaintiff's interest in the public square, and half of the cases do not. What is intriguing is that most of these cases litigated in federal courts concern public school forums, indicating perhaps a larger trend of individual students seeking to distribute evangelical Christian materials, such as "Issues and Answers," or the Gideons and similar groups wishing to distribute the Bible to public school students.

Access for Religious Clubs in Schools

Whether religious groups organized by students can be allowed to meet in public school facilities has been a national political issue since at least the early 1980s. In the wake of *Widmar v. Vincent*, in which the high court extended public forum doctrine to protect religious expression in public universities, federal courts began to adjudicate disputes concerning religious expression, student groups, and secondary public schools.[94] Some courts extended *Widmar's* protections to secondary schools; other courts did not. In response, Congress enacted the Equal Access Act (EAA) so that schools that receive federal funding and allow "noncurriculum" student groups to meet on campus after hours must allow most types of students groups, including religious groups, to meet as well. The Supreme Court ruled the EAA constitutional in *Board of Education v. Mergens*.[95] The EAA, and more generally the presence of religious student groups in public schools, polarizes opinion on religious expression and the links between church and state. "People who applaud the Equal Access Act tend to charac-

terize the clubs as the spontaneous result of student interest," as
one scholar notes. Student groups voluntarily organize, seek access, set their own goals, and so forth, and schools should encourage and foster such important student development. Yet,
opponents see the law, and student religious groups, "as a plot by
outside evangelical ministries to establish beachheads in public
schools."[96]

Public high schools feature prominently in these types of cases,
since 77 percent of the disputes concern attempts by student
groups to use high school facilities. There are only thirteen district
court cases that deal with religious group access to public schools
however, indicating that most disputes between religious groups
and public schools are probably resolved amicably under the terms
of the EAA. *All* of the cases arose after Congress enacted the
statute, but only seven of the thirteen cases are based on the act.
The remaining six disputes concern schools that raise an Establishment Clause defense to allowing religious groups on campus.
Importantly, if a school does not designate itself as a limited public forum—that is, if it closes its forum to all student groups that
are not related to specific school curriculum—then the school is
not bound to the terms of the EAA at all. The sole empirical study
to date on the Equal Access Act concludes that the *Mergens* decision sustaining the statute "did not trigger a tidal wave of religious
evangelizing in public schools. Nor did it result in an upsurge of
sectarian controversy or public conflict," even though most
schools in this (limited) study had Christian clubs, "usually of a
Protestant nature," as the only advocacy oriented student
groups.[97]

Local congregations and ministers often organize active religious student groups in public schools. One group, the "First Priority" organization, seeks out local youth ministers to organize
student groups, although maintaining that groups must be student
initiated in order for schools to accept them.[98] Other groups, such

as the Good News clubs, are also loosely based on materials distributed by a national organization, but also depend upon local groups to give the clubs a specific local context. Student groups seeking access to public school facilities will often have the goal of "returning" religious speech to public schools, and indeed form part of a larger agenda along those lines. As one scholar notes, conservative groups such as the Christian Coalition, the Family Research Council, and Focus on the Family see student groups as one way to return devotionals to public schools.[99]

There are few empirical studies of religious groups and their success rate in gaining access to public school facilities, and it is hard to tell if the litigation observed represents the bulk of disputes, or whether most disputes over access are resolved without resort to lawsuits. What is clear, though, is that student religious groups that litigate are predominantly evangelical Protestants, and most are affiliated with one of the national organizations such as First Priority or Good News. Thus, the impetus to litigate may not necessarily stem from the students (or parents, or ministers) themselves, but from an organization not specifically connected to the specific school district or community in question.

Religious Displays

Almost 14 percent (n=17) of the Christian speech cases concern the display of religious symbols, such as crosses, crèches, or nativity scenes, in public spaces in order to remind viewers and passersby of the religious significance of certain holidays such as Christmas and Easter. District courts are divided on how such cases should be resolved, with approximately half of the courts deciding that the First Amendment Free Speech Clause protects the public display of religious symbols, and the other half ruling against such displays.

Importantly, the Supreme Court has decided two religious display cases, *Lynch v. Donnelly* and *Allegheny County v. ACLU*. In

Lynch, the nativity scene at issue was sponsored by a municipal government; in *Allegheny County* the nativity scene and menorah in question were sponsored by private organizations. In both cases, the religious symbols were placed on public property. The Supreme Court decided both cases under the Establishment Clause, and in *Lynch* determined that Pawtucket, Rhode Island's display of a crèche did not impermissibly advance religion. In *Allegheny*, the Court concluded that the prominent display of a crèche did violate the Establishment Clause, but the display of a menorah mixed with secular objects of the Christmas holidays was constitutionally allowable. Both decisions are confusing, to be sure, but it is important to note that neither case involved public forum doctrine to justify placing religious symbols in the public square.

In the *Lynch* case, the federal district court that first decided the dispute noted that although the town's display of a nativity scene violated the Establishment Clause, it did not mean that privately motivated religious speech was similarly banned.

Having spent considerable time exploring what this case is about, the Court feels compelled to add a few words about what it is not about. It is not about an infringement of the right of Christians freely to express their belief that Christmas is the day on which the Son of God was born. This decision has nothing to do with the ability of private citizens to display the crèche in their homes, yards, businesses, or churches. However, the right to express one's own religious beliefs does not include the right to have one's government express those beliefs simply because the believers constitute a majority.[100]

Thus, there is a clear difference between government-sponsored religious displays, and those backed by private individuals or groups. All of the district court cases concerning religious displays concern privately sponsored displays in the public square.

One early case is *McCreary v. Village of Scarsdale* from 1983, which concerned whether the refusal of Scarsdale, New York, to allow the display of a nativity scene during Christmas in a town-owned park violated the free speech rights of group of private citizens known as the Scarsdale Crèche Committee. For over twenty years the committee was allowed to sponsor a crèche display in the park in order to convey the "real significance of Christmas," but the display was discontinued when the town trustees voted to stop the practice. The district court determined that the town's refusal did not violate the free speech rights of the individuals involved with the crèche committee. The court touched upon some of the pertinent issues involved with religious symbols in the public square.

> Allowing plaintiffs' crèche to stand . . . would have the direct and immediate effect of advancing religion in two related ways. First, in contrast to cases like *Widmar [v. Vincent]* where speech derives from the simultaneous efforts and actions of those who have gathered to engage in it, when a symbol is placed on public land the land performs an added and enhanced *function*. No longer is the land just a place from which a message can be proclaimed; when a symbol is left on public land the land actually becomes the message bearer. This means that public resources are substituted for personal conduct as a way of generating speech. . . . state resources are relied upon and used to advance religion.[101]

Although the district judge determined that the town park in question was a traditional public forum open to expressive activity, the privately sponsored display of a nativity scene is still pro-

hibited by Establishment Clause prohibitions on government endorsement of one religious message.

Further public display cases concern slightly different types of
exhibits. In *Doe v. Small*, for instance, at issue was a display of sixteen religious paintings depicting the life of Christ put up in a city-
owned park by a local Jaycees organization during the Christmas
holidays in Ottawa, Illinois. The display has been erected annually
over the course of several decades. Although the paintings were
privately owned, neither the city nor the Jaycees knew exactly
who owned them. Moreover, the paintings were often placed in
the park soon after Thanksgiving holidays (late November), and
remained on display until February or March because, as the
Jaycees put it, "the ground had frozen, making removal impracti-
cal until warmer weather ensued."[102]

The district court determined that the city's continual grant of
access to the Jaycees for the display of the religious painting violates the Establishment Clause: "thus City Defendants may—and
must—regulate religious speech [in the park], including that of
Jaycees, if such speech presents the danger of a violation of the
Establishment Clause." Moreover, the Jaycees "are the *only* group
that has regularly taken advantage of the forum for an expressive
activity of any length. Other private uses of the park . . . do not
result in the same kind of sustained statement of a message . . .
here there is unrefuted empirical evidence that religious groups
will dominate [the] open forum for Jaycees' religious display has
dominated the Park, with a few interruptions, for over 30
years."[103]

Another case concerning the display of a religious symbol
demonstrates the blurred boundaries that can often exist in these
types of disputes between private expression in the public square
and government endorsement of the speaker's message. *Doe v.
County of Montgomery, Illinois* concerned the display of a neon
sign reading "The World Needs God" in foot-high letters. The

sign, located over the entrance to the old county courthouse in Montgomery County, Illinois, was paid for in 1940 by the Federated Women's Bible Club (now defunct), and over the course of decades ownership of the sign passed to the county government. It was removed in the 1960s when the courthouse was cleaned, and was replaced in 1968 at the request of several local religious groups. What started as a privately owned and motivated religious display developed, by the 1990s, into government ownership of the sign and therefore government endorsement of the sign's message.

Applying Establishment Clause jurisprudence, a federal district court ordered the sign removed from the government building, as it effectively endorsed one religious message and thus violated the separation of church and state.[104] Importantly, though, had ownership of the sign not passed to the government, the litigation dynamics may have been slightly different, in that the owner of the sign, presumably a private speaker (not affiliated with the government), could have articulated a clearer free speech argument based on access to a public forum. As it were, the government's ownership of the sign made it the "speaker," and thus its message was carefully scrutinized and forbidden under the Establishment Clause.

To be sure, the public display of religious symbols, whether by private speakers or government entities, tends to raise more Establishment Clause concerns than other public access disputes. "The land actually becomes the message bearer," as the district court put it in the *McCreary* case discussed above, meaning that it is often difficult to disentangle the privately motivated speech surrounding a religious symbol from the public land on which that symbol is located.

CONCLUSION

Understanding the dynamics of litigation in religious speech and public forum disputes shows the context in which district courts must decide these cases. That most of the cases involve local forums owned by county or city governments, or even local school boards, is perhaps not surprising. As scholars of religion and politics commonly point out, many of our disputes over the intermingling of religion and government occur at the local level. Thus, district courts primarily respond to more localistic concerns about when and how governments manage public properties under their control. The predominantly local nature of the public square fits into more theoretical arguments that view the metaphorical public square defined by Richard Neuhaus as comprised of mini public squares that contribute to a larger national dialogue between religion, politics, and society. In terms of litigation, this dialogue takes place at the most local level, in municipal libraries, public schools, and public parks. Indeed, those local public forum disputes that are not litigated perhaps do not contribute as much to our understanding of religious speech in public places, simply because we do not know about them and cannot understand the interplay of pressures, from religiously motivated expression to the needs of the government in regulating and maintaining forums in a certain manner.

The types of religious interests and types of expression seeking access to the public forum also illuminate the policymaking role of courts. Compared with religious liberty litigation in general, there are far fewer religious voices using the Free Speech Clause and public forum doctrine in the First Amendment to get their messages to the public. Whereas a plethora of faiths and religious groups seek protection for their religious beliefs through Free Exercise Clause litigation, only a few types of faiths seek to protect their specific religious message and gain access to the public square through public forum litigation. Significantly, the vast majority of religious speech claims are brought by Christian speakers, and arguably the law on religious speech and public forums is developing in the context of one specific faith-based message. The ramifications of this are discussed in subsequent chapters.

CHAPTER 4

"The Land Becomes the Message Bearer": Locations of the Public Square

LITIGATION DYNAMICS SHOW THE KINDS of messages and types of expression that speakers seek to place in the public square. As chapter 3 illustrates, the motivations of religious speakers range from Krishna solicitations for money and the distribution of Christian literature by evangelical public school students to the vocal proselytism by preachers such as James Gilles who sought to use Virginia Tech's drill field to preach to the masses of college students filing by. Many different types of expression and religious messages are bundled together in religious speech and public forum disputes. Yet, several questions remain unanswered. Where is all this religious speech going? What venues and public squares do speakers choose to litigate? Moreover, how do district courts define the contours of forums in their policymaking?

To a large extent, how judges approach the content of a public forum depends on the category and spatial dimensions of the forum itself. Prior to any discussion of whether the government may regulate the content of speech in a public place is a determination of whether the space is actually open to speech and expressive activities. Defining or categorizing the public forum is the first step, and here courts focus on the spatial dimensions of the public area in question and its historical and customary usages. As the Supreme Court put it in *NAACP v. Cornelius*, "the extent to which the Government can control access depends on the nature of the relevant forum."[1] Justice Felix Frankfurter points out that the crux of public forum questions concern the spatial and geographical characteristics of the public property in question. His concurring opinion in *Niemotko v. Maryland* is instructive, as he notes, "Where does the speaking which is regulated take place? Not only the general classifications—streets, parks, private buildings—are relevant. The location and size of a park; its customary use . . . the facilities . . . readily available in a community for airing views, are all pertinent considerations."[2] Similarly, in *Grayned v. City of Rockford* the Supreme Court observes "the nature of a place, the pattern of its normal activities, dictate the kinds of regulations of time, place, and manner that are reasonable. Although a silent vigil may not unduly interfere with a public library, making a speech in the reading room almost certainly would. That same speech should be perfectly appropriate in a park. The crucial question is whether the manner of expression is basically incompatible with the normal activity of a particular place at a particular time."[3] Questions of the precise location and type of forum are important, then, to understanding court policymaking concerning speech and expression in public places. Analyzing the forums open to religious speech generates a more nuanced inquiry into how religious speech interacts in the public square and the policymaking role of federal district courts in defining public properties under forum analysis.

One district court case, *Travis v. Owego-Apalachin School District*, offers a nice example of how district judges initiate the forum inquiry prior to assessing the constitutionality of government limits on speech within the public space at issue. Here, Toby Travis, a professional magician and evangelist for the Christian evangelical group Youth for Christ, Inc., wanted to use the Owego-

Apalachin Middle School auditorium for a fundraising magic show, the proceeds of which would benefit the pro-life crisis pregnancy center Birthright of Owego. Birthright of Owego initially made the request for access, and the school board granted permission. However, when Birthright sought to reschedule the magic show because it conflicted with Owego's Strawberry Festival (which would negatively affect the magic show's audience draw), the school board denied the request for use because "Travis would engage in religious and/or political activity during the course of the performance." New York State law allows local schools to open their facilities to their communities for certain activities, but it expressly prohibits usage in which admissions fees are charged "for the benefit of a society, association or organization of a religious sect of denomination," and facilities may likewise not be used for the teaching of religious doctrine.[4] Travis sued, contending that denial of access violates his free speech under the First Amendment.

Federal District Judge Thomas J. McAvoy agreed. In his analysis, the school district operated a limited forum under state law by allowing other community groups to use its facilities. Moreover, the school previously allowed other religious groups to hold community Christmas programs, and the magic show that Travis proposed is more akin to a "social, civic or recreational meeting or entertainment pertaining to the welfare of the community open to all," a type of forum access that is explicitly permitted by New York state law.[5] In arriving at his conclusion Judge McAvoy traverses public forum doctrine and his analysis is illustrative of the kinds of issues and questions with which district judges must contend.

The Owego-Apalachin school facilities are considered limited public forums, designated and opened by the government specifically for expressive activity, and are thus not traditional forums historically and customarily open to speech-related conduct. As

Judge McAvoy explains, the Supreme Court's public forum doctrine provides the framework for assessing "the competing interests regarding the use of government property.... [in order] to balance the government's interest in limiting the use of its property against the interests of those who wish to use the property for expressive activity." Figuring out if the government—here, a school board—designates a space as a public forum is tricky, and hinges upon several issues. Again, for Judge McAvoy, "the policy and practice of the government has substantial bearing on whether it has intended to designate a place not traditionally open to assembly and debate as a public forum. Also pertinent to ascertaining the government's intent is the nature of the property and its compatibility with expressive activity."[6] Not only must judges inquire into how the government views and treats a public space under its control; the nature of the space must also be considered. The actual physical characteristics of the property are relevant, as is the actual usage of the space as well. "Forum classification and denial of access are distinct issues," as McAvoy stipulates, thereby framing part of the district court policymaking role. Courts must first delve into the physical, spatial dimensions and usages of public spaces to determine whether they are traditional, limited/ designated, or nonpublic forums, with consequent ramifications on access for speech and expression.

A brief review of public forum doctrine sets the terms for how district courts make policy for religious speech in the public square. For the Supreme Court in *Perry Educational Association v. Perry Educator's Association*, "the existence of a right of access to public property and the standard by which limitations upon such a right must be evaluated differ depending on the character of the property at issue."[7] Recognizing that the "character" of public properties can differ markedly, the Court created three different categories of forums to serve as a framework for balancing the right of free speech with the regulatory interests of the government.

The first category, the traditional public forum, concerns spaces such as streets and parks that historically and customarily are devoted to speech activities and public debate. Government regulations on the content of speech in the forum must be justified by a compelling interest that overrides the rights of the speaker, and the regulations must be as narrowly defined as possible. Time, place, and manner restrictions—regulations on when the speech takes place, precisely where it occurs, and how the message is expressed—are constitutional as long as they again are narrowly drawn, are justified by a significant state interest, do not interfere with the content of the speech, and leave open alternate means of communication.

Traditional forums are always "open," but limited or designated public forums are not. Designated forums are those public spaces opened by government policy or mandate to speech and expressive activity. Governments may open and close designated forums, but once open the rules of the traditional forum apply in that all restrictions on speech must meet the compelling interest test. When the government designates a place as a public forum, it subsequently loses much of its regulatory power over it, and its ability to limit access to it is restricted in the same way as with traditional public forums.

Finally, public property that is not a traditional or designated forum is open to speech, but the government may regulate access to it under a more relaxed reasonableness standard, meaning that restrictions on speech do not have to be justified by a compelling interest, but only have to be reasonable in light of the forum and the circumstances surrounding it. This last category with its deferential approach to government regulation reflects that some government property is simply not amenable to expressive activity and public debate, and "[t]he State, no less than a private owner of property, has power to preserve the property under its control for the use to which it is lawfully dedicated." Nonpublic forums include places such as military installations, some government buildings, letterboxes, and United States Post Offices.

LOCATION, LOCATION, LOCATION

Only a few types of public properties are litigated in religious speech/public forum disputes, and almost all of them, as chapter 3 notes, fall under local government jurisdictions. Absent are locations such as federal military bases and other installations, state and federal government laboratories or other types of research centers, and other types of government buildings and lands that are not generally open to the public anyway. As table 4.1 shows, five main types of forums are prominent in district court cases. Much district court attention is focused on only two specific types of forums, however. Schools, public parks, and other open spaces are most prominent in litigation, and combined account for approximately 75 percent of all cases, with schools accounting for about 38 percent of forums and parks 37 percent.[8] Moreover, schools and parks are more than likely to fall under local government control, with 92.4 percent (n=61) of the schools falling under local school board control, and 72 percent (n=46) of the parks coming under local control. The remainder are regulated by state and federal agencies. With schools, for instance, public universities involved in forum litigation are regulated by state governments. As for parks, state agencies often regulate state fairgrounds, the federal government has oversight of litigated places such as the Washington, D.C., Mall, and even National Forest lands that may serve as public forums open to speech and expression. That three-fourths of the forum locations are schools or parks falling under local government jurisdiction again demonstrates the important role that sub-national governments play in how the law develops.

Other forum locations are travel terminals, government buildings, and public spaces that simply defy easy definition. Travel terminals are logically public places where speakers can get their messages out to large numbers of people, yet they only account for 8 percent of disputes filed in district courts. Disputes over travel forums may concern airports, as in *ISKCON v. Engelhardt* in which Krishnas sought to practice *sankirtan* at Kansas City International Airport.[9] Other travel places include the Washington, D.C. Metro system or commuter trains in the Boston area.[10]

In addition, government buildings, such as the Rhode Island legislature's rotunda in Sister Mary Reilly's dispute, only comprise 9 percent of the cases. Examples of government buildings include *U.S. v. Boeswetter*, in which several Krishnas were prosecuted by the federal government for violating regulations against soliciting in the Kennedy Center for the Performing Arts in Washington, D.C.,[11] or the display of the Ten Commandments by a Texas State judge in his courtroom.[12] Local government buildings are affected too, for instance with groups that wish to hold worship services in government buildings, village halls, and even local library meeting rooms.[13]

Finally, a catch-all category called "other" consists of public places that do not fit the above categories and includes 8 percent of the cases. This type of forum defies easy categorization. For instance, several cases concern whether radio waves are public forums, and if so whether litigants have a First Amendment right to broadcast religious programs without licenses from the federal government.[14] Other disputes include whether state license plates are public forums open to religious expression as well.[15]

Traditional Public Forum

Hague v. CIO, 307 U.S. 496, 515–16, (1939).

Wherever the title of streets and parks may rest, they have im-

memorially been held in trust for the use of the public and, time out of mind, have been used for purposes of assembly, communicating thoughts between citizens, and discussing public questions. Such use of the streets and public places has, from ancient times, been a part of the privileges, immunities, rights, and liberties of citizens. The privilege of a citizen of the United States to use the streets and parks for communication of views on national questions may be regulated in the interest of all; it is not absolute, but relative, and must be exercised in subordination to the general comfort and convenience, and in consonance with peace and good order; but it must not, in the guise of regulation, be abridged or denied.

Perry Educational Association v. Perry Educators' Association, 460 U.S. 37, 45 (1983).

In these quintessential public forums, the government may not prohibit all communicative activity. For the State to enforce a content-based exclusion, it must show that its regulation is necessary to serve a compelling state interest and that it is narrowly drawn to achieve that end. The State may also enforce regulations of the time, place, and manner of expression which are content-neutral, are narrowly tailored to serve a significant government interest, and leave open ample alternative channels of communication.

Limited or Designated Public Forum

Perry Educational Association v. Perry Educator's Association, 460 U.S. 37, 45 (1983).

A second category consists of public property which the State has opened for use by the public as a place for expressive activity. The Constitution forbids a State to enforce certain exclusions from a forum generally open to the public even if it was not required to create the forum in the first place. Although a State is not required to indefinitely retain the open character of the facility, as long as it does so, it is bound by the same standards as apply in a traditional public forum. Reasonable time, place, and manner regulations are permissible, and a content-based prohibition must be narrowly drawn to effectuate a compelling state interest.

Police Department of the City of Chicago v. Mosely, 408 U.S. 92, 96, (1972).

. . . government may not grant the use of a forum to people whose views it finds acceptable, but deny use to those wishing to express less favored or more controversial views. And it may not select which issues are worth discussing or debating in public facilities. There is an "equality of status in the field of ideas," and government must afford all points of view an equal opportunity to be heard. Once a forum is opened up to assembly or speaking by some groups, government may not prohibit others from assembling or speaking on the basis of what they intend to say. Selective exclusions from a public forum may not be based on content alone, and may not be justified by reference to content alone.

Nonpublic Forum

Perry Educational Association v. Perry Educator's Association, 460 U.S. 37, 46 (1983).

Public property which is not, by tradition or designation, a forum for public communication is governed by different standards. We have recognized that the "First Amendment does not guarantee access to property simply because it is owned or controlled by the government." In addition to time, place, and manner regulations, the State may reserve the forum for its intended purposes, communicative or otherwise, as long as the regulation on speech is reasonable and not an effort to suppress expression merely because public officials oppose the speaker's view.

<u>Greer v. Spock</u>, 424 U.S. 828, 836 (1976).

. . . *whenever members of the public are permitted freely to visit a place owned or operated by the Government, then that place becomes a "public forum" for purposes of the First Amendment. Such a principle of constitutional law has never existed, and does not exist now. The guarantees of the First Amendment have never meant that people who want to propagandize protests or views have a constitutional right to do so whenever and however and wherever they please. The State, no less than a private owner of property, has power to preserve the property under its control for the use to which it is lawfully dedicated.*

Traditional Public Forums

Examples: Public Parks, Streets, Sidewalks, other Thoroughfares

Means of Regulation: Compelling Interest Test; Content-Neutral Time, Place, and Manner Regulations that are Narrowly Defined.

Limited or Designated Public Forums

Examples: Public Schools, Government Buildings, Travel Terminals

Means of Regulation: As long as the forum is open, the compelling interest test applies as with Traditional Public Forums; Content-Neutral Time, Place, and Manner Regulations that are Narrowly Defined.

Nonpublic Forum

Examples: Letterboxes, U.S. Post Office Facilities, U.S. Military Facilities, Some Government Buildings

> **Means of Regulation:** Reasonable regulations on speech are allowable as long as regulation is not an effort to suppress the speaker's viewpoint.

Public School Forums

Public school forums serve as outlets for many types of religious speech and expression, as chapter 3 pointed out. Local churches and other religious groups use school facilities to hold worship services or other religious gatherings during nonschool hours, and students themselves often seek to distribute religious literature or organize religious clubs. District court policymaking must account for a wide variety of schools as forums, from elementary schools to public university facilities. In addition, religious speech occurs not only in facilities devoted to expressive activities such as auditoriums and performance halls; it also occurs in school hallways, between classes, and outside on school grounds.

For the past two decades public schools have been a real battleground for religious activists, especially evangelical Christians from the so-called Christian Right. As scholars of religion and politics frequently note, Christian activists charge that public schools "promote anti-Christian values and [threaten] the ability of conservative Christians to inculcate their values in their own children."[16] The focus of their complaints are often curriculum related, and target "secular-humanist" textbooks that denigrate evangelicalism, ignore creationism, or promote multiculturalism hostile to basic Christian beliefs.[17] There is, then, a deeper context for religious speech and public school cases. However, Christian activists who target public schools often do so not through public forum litigation, but instead through school board elections or lawsuits over curricula matters and textbooks. The religious speech and public forum cases represented in this study do concern individuals and churches that wish to use public school facil-

Location of Forum		Traditional Forum	Designated Forum	Nonpublic Forum	Total
Public School	Count	2	59	5	66
	% within Location of Forum	3.0%	89.4%	7.6%	100.0%
	% within Type of Forum?	4.7%	57.3%	17.2%	37.7%
Travel Terminal	Count	3	10	1	14
	% within Location of Forum	21.4%	71.4%	7.1%	100.0%
	% within Type of Forum?	7.0%	9.7%	3.4%	8.0%
Government Building	Count	1	13	2	16
	% within Location of Forum	6.3%	81.2%	12.5%	100.0%
	% within Type of Forum?	2.3%	12.6%	6.9%	9.1%
Public Park, Other Public Space	Count	37	16	11	64
	% within Location of Forum	57.8%	25%	17.2%	100.0%
	% within Type of Forum?	86%	15.5%	37.9%	36.6%
Other	Count		5	10	15
	% within Location of Forum		33.3%	66.7%	100.0%
	% within Type of Forum?		4.9%	34.5%	8.6%
Total	Count	43	103	29	175
	% of Total	24.6%	58.9%	16.6%	100.0%

TABLE 4.1
Location of Forum by Classification of Forum. Federal District Courts, 1974–2001.

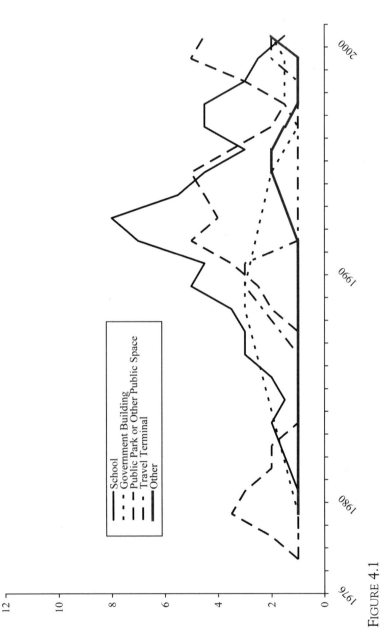

FIGURE 4.1

Types of Forums, by Two-Year Moving Averages. Federal District Courts, 1974–2001.

ities for speech-related purposes, but in many of the cases it would be difficult to discern a hostility to public education in general, and indeed a linkage to this broader trend of Christian activists targeting public schools. The local, nondenominational church that wishes to use school facilities to hold a worship service, for instance, is more likely seeking adequate space for its congregation, and is not engaged in some kind of conduct to reform and rid schools of secular humanism. Likewise for individual students who wish to distribute religious literature on a school campus, or form a religious student group and meet in school classrooms. They may be evangelical or fundamentalist Christians linked to the broader Christian right political movement so hostile to public schools, but they are more likely acting as private, individual religious speakers (and evangelists, in a sense) than as spokespeople and activists for a larger social and political cause.

Public school forums account for slightly more than one-third of the district court cases. Of those disputes, elementary schools comprise 21.5 percent (n=14), junior high or middle schools 9.2 percent (n=6), high schools 55.4 percent (n=36), university facilities 6.2 percent (n=4), and other types of schools 7.7 percent (n=5). The vast bulk of religious speech goes into high school forums, with elementary school forums coming in second. For primary and secondary schools, all types of expressive content are involved in litigation, from student-initiated evangelism to the use of facilities for religious services after school hours by non-school groups. Some schools defy easy definition, and are simply categorized as "other." One good example of an "other" school is the case *Herdahl v. Pontotoc County School District*, which concerns Bible reading and prayers over the school intercom in the North Pontotoc Attendance Center of Pontotoc County, Mississippi. The attendance center is a single facility housing kindergartners through twelfth graders.[18] Since the single facility is a combined primary and secondary school, it is simply categorized in a different manner.

The Supreme Court's guidance on public schools has been reasonably consistent. Summarizing its approach to school forums in *Hazlewood School District v. Kulhmeier*, the Court notes that

> Public schools do not possess all of the attributes of streets, parks, and other traditional public forums that time out of mind, have been used for purposes of assembly, communicating thoughts between citizens, and discussing public questions. Hence, school facilities may be deemed to be public forums only if school authorities have by policy or by practice opened those facilities for indiscriminate use by the general public, or by some segment of the public, such as student organizations. If the facilities have instead been reserved for other intended purposes, communicative or otherwise, then no public forum has been created, and school officials may impose reasonable restrictions on the speech of students, teachers, and other members of the school community.[19]

Likewise in several cases concerning public universities[20] and secondary and primary schools[21] the Court consistently places schools in the designated or limited public forum category.

In categorizing and defining the contours of public school forums, district courts evidence a high level of consensus. Almost 90 percent of all courts agree that public schools by and large are designated public forums. Schools are not forums historically and customarily open to speech and expression, nor are they usually nonpublic forums closed to expressive activity in general. That district courts categorize them as designated forums means that local school boards or other agencies in charge of a school system may open their schools to speech-related activities. Once open as a designated forum, though, local oversight and regulation of access must conform to the strict standards of the compelling interest test. The primary question in defining the contours of schools as forums is whether a school board has expressly opened its facilities to speech and expressive conduct. Thus, courts inquire into specific school policies on access as well as past usages of school facilities by student and community groups. In sum, district court policymaking demonstrates that public forum law governing public schools as *forums* is clear: schools at all levels—primary, secondary, university—are designated public forums that must initially be opened to expression by their governing bodies.

Importantly, as chapter 3 highlights, 98.5 percent of the public school cases concern Christian-based speech, often in the form student-sponsored religious clubs, the distribution of religious literature, or the use of school facilities (after hours) by local religious congregations to hold worship services or other types of religious meetings. Moreover, approximately 50 percent of the cases concerning Christian speech focus on public school forums. The specific type of message seeking access to a forum is more properly assessed in the context of court policymaking on the *content* of forums, which is the subject of the next chapter. Yet, how messages link with specific locations is introduced here to frame district court policymaking on the *contours* of the forums and locations in question. As noted above, district courts by and large agree that public schools are designated public forums. In the cases where district courts departed from the designated forum category, with few exceptions the public school as issue was almost always an elementary school. For example, in *May v. Evansville-Vanderburg School Corporation*, several school teachers sought to hold weekly prayer meetings in their elementary school. Ultimately, a district court determined that the school board's refusal to allow the meetings was constitutional, since the local school board had taken no action to designate and open the elementary school as a public forum. The court did note that although the school district adopted a new policy signifying compliance with the then-new Equal Access Act, "the evidence is clear that the Act applies to student, rather than teacher groups; [and] that the Act is directed to secondary, rather than elementary schools."[22] Similarly, in C. H. v. Oliva et al. and Medford Township Board of Education, at issue was whether an elementary school child could read from a children's Bible to his classmates during class time allotted to such activities. The child's teacher and principal denied permission, and a district court ultimately rejected the child's First Amendment free speech argument, noting that classrooms in elementary schools are not public forums.[23] Many district courts narrowed their categorization of public schools by pointing out that the high court's decisions mainly concerned public universities and high schools, and did not incorporate elementary schools.

To be sure, secondary and primary schools pose an interesting contrast. Elementary or primary schools may be designated as forums by school boards, and recognized as such by district courts. Yet, only rarely are they open to religious speech, as in approximately 75 percent of the elementary school cases district courts refuse to allow access to a religious speaker. Secondary schools such as high schools may be designated forums too, but the situation is reversed, in that district courts allow religious speech and expression in almost three-fourths of the cases. District court policy-making refuses to analogize principles protecting religious speech announced in the context of secondary schools to the primary and elementary school level, and in a sense courts treat those schools and younger students as much more impressionable than older, more mature students at the secondary level. Thus, religious speech may be allowable in schools with older students simply because those students are more mature and will not be easily misled or coerced by religious messages. Elementary students are different, and there are thus higher barriers to religious speech at the primary level than at the secondary level.

However, the Supreme Court entered this policy fray and extended the full protection of its forum categories down to elementary schools. It did so, albeit indirectly, in *Good News Club v. Milford Central School*. Although the seven-justice majority did not specifically categorize the elementary school at issue as a designated forum, Justice Thomas for the majority noted that "because the parties have agreed that Milford created a limited public forum when it opened its facilities in 1992 . . . we need not resolve the issue here. Instead, we simply will assume that Milford operates a limited public forum."[24] In addition, the elementary school at issue was determined to be open to speech and expressive activities—here, an after-hours religious group for students—indicating that the Court now supported religious speech at the lower level of the public school system. However, it is too soon to tell if the Court's oblique designation of elementary schools as public forums has cleared up any lingering confusion in lower district courts.

FEDERALIZING THE PUBLIC SCHOOL FORUM

Unlike with other forums, the federal government has addressed concerns with public schools and access for religious speakers. In 1984 Congress passed the Equal Access Act mandating that when a public school allows "noncurriculum" related student groups to meet on campus either before or after school hours (during "noninstructional time"), the school has created a limited open forum and must allow access to religious, political, philosophical, or other types of groups as well.[25] The Supreme Court determined the act constitutional in *Board of Education v. Mergens*.[26] As the Court put it, the statute simply extended its *Widmar* decision protecting religious speech in a forum maintained by a public university down to the secondary school level. The statute did not

violate the Establishment Clause either. Although there is debate
over the efficacy of the Equal Access Act itself, it is clear that the
statute has rarely been litigated in federal district courts.[27] In the
context of this study, there are only sixteen cases (9.1 percent of
the total) invoking the Equal Access Act to gain admittance to a
public school forum. There is very little research on the application of the act by public schools, but what does exist indicates that
public schools are aware of the statute and do try to follow it.[28]

Figure 4.1 demonstrates that public school forum cases peaked
around 1993, a few years after the Court's *Mergens* decision sustaining the Equal Access Act, and have declined since. Explain-
ing the decline of school litigation is beyond the scope of this
work, but a few observations are in order. To be sure, the Equal
Access Act probably worked to allow religious student groups into
school forums. The absence of litigation based on the act in federal district courts indicates that public schools were perhaps following the law and devising policies of access that recognized
religious student groups as any other type of group, and thus deserving to use public facilities just as any other private speaker.
Some school districts probably allowed religious student groups access anyway and simply justified their preexisting policies under
the new federal law.

Another more noteworthy development concerns the United
States Department of Education's instructions to public schools in
the 1990s that clarified First Amendment law and the schools' re-
sponsibilities toward students. In 1995, and again in 1998, Secretary of Education Richard Riley issued presidential guidelines on
religious expression to all public school districts in the United
States. The guidelines succinctly state the applicable First
Amendment principles concerning student religious expression.
As the secretary stipulates, "these guidelines continue to reflect
two basic and equally important obligations imposed on public
school officials by the First Amendment. First, schools may not

forbid students acting on their own from expressing their personal religious views or beliefs solely because they are of a religious nature. Schools may not discriminate against private religious expression by students. . . . [Second] schools may not endorse religious activity or doctrine."[29] There is some evidence that the federal government's guidelines have had some effect. For instance, an informal study of school boards conducted by the American Jewish Congress concludes that 80–90 percent of school districts have policies in place that allow students to access public school facilities for religious speech and meetings.[30] Similarly, the National School Boards Association indicates that the secretary of education's guidelines "have been successful in reducing conflict, mainly in a preventive way."[31] Lawyers who litigate school issues likewise point out that the EAA and federal guidelines often allow disagreements to be settled through negotiation and compromise, and without resort to federal courts and litigation.[32]

Federal guidelines on student religious expression in public schools coincide with the drop in public school litigation in the mid-1990s, and participants in school disputes by and large note that the guidelines in conjunction with the Equal Access Act help resolve conflicts over access to schools for student religious groups and individual speakers. The high level of agreement among district courts as to how schools should be typed under public forum analysis—the contours of the forums in question—suggests that the main issues of contention and policy divergence among courts concerns the content of public school forums, and the extent to which local school boards may regulate access to their facilities. It may be, though, that only the most extreme cases are litigated in district courts, cases that are simply not resolvable under the federal guidelines and the EAA. Therefore, even though there is a high agreement among judges on how public schools should be categorized as forums, some content-related issues may be too difficult to resolve under the federal guidelines in place. Importantly, cases concerning other forums have not demonstrated the sharp decrease found with public schools. Indeed, litigation concerning public parks and other open spaces evinces a sharp upturn just as school litigation is declining. Relative to other types of forums, the decline in number of school cases is painted in even bolder relief, and to be sure the federal government has not devoted any attention at all to religious speech in other types of public properties. It has not offered guidelines to local governments, for instance, on how locally owned public squares are to be managed for speech activities. The Education Department's statement of principles of public schools is unique, then, and the end result is that schools and potential litigants seeking access to school facilities probably resolve any disputes over school usage without resorting to district court litigation.

TRAVEL TERMINALS

Although not generating as many cases as public schools, disputes over religious speech in travel terminals produce similar consensus among district courts about their categorization as designated public forums. Travel terminals consist of railway stations,[33] airports,[34] and bus stations.[35] Chapter 3 discussed how the Krishnas targeted much of the religious speech in the form of *sankirtan* at forums such as large airports and state fairs where high numbers of people gather, and here approximately one-half of the cases concerning travel terminals are filed by Krishnas seeking to undercut regulations on their ability to solicit others in airports and other places. Other cases are filed by the Jews for Jesus contesting airport regulations limiting their ability to distribute religious literature, and the Chabad-Hassidim wishing to exhibit a menorah next to a Christmas display in a busy airport.

That slightly more than 70 percent of travel terminals are considered designated public forums indicates the high level of policy consensus among district courts. This consensus, though, does not mirror the Supreme Court's policy represented by *ISKCON v. Lee* in which a six-justice majority sustained the Port Authority of New York's prohibition against solicitations in La Guardia and JFK airports. Chief Justice Rehnquist notes for the majority that airports generally are not forums open to expression at all.

> But given the lateness with which the modern air terminal has made its appearance, it hardly qualifies for the description of having "immemorially . . . time out of mind" been held in the public trust and used for purposes of expressive activity. Moreover, even within the rather short history of air transport, it is only [i]n recent years [that] it has become a common practice for various religious and nonprofit organizations to use commercial airports as a forum for the distribution of literature, the solicitation of funds, the proselytizing of new members, and other similar activities. Thus, the tradition of airport activity does not demonstrate that airports have historically been made available for speech activity. Nor can we say that these particular terminals, or airport terminals generally, have been intentionally opened by their operators to such activity; the frequent and continuing litigation evidencing the operators' objections belies any such claim.[36]

Figure 4.1 indicates a rise in district court cases on travel terminals in the mid-1980s, a progression that quickly halted in the early 1990s. The Court's decision in *ISKCON v. Lee* defining public airports as "nonforums" most likely stopped groups and individuals from litigating cases concerning religious expression in airports. As well, the *Lee* decision coincided with the collapse of ISKCON's litigation efforts over *sankirtan* due to the movement's internal conflicts. Rarely do other groups or individuals seek to use airports as outlets for their religious speech, thus with the absence of the Krishnas district courts no longer focus on speech conflicts concerning airports as public forums.

However, an important caveat to the Supreme Court's *Lee* decision is *International Society for Krishna Consciousness of California v. the City of Los Angeles*, which concerns whether Los Angeles International Airport (LAX) is a public forum under *California* state law. The Los Angeles city council passed a sweeping ordinance in 1997 that effectively banned all solicitations in LAX terminals. ISKCON sued, claiming a violation of its free speech rights under the California Constitution. District Judge John G. Davies notes that the protections for free speech in the Californian Constitution are much more sweeping than in the First Amendment to the U.S. Constitution. Moreover, "public forum analysis under California law is different than under federal law. Therefore, the Supreme Court's decision in *Lee* does not dictate any conclusions here."[37] The Los Angeles city government argued that soliciting in LAX must be banned outright, due to the congested, crowded nature of the space, and due to the aggressive and annoying tactics of solicitors who often confront harried travelers who will be much more susceptible to giving away money.

Applying California law, the district judge notes that there are less restrictive means to protecting travelers from aggressive solicitors in the airport.

The Court finds that solicitation is not basically incompatible with the purpose of LAX because there is no evidence that the problems purportedly caused by solicitors could not be effectively controlled by use of less restrictive measures. That is, under California law, when banning a protected speech activity in a forum open to the general public, the City bears the burden of establishing that the activity is basically incompatible with the purpose of that forum. A protected speech activity is not basically incompatible with the purpose of a forum if the disruption it causes could be controlled by measures short of a complete ban on the activity. The Defendants have not shown that the problems purportedly caused by solicitors at LAX could not be effectively managed by less sweeping measures. Therefore, the Ordinance is inconsistent with the Liberty of Speech Clause of the California Constitution.[38]

The few travel forum cases after *Lee* indicate that district courts tend to follow the principle that airports are not public forums, and regulations on expressive activity in them need only be reasonable in light of the exigencies of the public space in question. Thus, governments charged with monitoring and regulating access to travel terminals are accorded significant deference in how they manage and operate them. *ISKCON v. Los Angeles* poses an intriguing counter to *Lee*, however, and may indicate that similar public forum cases are perhaps litigated now in *state*, as opposed to federal, courts. Since almost all airports in question will fall under some kind of local or state jurisdiction, it may be that litigants who turn to state constitutional law instead of the First Amendment will be more successful and will in fact override the restrictive *Lee* decision.[39]

GOVERNMENT BUILDINGS

Government-owned buildings as forums include places such as the Rhode Island legislative rotunda, the United States Capitol building, the United States Supreme Court building, and local courthouses and public libraries. Religious speakers seek access for a range of expression too, from leading a "prayer tour" of the U.S.

Capitol[40] to using public library meeting rooms to hold a Genesis
Commission Meeting to educate the public about creationism.[41]
Again, as with travel terminals and public schools, district courts
generally agree that government buildings are designated forums,
open to speech and expression only when the government specifically enacts a policy to that effect. In 81 percent of the cases government buildings were declared limited public forums. Generally,
district courts apply the *Perry* and *Cornelius v. NAACP* precedents
that define the categories of public forums and how they are applied. Thus, as Justice Sandra Day O'Connor notes in *Cornelius*,

> The government does not create a public forum by inaction
> or by permitting limited discourse, but only by intentionally
> opening a nontraditional forum for public discourse. Accord-
> ingly, the Court has looked to the policy and practice of the
> government to ascertain whether it intended to designate a
> place not traditionally open to assembly and debate as a pub-
> lic forum. The Court has also examined the nature of the
> property and its compatibility with expressive activity to dis-
> cern the government's intent.[42]

William Books v. City of Elkhart poses an interesting departure from
district court policymaking, however.[43] Represented by the Indiana Civil Liberties Union, Books asked a district court to order the
removal of a Ten Commandments display from the lawn surrounding the City Municipal Court building in Elkhart, Indiana.
Although this case could easily be categorized as religious speech
occurring in a public park or other public space, the district judge
conducted the forum analysis in the context of the courthouse
building. The display was given to the city in 1958 by the local
chapter of the Fraternal Order of the Eagles as part of its national
Youth Guidance Program.[44] The display is ruled constitutional
under the Establishment Clause of the First Amendment, but Dis-

trict Judge Allen Sharp does address the public forum argument since the litigants in the case raised it. Relying on *Capitol Square Review & and Advisory Board v. Pinette*, in which the Supreme Court define the plaza surrounding the Ohio Statehouse as a traditional public forum, Judge Sharp notes that

> The City of Elkhart has chosen to keep the Ten Commandments monument as part of its general policy to display objects of cultural and historical significance on public property. Nothing in the record indicates that the City has ever refused to accept and display an object on its property for a content-based or discriminatory reason. Therefore, the City has met the requirement of strict neutrality for displays of private speech on public property. By accepting the monument in the 1950s the city effectively turned its Courthouse lawn into a public forum open to private speakers. And, the city has not regulated the forum to exclude speech for content-based reasons.[45]

PUBLIC PARKS AND OTHER PUBLIC SPACES

In articulating early principles of public forum doctrine, the Supreme Court observed in *Hague v. CIO* that "wherever the title of streets and parks may rest, they have immemorially been held in trust for the use of the public and, time out of mind, have been used for purposes of assembly, communicating thoughts between citizens, and discussing public questions. Such use of the streets and public places has, from ancient times, been a part of the privileges, immunities, rights, and liberties of citizens."[46] Parks and other open spaces have an exalted status in public forum law in the sense that they are the most traditional type of forum open to public debate and the exchange of ideas. To be sure, public forum doctrine originated within the context of parks and open spaces in *Hague* and modern doctrine has its roots in the notion that spaces owned by the government are often open to the free exchange of ideas.

As with public schools, parks and similar type places comprise slightly more than one-third of district court cases. However, district courts do not show the kind of policy consensus on how parks should be categorized as forums, unlike with public schools, government buildings, and travel terminals. About 58 percent of parks are typed as traditional public forums, 25 percent are designated public forums, and 17 percent are considered nonpublic forums.

Deegan v. City of Ithaca is a good example of a traditional public forum.[47] Kevin Deegan and others proclaimed their Christian faith to passersby on Ithaca Commons, an outdoor pedestrian mall in Ithaca, New York. A police officer informed them that Ithaca ordinances prohibit sound on the mall that can be heard twenty-five feet away, and requested that they lower the volume of the speech. Although he was not prosecuted for violating the ordinance, Deegan sued to enjoin its enforcement, contending that limiting the volume of his religious speech violates the free speech and free exercise clauses of the First Amendment. Typing the Ithaca Commons as a traditional forum was not a difficult task for the district judge, since it was a public place open to pedestrians. As well, the noise restrictions did not substantially impede Deegan's ability to express his message, since the local government did not seek to regulate the content of his speech, and other ways of communicating his message remained open. Areas open to pedestrian access are generally considered traditional public forums, as are streets and in some instances roads. For instance, in *Bischoff v. Osceola County, Florida* several religious activists picketed Walt Disney World to protest what they considered to be the Disney Corporation's pro-homosexual personnel policies. Their expressive conduct took place at a busy intersection near the theme park, and as District Judge G. Kendall Sharp pointed out, activists occasionally crossed several lanes of traffic to distribute literature to motorists. Applying Supreme Court dicta from *ISKCON v. Lee*, Judge Sharp notes that "modern roadways constitute a traditional public forum for the discourse of ideas."[48] Yet, Florida law regulating and prohibiting pedestrian access to certain roadways protects the public, thus even though the protestors were expressing their message in a traditional public forum—a modern roadway—their speech could still be limited by the government's need to maintain the safe and orderly flow of traffic.

Although not exactly public parks per se, many disputes concern county and state fairs. In *Heffron v. ISKCON*, a Krishna *sankirtan* case, the Supreme Court labeled state fairs as designated public forums since they are temporary events open to the public for short periods of time. District court policymaking in similar disputes follow the high court's reasoning.[49] Other open public spaces as designated forums are more confusing. In *Chabad-Lubavitch of Georgia v. Harris*, for example, a Lubavitch group sought to place a menorah in the plaza surrounding the Georgia Statehouse. District Judge Orinda Evans noted that the Georgia attorney general in an opinion letter "admits that the plaza in question has been designated a public forum."[50] Thus, the judge seems to indicate that Georgia has opened the plaza to speech-related activities, thereby making it a designated forum. However, the Supreme Court's decision in *Capitol Square Review & Advisory Board v. Pinette* contradicts the district court policy in the Georgia Statehouse, as in *Pinette* the Capitol Plaza surrounding the Ohio Statehouse was declared a traditional public forum since it had been open to expressive conduct for well over a century.[51]

Warren v. Fairfax County offers another example of an open space as a designated public forum. Here, the plaintiff sought to display a crèche and cross on the grassy area enclosed by the horseshoe driveway in front of the Fairfax County, Virginia, Government Center Complex. The landscaped area in question is called the "Center Island," and the county allows speech-related activities to take place by permit only. All permits require that displays must not be left unattended. For District Judge T. S. Ellis, "It is readily apparent that the Center Island is not, as plaintiff suggests, a traditional public forum. It is, by definition, neither a street nor a sidewalk. It is also not a park, at least in the traditional sense of that term. It is an enclosed median between the two legs of a U-shaped driveway. As such, it cannot be said that the Center Island is the type of area 'immemorially . . . held in trust' for the public's use. Indeed, areas of this sort are designed more for aesthetic purposes such as plantings than for public expressive activity."[52]

In one case concerning ISKCON's practice of *sankirtan* and the public sidewalk in front of the United Nation's buildings in New York City, a district judge categorized the area in question as a nonpublic forum. In *ISKCON v. City of New York*, several Krishnas wished to practice *sankirtan* at the Visitors' Gate to the U.N. area due to the high number of people normally gathered there. Moreover, they especially targeted the Visitor's Gate because it provided "access to the particular audience that comprises United Nations visitors because of the international character of the group." In addition, the high number of tourists passing through the gate was important, too, since Krishnas also viewed "tourists as people who are at leisure, not going to and from their places of employment, and therefore more receptive to . . . [their] religious message."[53] New York City banned all speech and expressive activity within a hundred feet of the Visitor's Gate to ensure the orderly flow of crowds, and to further guarantee the security of the U.N. complex. The judge noted the unique circumstances of the United Nations presence in New York, pointing out that under the so-called Headquarters Agreement between the United States and the United Nations, New York was obligated to ensure the "tranquility" of the headquarters district surrounding the U.N. Moreover, it was undisputed that New York had the authority to regulate usage of public streets in the "immediate vicinity of the U.N." New York showed that it had a "weighty" responsibility to provide security around the U.N. complex, even if its security policies interfered with the exercise of First Amendment rights. As the district court noted, "The mere fact of public ownership does not by itself require that a place be available as a public forum," and the "exclusion of plaintiffs from the immediate vicinity of the Visitors' Gate is a reasonable accommodation of the conflicting interests at stake, well-tailored to the exigencies presented at this heavily trafficked entry point to the U.N. Headquarters."[54]

OTHER TYPES OF FORUMS

Some public spaces are simply not easy to define. These types of cases often fall under the so-called metaphysical type of public space noticed by the Supreme Court in *Rosenberger v. University of Virginia*. There, a religious student group at the University of Virginia published a magazine for the university community called *Wide Awake*, and sought access to university monies allocated to fund student publications for the university community. In striking down the university's refusal to fund the religious publication due to Establishment Clause concerns, Justice Kennedy explains for the high court that the funding system for student publications "is a forum more in a metaphysical than in a spatial or geographic sense, but the same principles [of traditional public forum law] are applicable."[55] Thus, the university's refusal to finance the group's religious publication discriminated against the group's message because of its viewpoint, which is an unconstitutional infringement of free speech.

One such example is *U.S. v. Any and All Radio Station Equip-*

ment.[56] In this case, Radio Mission Evangelista operated a Spanish-language Christian evangelical radio station in New York City without a broadcast license from the Federal Communications Commission. After two warning letters requesting the station to cease its broadcasts, the federal government seized the broadcast equipment and instituted forfeiture proceedings against it. The radio station, owned by the church Inglesia Pentecostal El Fin Sen Acera, asked the district court to halt the proceedings. The church argued the radio station was part of their religion: "it is a central tenet of Christianity and especially the Pentecostal sect, that the church member share the teachings of Jesus Christ to convert humankind to act and believe in accordance with the one true philosophy and view of the world, the teachings of Jesus Christ. Claimants assert that the FCC regulation prohibiting the distribution of [low-level broadcast] licenses significantly inhibits a central tenant of their belief—spreading the word of Jesus Christ as thoroughly and profoundly as possible—because they cannot afford to obtain a Class A, B or C broadcast license." For the church, then, the FCC's refusal to grant noncommercial broadcast licenses for low-level, limited-range transmitters effectively interfered not only with their right to free speech, but also the free exercise of religion. District Judge William H. Pauley relied on a Second Circuit Court decision concerning the Federal Communications Act, and pointed out that "the Government's allocation of the radio spectrum is not subject to public forum analysis. Regulation of protected expression in a nonpublic forum is reviewed for reasonableness so long as it is viewpoint neutral. Here, the licensing scheme set forth in FCA is viewpoint neutral."[57] Radio waves do not fall under public forum analysis at all.

However, state-issued license plates are different. Like many states, the Commonwealth of Virginia sells personalized automobile license plates—so-called vanity plates—and allows automobile owners to spell out messages on their plates with words or

numbers, except for words and phrases that concern the "drug culture," are obscene, or refer to deities. In *Pruitt v. Wilder*, Reverend
Dan Pruitt wanted a Virginia license plate with the phrase
"GODZGUD." Under its "no deities" policy, the state refused.
Pruitt sued, claiming violations of the free speech and free exercise
clauses of the First Amendment. "The portion of the [state] policy
which bans references to deities represents a viewpoint-based regulation of speech in a nonpublic forum," District Judge Richard L.
Williams asserts, "and therefore violates the Free Speech Clause of
the First Amendment."[58] In addition, Virginia's license plate policy "allows references to religion in general," and in practice the
state "has granted applications for plates which refer to religion in
general, plates such as 'BIBLE,' 'ICOR14' and 'PSALM96.'" Thus,
as the judge concluded,

> The fact that the . . . policy purports to treat all references to
> deities the same does not mean that the policy is viewpoint
> neutral. To the contrary, by allowing one subset of religious
> speech—that not directly referring to a deity—to be placed
> on [license plates], while denying another sub-set of religious
> speech—that referring to deities—the . . . policy discrimi-
> nates on the basis of the speaker's viewpoint. This is particu-
> larly evident when it is considered that some religions, such
> as Buddhism, do not make reference to a deity, whereas oth-
> ers, like Christianity, center on a deity or deities.[59]

Virginia's attempt to limit religious messages on personalized license plates constituted viewpoint discrimination; it discriminated against religious messages that referred to deities, but not
religious messages that made reference to other things such as the
Bible.[60]

THE PARTISAN PUBLIC SQUARE?

In categorizing the contours of public squares under public forum doctrine, district courts evince a high level of agreement. Their policymaking is relatively consistent across specific locations, from public schools to public parks. There are variations to be sure, but in general district court policies are predictable. Scholarship on federal district courts often highlights the importance of partisanship for court policymaking. Thus, one important question here: is there a noticeable difference between how Republican and Democratic district judges categorize public squares?

It is commonly understood that presidents appoint judges who reflect a specific political ideology. As C. K. Rowland and Robert Carp highlight in their extensive study of several decades of federal district court policymaking, "twenty years of scholarship depict a consistent link among sociolegal environments, highly politicized presidential appointments, and aggregate patterns of political jurisprudence."[61] Moreover, civil rights and civil liberties issues, especially freedom of religion and freedom of expression, "provoke high levels of partisanship among U.S. trial judges."[62] Although a somewhat inelegant measure of a trial judge's political ideology, many scholars use the political ideology of the appointing president to categorize large samples of trial court data. Again, for Rowland and Carp, "the values of the nominator [president] can and do make a difference in the way decisions are subsequently made on the trial bench. The appointees of Democratic presidents are clearly more liberal in their decision making than are judges chosen by Republican chief executives."[63]

Are there partisan differences in how judges type public squares as traditional, designated, or nonpublic forums? To a certain extent there are. As table 4.2 spells out, Democratic and Republican judges do sometimes approach public spaces differently in terms of how a specific local is categorized. For instance, Republican judges almost always classify public schools as designated public forums (96 percent), whereas Democratic judges use that category only slightly less (79 percent). Is this partisan disparity significant? Probably not, since both Republican and Democratic judges generally view public schools similarly, thus indicating a strong policy consensus across political boundaries. There is some partisan difference on the status of travel terminals, with Republican and Democratic judges disagreeing over whether they are traditional or designated forums. Here, though, the small number of cases cautions against drawing hard and fast conclusions.

The most noticeable partisan difference occurs with public parks and other open public spaces. Republican and Democratic judges seem to disagree over whether parks are traditional or designated forums. Republicans categorize parks as traditional forums in about 63 percent of cases, but in only slightly more than 50 percent of cases do Democratic judges do so. Again, though, some caution here is warranted, simply because these differences could be accounted for by the special exigencies of the public properties in question, especially with public parks and other open spaces. As the discussion on parks above makes clear, not all of them fall under the Supreme Court's views of places open to speech since time immemorial.

Republican judges are usually more conservative than their Democratic cohorts on the federal bench. Between 1933 and 1987, as Carp and Rowland point out, "Democrats on the trial bench were 1.42 times more likely to decide cases in a liberal direction than were their Republican colleagues."[64] Democrats are more likely to rule in favor of a criminal defendant, uphold a free speech or free exercise of religion claim, rule in favor of a right to privacy claim, and so forth. With this in mind, it is difficult to determine how categorizing public properties under public forum analysis breaks down along "liberal" or "conservative" lines. That is, do liberal judges more often state that a specific location is a

Location of Forum		Traditional Forum	Designated Forum	Nonpublic Forum	Total
Public School	Count	2	59*	5*	66
	Republican Judges		43 (95.6%)	2 (4.4%)	45 (100%)
	Democratic Judges	2 (10.5%)	15 (78.9%)	2 (10.5%)	19 (100%)
Travel Terminus	Count	3	10*	1	14*
	Republican Judges	2 (33.3%)	3 (50%)	1 (16.7%)	6 (100%)
	Democratic Judges	1 (14.3%)	6 (85%)		7 (100%)
Government Building	Count	2	12	2	16
	Republican Judges	1 (16.7%)	4 (66.7%)	1 (16.7%)	6 (100%)
	Democratic Judges	1 (10%)	8 (80%)	1 (10%)	10 (100%)
Public Park, Other Public Space	Count	37	13	14	64
	Republican Judges	22 (62.9%)	5 (14.3%)	8 (22.9%)	35 (100%)
	Democratic Judges	15 (51.7%)	8 (27.6%)	6 (20.7%)	29 (100%)
Other	Count		5	10	15
	Republican Judges		2 (33.3%)	4 (66.7%)	6 (100%)
	Democratic Judges		3 (33.3%)	6 (66.7%)	9 (100%)

*One case missing due to missing variables.

Table 4.2

Location of Public Forum by Type of Forum and Judges' Political Background as Defined by Appointing President. Federal District Courts, 1974–2001.

traditional public forum in which speech is almost certainly regulated? Do conservative judges more generally use the designated forum status, or even nonpublic forum category, in order to allow the government more leeway in regulating speech within specific public spaces? The data above do not easily answer this question.

However, introducing another variable does show real partisan differences in judicial policymaking. It is one thing for a judge to categorize a public space as a traditional, designated, or nonpublic forum. It is quite another issue for the judge to determine if that forum is open to speech-related activities. For instance, all of the public spaces typed by judges as traditional public forums were also determined to be open to speech and expressive activity. Yet, 74.8 percent of designated public forums were subsequently open to speech, and only 24.1 percent of nonpublic forums were open to speech related activities. Democratic and Republican judges agree in all traditional forum cases that once a traditional forum is declared, it is presumptively open to speech and expression. Yet, Democrats and Republicans disagree about designated forums and nonpublic forums. For instance, in cases involving designated public forums, Democratic judges determine the forum open to speech 77 percent of the time (n=33) whereas Republican judges open the forum to speech 74 percent of the time (n=43). With nonpublic forums, Republican judges opened the forum to expression anyway 13 percent of the time (n=2), and Democrats declared them open to speech 38 percent of the time (n=5).

Controlling for pro-forum decisions referenced by the specific location of the forum, it is evident that partisan differences affect district court policymaking. For example, of sixty-six cases concerning public schools, almost all of which were categorized as designated public forums, forty-five were declared open to speech and expression. Republican judges were somewhat less supportive of declaring schools open to expression than Democratic judges. Republicans declared schools as forums open to expression 66.7 percent of the time, and Democrats did so 78.9 percent of the time. Republican judges could be signifying a more deferential approach to local school regulation of access to forums, in that they are more inclined to declare a public school not open to speech and expression. Democrats, on the other hand, evidence a greater willingness to override local school board decisions about whether its schools are open to speech, and thus are more willing to side with the speaker seeking access. That the underlying context of these cases concerns religious speech, and exclusively a Christian-based religious speech, is interesting. By supporting the open forum for schools more, Democrats are implicitly suggesting that religious speech in public schools is perhaps allowable. Or, Democrats are at least lowering one threshold to protecting religious speech in public schools. By declaring that a public location is in general open to speech, judges answer one threshold issue concerning access, which is simply whether speech is allowed into the forum or not. It would be easy for a Democratic judge to simply declare—in the context of religious speech cases—that a school is a designated public forum that has not been opened to speech by its governing body. Republican judges, appointed by more "conservative" Republican presidents, are presumed to be more supportive of religious expression in public spaces due to their perceived support for more government and public recognition of religious exercises in general. Yet, although Republicans opened schools to speech in two-thirds of the cases in which religious speech was an underlying subtext, they nonetheless demonstrated slightly less support for speech-related activities in public schools than Democrats. This smaller and more nuanced case population of religious speech and public forum disputes indicates partisan results different than those observed by larger studies of district courts across time and policy areas.

Rowland and Carp's study indicates that between 1977 and 1987 Democratic Judges upheld a free expression claim in 67 percent of their cases, whereas Republicans protected free expression in 51 percent of their cases. For freedom of religion broadly construed to include the Free Exercise and Establishment Clauses, Democrats either protect a free exercise claim or rule that a government violated the Establishment Clause 60 percent of the time, compared with Republican support for religious liberty claims 36 percent of the time.[65] Over time, and with a much larger population of district court cases, significant differences between Democratic and Republican district judges are noticeable.

Partisanship may be less noticeable in religious speech and public forum disputes, although it is still present. Yet, the intriguing point is not the relative absence of partisanship affecting district court policymaking, but the partisan agreement present in religious speech cases in contrast to the real differences among Democratic and Republican judges noticed by Rowland and Carp in their much larger study. Since this analysis presently concerns district court policymaking that categorizes public spaces under public forum law—with no regard to the *content* of those forums—there is a strong argument to be made that the settled law on how to categorize places as traditional, limited, or nonforums tends to erode and negate differences between Democrats and Republicans at least as far as categories of forums go. The high court's policy guidelines on how spaces should be categorized are relatively clear and precise, and district courts simply apply the existing categories to specific forums involved in litigation. Of course, the partisan agreement observed in how courts define the contours of forums may not be present when courts determine the *content* of public forums, especially in religious speech cases. Chapter 5 discusses that issue in turn.

As figure 4.2 points out, Democratic judges tend to open forums to expression more often than Republican judges. Partisanship, as measured by the difference between Democratic and Republican support for pro-forum decisions relative to specific locations, is

		School	Travel Terminus	Government Building	Public Park, Other Public Space	Other	Total
Republican Judge	Count	30	4	4	29	3	70
	% Within Political Background of Judge	66.7%	66.7%	66.7%	82.9%	50%	100.0%
Democratic Judge	Count	15	5	7	26	3	56
	% Within Political Background of Judge	78.9%	71.4%	70.0%	89.7%	33.3%	100.0%
Total	Count	45	9	11	55	6	126
	% Within Location of Forum	100.0%	100.0%	100.0%	100.0%	100.0%	100.0%
	% Total	35.7%	7.1%	8.7%	43.7%	4.8%	100.0%

Table 4.3

Pro-Forum Decisions by Political Affiliation of District Judge and Location of Forum. Federal District Courts, 1974–2001.

greatest with public schools and other types of forums. Partisanship is less significant with public parks, government buildings, and travel terminals. With public schools, for instance, the partisan difference is 12.2 percent, with Democrats indicating more willingness to determine a school open in general to speech and expressive activities. Interestingly, Republicans are more willing to decide that other types of spaces are open to speech and expressive activities, and the percentage difference is greater than with public schools. Republican judges then seem more sympathetic to public forum disputes involving novel types of forums that are not necessarily covered by existing public forum doctrine. Across the remaining types of spaces—travel terminals, public parks, government buildings—it is fair to argue that the partisan difference is not significant.

CONCLUSION

The high level of policy agreement among district courts on how specific public spaces are categorized under public forum doctrine indicates that the law, and how it is applied, is relatively stable. The policy guidelines from the Supreme Court are relatively clear on how to categorize places as traditional, designated, or nonpublic forums. To be sure, there is dissent among the justices on the application of public forum doctrine, but that disagreement does not seem to have affected in a measurable degree how district courts define the contours of forums open to expression. Courts are faced with a heterogeneous system of public forums, represented by the many different types of places where religious speakers seek to place their messages. From international airports such as John F. Kennedy Airport in New York City, to the Visitor's Gate at the United Nations, to the North Pontotoc Attendance Center in the Pontotoc County, Mississippi, School District, district

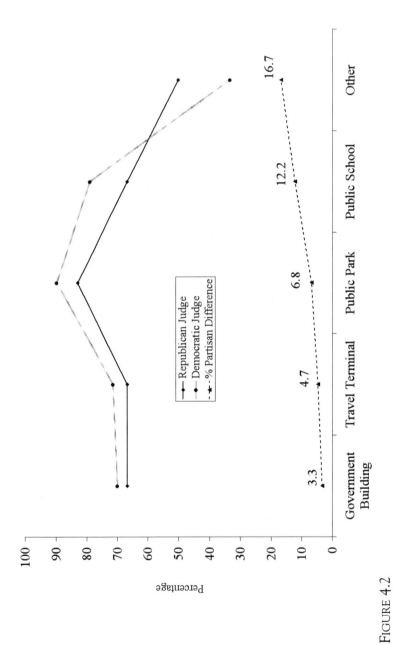

FIGURE 4.2

Pro-Forum Decisions by Political Affiliation of District Judge and Location of Forum. Federal District Courts, 1974–2001.

courts must somehow determine how this plethora of publicly owned spaces fall under First Amendment public forum categories. It may well be that no two forums are quite alike, and if this is the case, district courts do an admirable job at synthesizing and applying public forum doctrine in a coherent and generally predictable manner.

However, it is one thing to categorize a public space as a traditional, designated, or nonpublic forum. It is quite another issue to determine whether that forum, once typed, is indeed open to speech and expression. And, if so, is it open to *religious speech and expression?* To return to District Judge McAvoy's point in *Travis v. Owego-Apalachin School District,* forum classification and access issues are two separate things. Courts not only must determine how a public space is defined under public forum classifications; they must also determine when and under what conditions speech and expression are allowed access to the forum. Policing the content of the public square—determining when the government may regulate access to the square for religious speech, and when it may not—becomes a very significant policymaking role for district courts.

CHAPTER 5

Sacred Messages, Public Places, and the Content of the Public Square

THE GIDEON BIBLE (KING JAMES VERSION) is a ubiquitous feature of hotel room accoutrements throughout the United States, and perhaps the world. Its presence reflects the Gideon Bible Society's long-standing tradition of distributing Bibles to the public. Robert Alley notes that hotel rooms are only one target of the Gideons: "for some thirty-five years the Gideons have been distributing, on a selective basis, Bibles in public schools."[1] The Gideons' conduct sometimes leads to litigation, usually against school boards, that focuses on whether the Establishment Clause prohibits public schools from allowing Bible distribution, especially when the Gideons enter classrooms, school hallways, or other facilities to do so. Yet, as Alley points out, the Gideons have of late gone on the offensive, and instead of trying to defend their conduct (or, more appropriately, the school's conduct) under the Establishment Clause, they rely on the Free Speech Clause of the First Amendment to argue that freedom of expression includes the right to distribute religious literature in public forums such as schools. In one recent case, a federal district judge sided with the Gideons and sustained their free speech right to distribute Bibles in a rural public school district, noting that "the Gideons' passing out Bibles was no different from baseball coaches' passing out Little League brochures."[2] If the school allowed community groups such as the Boy Scouts or Little League to hold meetings and recruit students, then it likewise had to allow the Gideons to distribute their Bibles.

Recall that public forum disputes involve courts in a two-part reasoning process. First, courts must determine how the public space in question is categorized under public forum law and whether it is open to speech and expression in general. Second, courts must also address whether religious speech can be allowed into the forum. As chapter 4 explains, district court policymaking on the contours of public forums—whether they are traditional, designated, or nonpublic—is relatively stable, and demonstrates that judges reach a high level of agreement on how specific locations are typed under public forum law. Although courts disagree about how public parks are categorized, there is relatively little divergence among courts that public schools are designated forums, for instance, and the same too for travel terminals. Defining the contours of the forum is the easy part, however. District court consensus on how public spaces are typed does not carry over into when and where religious speech in those forums is allowed. That is, district courts may agree on the contours of public forums, but they do not agree over their content.

It is important to recall the heightened protection for religious speech that the First Amendment seemingly provides. Many legal scholars and Supreme Court justices generally concur that religious speech and expression should be as protected under the First Amendment as other types of private speech. Douglas Laycock, a noted scholar of religious liberty jurisprudence, argues that "religious speech is central to the First Amendment because religion is central to the First Amendment. Religious speech is twice protected, once by the Free Speech Clause and once by the Free Exercise Clause. We can infer from the religion clauses that disagreements about religion . . . are of special constitutional significance."[3] The Supreme Court indicates as much, and notes that religious speech garners significant protections under the First Amendment Free Speech Clause. In *Lamb's Chapel v. Center Moriches Union Free School District*, for example, the Court unanimously ruled that the free speech rights of an evangelical church were violated by a public school district that refused access to its auditorium to the church for the showing of a religious movie. As Justice White argued for the Court, "The showing of this film would not have been during school hours, would not have been sponsored by the school, and would have been open to the public, not just to church members. . . . There would have been no realistic danger that the community would think that the District was endorsing religion or any particular creed, and any benefit to religion or to the Church would have been no more than incidental." In addition to the Establishment Clause argument, the school district also justified denial of access because of the "radical" nature of the church's speech. Justice White's response is to the point: "There is nothing in the record to support such a justification, which in any event would be difficult to defend as a reason to deny the presentation of a religious point of view about a subject the District otherwise makes open to discussion on District property."[4] *Lamb's Chapel* makes clear that if a public forum is basically open to community groups, then it should also be available to religious speakers such as an evangelical church. In addition, arguments that "radical" religious speech has no place in the public square and should be denied access are not credible, especially if that square or forum has been open to speech and expression in the past.

The Court articulates its heightened protection for religious speech in subsequent cases. In *Capitol Square Review & Advisory Board v. Pinette* the Court ruled 7:2 that the Ku Klux Klan's unattended cross in the Ohio Statehouse plaza was constitutionally protected speech. Justice Scalia writes for the majority, and points out that the cross was private religious expression, which "is as fully protected under the Free Speech Clause as secular private expression. Indeed, in Anglo-American history, at least, government suppression of speech has so commonly been directed precisely at religious speech that a free speech clause without religion would be Hamlet without the prince."[5] That same year in *Rosenberger v. University of Virginia* the Court overturned the University of Virginia's policy that denied funds from a mandatory student activities fee for student publications that centered on religious themes, even though other types of student publications could compete for monies from the student activity funds.[6] To refuse to fund religious publications was viewpoint discrimination, as the Court put it, which violated the Free Speech Clause.[7] In addition, the Establishment Clause did not serve as a compelling interest that allowed the university to prohibit funding to religious publications, contrary to its argument that by funding *Wide Awake*, it would in effect endorse the group's religious message.

Most recently, in *Good News Club v. Milford*, the Court returned to religious speech in public secondary schools. Unlike in *Lamb's Chapel*, which concerned a public high school auditorium, the contested forum in *Good News* was an elementary school. Writing for the six-justice majority (the Court voted 6:3), Justice Clarence Thomas notes the parallels between *Good News* and *Lamb's Chapel*, and essentially bases his decision on the *Lamb's Chapel* precedent.

The only apparent difference between the activity of Lamb's Chapel and the activities of the Good News Club is that the Club chooses to teach moral lessons from a Christian perspective through live storytelling and prayer, whereas Lamb's Chapel taught lessons through films. This distinction is inconsequential. Both modes of speech use a religious viewpoint. Thus, the exclusion of the Good News Club's activities, like the exclusion of Lamb's Chapel's films, constitutes unconstitutional viewpoint discrimination.[8]

That the school district denied forum access to the Good News Club solely because of the religious nature of its expression means, for the Court majority, that the school discriminated against the group because of the substance or viewpoint of its speech.

The Court's recent excursions into religious speech and public forums indicate that religious expression should receive heightened protection under the First Amendment. As one scholar of public forum jurisprudence notes, public forum disputes often involve courts in "a labyrinth of conflicting rules for determining how much deference ought to be accorded governmental decisions to limit public access to public property for speech purposes."[9] The Court's religious speech cases seem to make clear, however, that lower courts should rarely defer to government decisions limiting access to religious speech, and judges should inquire closely into the reasons for denying forum access so as to ensure that no viewpoint discrimination takes place. Courts must make sure that religious speech is not denied access to a forum because of the substance, content, or viewpoint that the speech espouses.

Federal District Court policymaking on religious speech does not mirror the high court's emphasis on giving religious speech heightened protection, and therefore more access, in public forum disputes. Arguably, the Supreme Court's emphasis on religious speech is perhaps of recent vintage, announced as it is in cases such as *Widmar v. Vincent* (1981), *Lamb's Chapel* (1993), *Rosenberg v. University of Virginia* (1995), *Pinette* (1995), and *Good News* (2001). Although in the two Krishna *sankirtan* cases *Heffron v. ISKCON* (1981) and *ISKCON v. Lee* (1992) the Court allowed local governments to regulate *sankirtan* in crowded state fairs and airports, the justices were quick to note that the Free Speech

Clause generally protected religious solicitations. To be sure, two-thirds of the district court cases arise after 1990, and even though the high court's increasing look at religious expression reflects rising litigation rates in lower district courts, lower courts should not necessarily reflect the Supreme Court's view of religious speech until after it is has addressed the issue in a string of cases. The Court's forays into protecting religious speech must be given time to filter down to the trial court level. Yet, district courts after 1989 only granted forum access to religious speech in slightly less than half of the cases (48.7 percent, n=57), and indeed after 1994 district court support for religious speech in public forums dropped further (44 percent of cases granted access to the forum, n=26). Thus, as the high court increased protection for religious speech, lower courts seemingly reduced it.

As figure 5.1 shows, district court support for religious speech is volatile, and demonstrates significant swings from year to year. In addition, district court policymaking shows a slight tendency against religious speech in public forums, shown by the five-year moving average data for decisions supporting religious speech. As the number of cases increases over time, district court support for religious speech drops. By the end of the time frame, 2000–2001, support for religious speech in public forums drops to around 40 percent of all cases. The five-year moving average indicates a general trend against religious speech, ranging from a high mark of 70 percent support for religious speech in the mid-1980s to 50 percent support by the year 2000. That courts support religious speech in about 50 percent of the cases is a trend that continued for a decade, indicating in the aggregate that perhaps courts have achieved some doctrinal stability in how the First Amendment free speech clause applies to religious expression. The data also indicate that as the Supreme Court emphasized the heightened protections for religious speech in a series of cases from *Widmar v. Vincent* to *Capitol Square Review & Advisory Board v. Pinette*, dis-

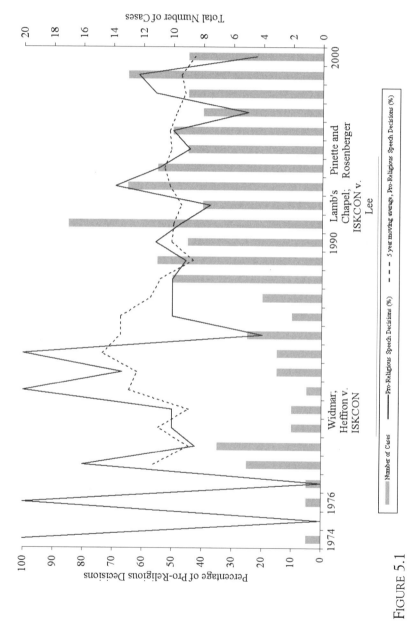

FIGURE 5.1

Pro-Religious Message Decisions by Federal District Courts, 1974–2000, with Supreme Court Case Markers.

trict court policymaking did not really change in response. That is, the support for religious speech remained relatively constant.

In addition to the relationship between district courts and the Supreme Court, district court policymaking on the content of public forums shows several trends. One, courts seem to favor certain locations for religious speech over others, and two, courts tend to protect certain types of religious expression more so than others. Courts are not consistent in granting access to religious speech across all types and locations of public forums litigated. Neither are they supportive of all types of religious expression, notwithstanding the Supreme Court's broad call to give religious expression a heightened sense of protection under the First Amendment.

For the following discussion the location and type of forums at issue are used as a framing device for understanding the conditions under which courts grant or deny access. Location is important, as the Supreme Court makes abundantly clear in its public forum jurisprudence: "the nature of the place, the pattern of its normal activities, dictate the kinds of regulations . . . that are reasonable . . . [The] crucial question is whether the manner of expression is basically incompatible with the normal activity of a particular place at a particular time."[10] Likewise, a right to access public property for speech purposes depends "on the character of the property at issue."[11]

However, locations are not the sole guiding factor in determining whether religious speech is granted access. As the discussion above shows, the Court of late increasingly affirms that religious speech, as speech, is entitled to significant First Amendment protections that may override concerns of forum location. Even though "the nature of the place, the pattern of its normal activities" affects whether speech is granted access to a public forum, the law has evolved to account specifically for religious speech as well, indicating that types of religious expression may be just as impor-

	% Forums Open to Speech	% Forums Open to Specific Religious Message	% Forums Open to Specific Religious Message, Controlling for Pro-Forum Decision
Location			
Public School	68.2	48.5	62.2
Travel Terminal	71.4	71.4	90.0
Government Building	68.9	56.3	81.8
Public Park	85.9	53.1	56.4
Other	40.0	20.0	33.3
Type of Speech			
Christian Speech	68.5	49.2	62.4
Jewish Speech	76.9	38.5	40.0
Muslim Speech	75.0	75.0	100
Krishna Speech	90.5	61.9	68.4
Other	88.9	55.6	62.5

TABLE 5.1

District Court Policymaking Across the Location of Forum and Type of Religious Speech According to Faith of Speaker. Federal District Courts, 1974–2001.

tant in gaining access as the specific location at issue. In addition to using forum locations as a framing device to assess district court policymaking, the type of expressive activity litigated is also used to outline and assess district court outcomes. The results are quite interesting, and indicate that district courts favor certain types of expression over others. Thus, even though location is important— that is, whether the speech goes into a public school, government building, or the like does matter—what seems to matter more is how the religious message is expressed.

Table 5.1 shows district court outcomes across several issues relating to religious speech and public forum cases. Starting with the public locations for speech, it is clear that district courts view most public places as essentially open to speech, except for those denominated as "other." For example, public schools are considered open to expressive activity almost 70 percent of the time, as are travel terminals and government buildings. Public parks and similar open spaces are adjudged open to speech in general in about 86 percent of the cases, indicating that district courts view parks and open spaces as places where expressive activity frequently occurs. Those locations not falling under the above categories are typed as "other," and noticeably are not as open to speech and expression as other public spaces. District court policymaking indicates that litigants in religious speech disputes tend to litigate public forums that are usually open to speech and related activities in general, although to varying degrees. Importantly, the locations of public forums indicate that religious speakers are seeking a kind of access available to nonreligious speakers, hence the fact that most forums at issue are considered open to speech.

Still, how district courts define the contents of the forums at issue is another matter. The example of public school forums is telling. Although over two-thirds of the public schools are considered open to speech by district courts, less than one-half (48 percent) are ultimately open to *religious speech*. A religious speaker may indeed win the first hurdle in public forum litigation by having a judge declare the forum at issue open to free speech, but as the table makes clear, just because that threshold burden is met does not guarantee access for religious speech. Indeed, controlling for the threshold issue of whether the forum is open to expression, it is clear that about two-thirds of religious speakers who successfully argue that the forum is open to speech ultimately gain access for their specific speech and message.

Public parks tell a similar story. Although a far higher percentage (85.9 percent) of parks and open spaces are declared open to speech and expression—indeed, district courts probably reflect the Supreme Court's doctrine that parks are historically open to the free trade of ideas—nonetheless religious speech is granted access by courts only slightly more frequently than with public schools. Overall, religious speech is protected in 53 percent of the cases. In those cases in which the park is considered an open forum, protection for religious speech is 56.4 percent, *below* that for public schools. That is, even though public parks and open spaces are considered open to speech and expression in almost nine out of ten cases, religious speech is granted access to those spaces slightly more than half the time, unlike with public schools in which religious speech is protected in almost two-thirds of the cases. This is an interesting dichotomy, in that public parks and other open spaces are considered the crux of public forum doctrine; they are, by far, usually the places traditionally, customarily, and historically open to free speech, whereas public schools historically have not been thought of as gathering places for nonschool related expression by the public at large. It may well be that the religious speech cases involving public parks often concern "extreme" forms of religious expression, such as aggressive solicitation of converts. It may also be that most disputes concerning religious speech and public parks are settled outside of courtrooms anyway, thus the disputes that are litigated are perhaps an exception. Nonetheless, it is clear that district courts treat parks differently than schools. Travel terminals and government buildings evidence the highest support for religious speech. Seventy percent of travel terminals are declared open to speech, and of those almost all (90 percent) are open to religious speech. Speakers have a good chance, then, of gaining access to travel terminals for their specific religious message. Disputes over government buildings as forums also show a similar trend. More than half of government buildings are considered by judges to be open to speech (56 percent), and of those, religious speech is granted access about 80 percent of the time. Again, this is an interesting result. As the Supreme Court indicates in the context of public airports, "as commercial enterprises, airports must provide services attractive to the marketplace. In light of this, it cannot fairly be said that an airport terminal has as a principal purpose 'promoting the free exchange of ideas.'"[12] Indeed, airports are often designed to "process and serve air travelers efficiently," and creating marketplaces for speech and expression are generally not part of airport planning. District court policymaking seems to counter the Supreme Court's view that travel terminals, and especially airports, are not usually considered public places open to expression.

Table 5.1 also indicates how district courts respond to the specific type of speech, in terms of the religious message underlying it. The specific faiths involved in litigation are discussed later in this chapter, but are introduced here to indicate another broad trend in district court decisions. Muslim speakers seemingly are the most successful in gaining access to the public forum, writ large, for their specific message. However, the small number of Muslim speech cases precludes consideration as to whether federal courts broadly protect this speech or not. Aside from Muslim speech, Krishna speakers are the most successful in gaining access to public forums for their specific message. District courts grant them access to public spaces about 61 percent of the time, which is probably a function of the types of spaces to which Krishnas seek access. They do not seek access to public schools, for instance, and generally confine their expressive conduct to places that are open to the public, such as parks and travel terminals. Interestingly, speakers falling into the "other" category win over 55 percent of their access cases, indicating that district courts are somewhat supportive of nontraditional religious messages in the public square. Christian speakers do not fair as well, as they gain access to public forums slightly less than 50 percent of the time. Finally, Jewish speakers gain access only 38 percent of the time, indicating that district courts, for various reasons, are less inclined to support their specific type of expression.

Table 5.2 shows district court support for religious expression relative to the specific type of expressive conduct and the location of the public forum. The broad trends are defined at the bottom of the table, and it is worthwhile to discuss how courts view the specific activities at issue first. As is evident, courts favor and grant forum access to some types of religious expression over others.

Preaching, which is simply defined as one litigant seeking to preach to passersby in a public forum, is only protected by district courts less than 40 percent of the time. In an early religious liberty case that involved elements of free speech, *Murdock v. Pennsylvania*, the Court noted that preaching was well protected under the First Amendment:

> spreading one's religious beliefs or preaching the Gospel through distribution of religious literature and through personal visitations is an age-old type of evangelism with as high a claim to constitutional protection as the more orthodox types. The manner in which it is practiced at times gives rise to special problems with which the police power of the states

is competent to deal. But that merely illustrates that the rights with which we are dealing are not absolutes.[13]

In dealing with public forum claims involving religious preaching, district courts seem to find that the regulatory power of governments in managing forums under their control outweighs the constitutional right to preach.

In contrast, though, distributing religious literature is more protected—about twice as much—than preaching. Courts protect the distribution of literature in 64 percent of the cases. Arguably, both types of expressive conduct seek to convert others directly, but courts are more willing to grant access to those who hand out religious literature versus those who seek a "soapbox" or temporary pulpit in a public space from which to expound religious teachings to others. As with distributing literature, soliciting others for donations to a religious cause (such as the Krishnas) or holding a worship service in a public forum, are similarly protected by district courts. Solicitations are protected speech about 62 percent of the time, and worship services are protected expressive activity in almost 65 percent of the cases. Of course, holding a worship service probably entails some kind of preaching or teaching activity as part of that service, so it looks as if district courts are somehow distinguishing between the "lone" preacher or itinerant evangelist who seeks to expound his or her faith to others, from the organized congregation that wishes to use a public space—often a school—in which to hold church services.

Interestingly, litigants who use public forum doctrine to gain access in order to give a prayer never succeed, although there are so few cases that no real trend in district court policymaking can be deduced. Courts do protect religious displays differently, though, and grant access to litigants seeking to place a religious display in a public forum in 40 percent of the cases. Other types of religious expression that do not neatly fit into the above categories are not

LOCATION	ACTIVITY RELIGIOUS SPEECH (%)	SUPPORT FOR	N Total N	% OF
SCHOOOL	Preaching	0%	2	1.1%
	Religious Club	38.2%	13	7.4%
	Distribute Literature	69.2%	13	7.4%
	Public Prayer	0%	1	.6%
	Enjoin religious Speech	22.2%	9	5.1%
	Religious Display	0%	1	.6%
	Worship Service	66.7%	24	13.7%
	Other	0%	3	1.7%
TRAVEL TEMINUS	Solicit Donations	100.0%	6	3.4%
	Distribute Literature	60.0%	5	2.9%
	Religious Display	0%	2	1.1%
	Worship Service	100.0%	1	.6%
GOVERNMENT BUILDING	Solicit Donations	100.0%	1	.6%
	Public Prayer	0%	1	.6%
	Enjoin Religious Speech	100.0%	1	.6%
	Religious Display	28.6%	7	4.0%
	Worship Service	100.0%	4	2.3%
	Other	50.0%	2	1.1%
PUBLIC PARK	Preaching	75.0%	4	2.3%
	Solicit Donations	46.7%	15	8.6%
	Distribute Literature	57.1%	7	4.0%
	Enjoin Religious Speech	33.3%	6	3.4%

	Count	Support %	Total %
Religious Display	17	58.8%	9.7%
Worship Service	7	42.9%	4.0%
Other	8	62.5%	4.6%
OTHER			
Preaching	2	0%	1.1%
Solicit Donations	2	50%	1.1%
Public Prayer	1	0%	.6%
Enjoin Religious Speech	1	0%	.6%
Religious Display	2	0%	1.1%
Worship Service	1	0%	.6%
Other	6	33.3%	3.4%
TOTAL			
Preaching	8	37.5%	4.6%
Solicit Donations	24	62.5%	13.7%
Religious Club in School	13	38.5%	7.4%
Distribute Literature	25	64.0%	14.3%
Public Prayer	3	0%	1.7%
Enjoin Religious Speech	17	29.4%	9.7%
Religious Display	29	41.4%	16.6%
Worship Service	37	64.9%	21.1%
Other	19	42.1%	10.9%
Total	175	50.3%	100.0%

TABLE 5.2

Locations of Public Forums, by District Court Support for Type of Religious Expression. Federal District Courts, 1974–2001.

necessarily denied protection by courts. Courts protect "other" types of religious expression in 42 percent of the cases. Finally, litigants who seek to drive a religious message out of a public forum are often successful, as district courts enjoin and prohibit religious speech from a public forum in about 70 percent of the cases, since 29.4 percent of requests for injunctions are considered pro-religious speech in that a court allows the religious message to remain.

However, a straightforward description of how district courts respond to certain types of religious expression is not all that illuminating, although it does establish very broad trends. More importantly, how those types of expression link up with specific forum locations is key to understanding the broader aspects of court policymaking. As table 5.2 also demonstrates, there are real differences in how courts protect religious expression vis-à-vis specific locations of the public forums at issue. Therefore, it is important to place religious expression within forum locations in more detail.

PUBLIC SCHOOLS

Scholars of religion and politics note the sustaining power of public schools on the issue agendas of religiously motivated interest groups. Public schools are constantly in the "religious spotlight," especially from the umbrella movement of the Christian Right that views public school curriculums in conflict with the attempts of Christian conservatives to rear their children within their own moral and religious framework. Others more capably dealt with the politicization of schools by Christian conservatives and little attention needs to be devoted to those debates here.[14] Importantly, as chapter 3 points out, almost all (98.5 percent) of the religious speech disputes concerning public schools focus on Christian-based speech.

Public schools figure prominently in public forum disputes concerning religious speech, as slightly more than one-third of district court cases concern schools as forums. Steven Gey links litigation over school forums to larger attempts by religious groups, especially those affiliated with the religious right, to reintroduce prayer and Christian morality back into American society. As he puts it, "the strategic use of free speech arguments has been especially prominent in Pat Robertson's group [American Center for Law and Justice] and others to reintroduce prayer into public schools. . . . in many of these cases, Establishment Clause concerns regarding state endorsement of religion have been avoided. . . . simply by treating the cases as indistinguishable from cases involving political, social, or artistic speech."[15] Thus, Gey notes a more pernicious trend of religious conservatives using free speech and public forum arguments to circumvent constitutional jurisprudence limiting public school support for religious expression and activities such as prayer. Furthermore, the line between government support for religion and private religious expression in government-owned forums becomes blurred in public school cases, and school boards act as "silent coordinator[s] of a religious exercise. That is, the government delivers an audience of potential recruits to a religious majority, which then uses the opportunity to proselytize."[16]

District court outcomes, however, do not necessarily reflect this view that schools may be captured by religious zealots intent on using the Free Speech Clause to protect conduct such as prayer, Bible reading, and other religious expression such as the distribution of Bibles or other religious materials. To be sure, court cases in no way encompass all of the disputes between individual speakers and schools. There is no doubt that many, if not most, disputes are resolved shy of litigation. As the discussion in chapter 4 on the U.S. Commission on Civil Rights hearings on free expression and public schools makes clear, speakers, schools, and attorneys all agree that most conflicts over religious expression are resolved without recourse to lawsuits. Either a school district has a general policy protecting religious expression broadly, or it is goaded into doing so by the intervention of attorneys and others.[17] The only way to definitively show how schools respond to requests for access to school facilities for religious speech is to undertake a substantive investigation that polls a representative sample of school board officials and others; so far, that has not been done.

Clearly, district courts favor certain types of expression in public schools over others. Preaching is disfavored, although there are only two court cases in which a free speech claim was attached to a preaching-related activity.[18] Litigants who claim a free speech right to engage in school prayer, or erect a religious display on school grounds, are also not successful. Those who have the most success are seeking access to school facilities to hold worship services or those who wish to distribute religious literature to the students.

District courts are very supportive of the free speech rights of congregations or other religious groups to use school facilities after hours. As the case outcomes show, district courts grant access for worship services two-thirds of the times, and in almost all of the cases courts do so because the school district allows community groups in general to use its facilities. Thus, schools open their facilities as designated forums, and by doing so must adhere to the strict standards of public forum jurisprudence that prohibit a school from denying access because of a speaker's viewpoint. By arguing that they were denied access because of their viewpoint, local congregations or other religious groups successfully gained entry into the public forum. When district courts deny access for worship services, they almost always do so because the school in question is not open to nonschool and community groups anyway. Thus, denials of access are either based on the nonforum nature of a specific public school, or on a school's reasonable attempts to regulate the time, place, and manner of religious speech. For instance, courts will generally defer to schools that limit religious group usage of facilities near the start or end of the school day. Courts often insist that a time barrier between the end of the school day and the use of facilities for religious purposes is necessary to prevent the perception that the school endorses the specific message at issue. Yet, in a real sense, by facilitating church and other religious group access to school forums, courts treat public schools as other types of government-owned gathering places that are often open to community groups.

One interesting case concerning worship service access is *Gregoire v. Centennial School District.* Greg Gregoire, regional director of Campus Crusade for Christ, sought use of a Pennsylvania public school's high school auditorium in order to hold a religious magic show. The school district refused access, claiming that the high school in question was not an open forum, and the Establishment Clause prohibited the religious content of the magic show. As District Judge Bechtle noted, the circumstances of Gregoire's use of the forum would not generally implicate the school in an endorsement of a religious message.

It is important to note at the outset that the activity here in question is not requested for use on the school premises during normal school hours at which members of the school student body would be the exclusive attendees or the principal attendees and at which teachers or other academic professionals would be present in some role. Rather, the activity is requested to take place on a weekend, after school hours, and the members of the public in the community of the school are those who are targeted for invitation, although many of these could very likely be, and indeed are presumably expected by the plaintiffs to be, students of the school system or persons of that age. No school personnel are expected to be present other than custodial employees. Those who attend would do so voluntarily. The plaintiffs have made application for this use as a result of the policy of this school district to allow groups in the community to apply for use of the school facilities after school hours for a broad spectrum of community activities, by all members of the community.[19]

Since the school is open to community groups in general, any discrimination against a group because of its message can only be justified by a compelling interest.

Adherence to the Establishment Clause, in the school's view, was the compelling interest. That is, to avoid endorsing a religious message, the school had no other option but to limit Gregoire's religious speech. However, as Judge Bechtle noted, "albeit with good intentions and possibly because it perceives its role to be an adversarial one in separating church and state, [the school] pushed too hard against the sometimes wavering wall of separation that must be held up between church and state. . . . Nothing in the Establishment Clause requires the State to suppress a person's speech merely because the content of that speech is religious in character." In addition, Gregoire's use of the forum would not implicate the school in an advancement of inhibition of religion at all, since the primary effect of forum usage is not state support of religion, but only private religious speech. Thus,

permitting plaintiffs the use they seek would not have as its primary effect either the advancement or inhibition of religion. The open speech forum at the school facilities during non-school days involving events that are not school employee initiated or led or primarily student attended does not confer any state endorsement or sponsorship of religious sects or practices. Any benefit a particular religious group, speaker, or religion may derive from defendant's open speech forum policy is merely incidental.[20]

Judge Bechtle enjoined Centennial School District from denying access to its facilities for the religious magic show, and the show did indeed go on.

However, after the magic show the school district changed its open forum policy ostensibly to close the forum for good. Greg Gregoire sued again, claiming that he might wish to use the facilities in the future, and the school's new policy violates the free speech clause and public forum law just as the old policy did. Judge Bechtle for a second time agrees, and orders the school to once more protect access for Gregoire's group, even though he had not yet sought to use the facilities again. He notes that the district's policy really has not changed at all, and the school board still designates some community groups as having access privileges to school facilities. As he points out, "this court held before, and it must hold again, that Centennial cannot continue to allow the designated groups and organizations to use its facilities, but exclude any applicant, such as plaintiffs, who seek to use the facilities to speak about religion, because that would once again be content-based discrimination against speech in an open forum."[21] Noting that the high school is "either an open public forum or it is not an open public forum," Judge Bechtle stipulates that the magic show's "Christian evangelical message is an explanation of . . . religious belief [and] that is a precise example of free expression of ideas that Centennial cannot prohibit, given the broad program of speech and expression offered to the community in its forum."[22] Thus, the school's change in its access policy was enjoined simply because it still discriminated against religious speech as speech.

District court policymaking granting access to local congregations, nondenominational churches, or other religious groups is also in keeping with larger trends concerning the relationship between churches and government entities. Mark Chaves and William Tsitsos demonstrate in their comprehensive study of church interaction with government agencies that "it is extraordinarily uncommon for congregations to be denied permission by government authorities to engage in the activities in which they wish to engage."[23] Chaves and Tsitsos investigate the success rate of churches in a nationwide study in getting permits and zoning approval for activities ranging from opening daycare centers, hosting bingo nights, or building new additions to their physical plant. By and large local or state authorities grant church requests. By supporting church, congregation, or other group access to public schools to hold worship services, district courts are engaging in a healthy interaction with churches similar to other, nonjudicial government agencies. As well, Chaves and Tsitsos's research indicates that government agencies almost always cooperate with churches in terms of permitting and zoning issues, and it is fair to speculate that public schools probably do as well. That is, schools that maintain open forum policies allow churches to use their facilities just as any other community group, therefore litigation concerning church access more than likely deals with exceptional cases in which access was denied.

Similar to the experience of churches or groups seeking access to school facilities to hold worship services, litigants wishing to distribute religious materials in public schools are also generally successful. District courts protect literature distribution in schools in about 70 percent of the cases. Although about half of the public forum disputes concerning religious literature take place within the context of public schools, and then again mainly within high schools and junior high schools. *Rivera v. East Otero School District* is a good example of these types of cases. Here, a student was suspended for distributing the evangelical Christian magazine "Issues and Answers" on his high school campus, and contested the school's action as a violation of his free speech right to distribute religious literature. District Judge Richard Matsch agreed with the student. Relying on the student free speech cases decided by the Supreme Court,[24] Judge Matsch noted that the school does not view student religious speech and the distribution of literature outside of the classroom as compatible with the school's mission. Yet, as Judge Matsch argued,

> The mission of public education is preparation for citizenship. High school students . . . must develop the ability to understand and comment on the society in which they live and to develop their own sets of values and beliefs. A school policy completely preventing students from engaging other students in open discourse on issues they deem important cripples them as contributing citizens. Such restrictions do not advance any legitimate governmental interest. On the contrary, such inhibitions on individual development defeat the very purpose of public education in secondary schools.[25]

Students have free speech rights, as Judge Matsch pointed out, and the distribution of religious literature is in keeping with those rights.

The school district raises an Establishment Clause defense, and argues that to allow distribution of "Issues and Answers" means the school effectively endorses its message in violation of the First Amendment. For Judge Matsch, it is more dangerous and entangling for the school to inquire into the content of religious literature than it is to allow it on campus: "permitting all lawful speech presents fewer entanglement risks than would be created by a policy of monitoring student speech, determining what was religious, and suppressing that speech." The school would violate the "excessive entanglement" prong of the *Lemon* test for the Establishment Clause if it closely monitored religious speech in order to protect itself from threats of endorsement.

Other district courts likewise follow suit and allow students to distribute religious materials. However, some courts do allow schools to limit the places where religious tracts may be distributed. For instance, students can be limited to certain areas when handing out their literature, and schools may prohibit distribution in classrooms and hallways—both of which are not normally considered open forums—provided there are other places available for this communicative activity.[26] One scholar notes that "in the school setting, public forum analysis grants school authorities almost unrestricted discretion in defining the permissible parameters of student speech."[27] District court policymaking does not support that assertion, at least with regard to the student distribution of religious literature. For other types of student expression, courts may tend to defer to school authorities that refuse or limit access, for instance in cases concerning student religious groups or student initiated prayer.

Student distribution of religious literature may be in keeping with the overall mission of public schools in promoting discourse and citizenship, but what about outside groups such as the Gideons who wish to distribute Bibles in public schools? Interestingly, courts generally allow the Gideons to do so, provided they confine their conduct to public sidewalks in front of a school, or do not actively confront students with Bibles for the taking. For instance, in *Bacon v. Bradley-Bourbonnais High School District No. 307*, a district judge allowed the Gideons to distribute Bibles in public areas and sidewalks near a school, since those areas are traditional public forums anyway, and the school can provide no evidence that the Gideon presence is hazardous or disruptive.[28]

In another case, the Gideons were allowed to actually place Bibles on a table in a public school foyer for students to pick up and take, if they wish, provided a prominent disclaimer is on the table stating that the school in no way endorses the Gideons' message.[29]

To be sure, district court policymaking does roundly support some types of religious expression in public school. Worship services and the distribution of religious literature are all protected to a high degree, and in comparison with other types of speech, such as prayer, preaching, and even access for student religious groups, worship services in school facilities after hours, or the distribution of religious materials during school, are significantly more protected. Interestingly, though, these expressive activities are not the types of activities necessarily favored by the Christian Right, or even criticized by those hostile to religious speech. That is, Christian conservatives and evangelicals who wish to "return" religion to public schools would certainly support worship services in school facilities and religious tracting on school grounds. Yet, Christian conservatives especially would like the return of school-sponsored prayers and Bible readings, both activities that are emphatically prohibited by the Establishment Clause. The impact of worship services by local congregations or groups after school hours does not exactly return religion to schools in the sense that the Christian Right would like. Handing out religious literature is in keeping with the Christian Right's desire to have more religion in schools, and indeed some of the materials handed out, such as the magazine "Issues and Answers," are produced by evangelical Christian organizations that may be linked, to a degree, with the Christian Right agenda. Yet, district courts overwhelmingly view the distribution of literature in general as a basic constitutional right, both for adults and students. Schools cannot prohibit religious materials due to their substance and content, although they may certainly regulate the time, place, and manner of its expressive activity.

Intriguingly, district courts are not very supportive of student religious groups that sue to use school facilities to hold religious meetings. To be sure, it is probably the case that public schools nationwide grant access to student religious groups more often than not, and lawsuits surrounding denials of facility usage are the exception.[30] But, when litigation does arise, district courts protect the religious speech of student groups in only 38 percent of the cases. In the wake of the Equal Access Act passed in the 1980s, the presumption was that courts would follow the terms of the federal statute and grant access to student religious groups on equal terms with nonreligious, curriculum oriented groups. In only 25 percent (n=16) of the public school cases did a litigant invoke the Equal Access Act as a means to gain entry to a public school forum, and district courts are essentially split over how the statute applies, with approximately half granting access under the statute's terms, and the other half denying access. Importantly, it is probably the case that public school boards abide by the statute's terms anyway, thus district court cases that do arise are again exceptions to widespread school policies granting meeting space for religious clubs. An in-depth analysis of district court statutory interpretation and the Equal Access Act is beyond the scope of this work, but suffice to say that the data show a study needs to be done.

GOVERNMENT BUILDINGS AND TRAVEL TERMINALS

Allowable religious speech in government buildings and travel terminals poses a real contrast to public schools. Again, to be sure, court cases reflect those instances in which the government and speaker could not, for whatever reason, reach a compromise on religious speech. In terms of how courts police the content of these public squares, though, it is clear that they are treated differently.

In both locations, district courts allow the solicitation of donations for religious causes, as well as the distribution of religious literature and the holding of worship services. To be sure, one main distinction between these forums and public schools is that schools are not a site for the solicitation of donations for religious causes such as ISKCON (Krishna). It is somewhat common sense as to why no litigants would seek access to a school for fundraising—school children probably do not have much money, and school officials will certainly protect their attendees from potentially fraudulent attempts to solicit for religious movements. In similar types of disputes concerning congregations and groups that seek government facilities for their worship services, or speakers who distribute religious literature, district courts are overwhelmingly supportive of access.

One interesting case is *U.S. v. Boesewetter et al.*, which concerns whether the National Park Service can limit Krishna solicitations in the semipublic areas of the Kennedy Center for the Performing Arts in Washington, D.C. Boesewetter and other Krishnas were arrested for violating Park Service rules prohibiting soliciting in the entrance hall to the center. The rules, as the Park Service noted, serve to protect the tranquility of the Kennedy Center and provide refuge from the "hustle and bustle" of daily life. Limiting expressive activity reflects that the "Kennedy Center is dedicated to the performing arts and has a close association in visitors' minds with the memory of a slain president."[31] District Judge Gasch disagreed, noting that the Court "must weigh heavily the fact that both speech and religious activity are involved. The crucial question with respect to the free speech claim is 'whether the manner of expression is basically incompatible with the normal activity of a particular place at a particular time.' *Grayned v. City of Rockford* . . ."[32] The Park Service did have reasons to regulate the time, place, and manner of speech in the Kennedy Center Entrance Hall. However, commercial vendors were allowed to ply their trade in the entrance hall. Thus, as Judge Gasch pointed out, "more closely analogous to the distribution at issue here is the

permitted commercial sale of souvenir programs and other com-
memorative items under similar circumstances. Having permitted
such activities to take place in the semi-public portions of the
Kennedy Center, the government cannot attempt to impose an
absolute ban on defendants' religious activities." The Krishnas
were entitled to solicit donations as long as commercial vendors
were allowed to make money by selling programs and the like.

In another religious speech dispute concerning a federal government building, *Bynum v. U.S. Capitol Police Board*, an individual sought to lead "prayer tours" through the Capitol Building in
Washington, D.C. The Capitol Police asked him to stop, since his
"tours" were deemed to be demonstrations, which are certainly not
allowed within the building.[33] Judge Friedman pointed out that
the U.S. Capitol Building had not been designated a public forum
by Congress, thus speech activities could be restricted by the more
relaxed reasonableness standard under the First Amendment.
However, the judge also noted that the Capitol Police Board's
control over expression is too broad, and allows the police to restrict behavior that is in no way disruptive of Congress' business.
Judge Friedman's ruling enjoined the Capitol Police "from restricting any acts that they believe constitute expressive conduct
that conveys a message supporting or opposing a point of view . . .
including the discrete act of bowing one's head, closing one's eyes
and clasping one's hands."[34]

Soliciting is protected by district courts in travel terminals too,
and most of these cases are initiated by Krishnas practicing *sankirtan* in crowded airports or bus and train stations. Their right of access is overwhelmingly protected by district courts, though, as is a
similar right of others to distribute religious literature. As well,
worship services are similarly protected, as in Sister Mary Reilly's
case involving the Rhode Island Legislature Rotunda.

The type of religious expression that district courts overwhelmingly refuse to protect is the display of religious symbols. Religious

displays in public parks receive some protection from courts, discussed below, but government buildings and travel terminals, both enclosed spaces, are not generally considered appropriate public places for the display of Christian crosses, Jewish menorahs, and the Ten Commandments. In *Shea v. Brister*, Texas state district court judge Scott Brister displayed a copy of the Ten Commandments in his courtroom in Houston, Texas. Daniel Shea, an attorney who litigates in the Houston area, sued Brister in federal district court to force the removal of the display. The display is 12.5 inches by 15.5 inches, and hangs in an unobtrusive place in the spectator's gallery. It cannot be seen from the main courthouse hallway, although Shea maintains that the display will influence juries "so that they may not follow their secular duty but might be swayed by the religious underpinnings of the display."[35]

Exercising judicial restraint, Federal District Judge Hittner ruled that Shea has no standing to bring his complaint. Although he is suing as a taxpayer, Judge Hittner points out that there is no public money supporting the display in the state courtroom. Likewise, Shea's contact with the display and the courtroom itself is "casual and remote," thus he is unable to demonstrate any real harm or threat of harm to constitutionally protected rights. By terminating the case on standing issues, Judge Hittner indirectly maintains access for the Ten Commandments in Judge Brister's courtroom.[36] Standing dismissals are rare in these types of cases, and it may well be that the district judge simply acted strategically to avoid a messy, protracted constitutional dispute involving a state court judge and state courtroom.

The Ten Commandments may remain in Judge Brister's courtroom by procedural default, but courts have been reluctant to allow other kinds of religious symbols in government buildings and travel terminals, and have addressed most other disputes on their merits. In *Lubavitch of Iowa v. Walters*, for instance, a Chabad-Lubavitch group in Des Moines wanted to place an unattended menorah on a landing adjacent to the Iowa State Capitol Building entrance. Arguing that a Christmas tree is historically erected on the site during Christmas, the Lubavitchers sought access for their specific message too. However, District Judge Vietor denied access for the menorah, noting the state capitol's policy against unattended displays in general is applied consistently, and in a manner that does not discriminate against the message or viewpoint represented by such displays. As well, Judge Vietor relies on the Supreme Court's *Lynch* decision that stipulates Christmas trees are secular,[37] not religious, displays of the Christmas holidays.[38]

In a similar dispute, Muslims sought to place a crescent and star symbol in the Manhattan General Post Office alongside existing Christmas tree and menorah displays. The postmaster refused their request, and they turned to the federal district court in Manhattan to protect their free speech claim. District Judge Sotomayer refused to grant access to their crescent and star, and pointed out that although the post office is a government building, it is "essentially a commercial enterprise—delivering mail and packages for its customers in return for payment . . . Its facilities are, in the main, reserved for the specific purpose of 'accomplishing the most efficient and effective postal delivery system.'"[39] The post office in this case is not a public forum, and its restriction of the Muslim display only has to be "reasonable," and not an attempt to suppress the speakers' point of view. For the court, the post office allowed Christmas trees and menorahs as more of a marketing measure to promote business, and its denial of access for the Muslim crescent and star was not due to disagreement with their symbolic message, but simply because those symbols did not fit the post office's marketing scheme during the holidays.

Some of the primary arguments against unattended religious displays such as menorahs, crèches, or even crescent and stars, is that such displays risk violating the Establishment Clause. By allowing religious displays, governments may be perceived as endorsing the specific religious message of a display, and thus violate the First Amendment. Establishment Clause arguments were raised in 59 percent (n=17) of the cases involving religious displays, and district courts rule against such displays in 58 percent of those cases. In 40 percent of the cases involving religious displays and public forums (twenty-nine cases total) courts protected religious displays by ordering government to grant entry, even though the government managing the specific forum at issue alleged an Establishment Clause violation. The vagaries of how the Establishment Clause links with religious speech are addressed at a later point in this chapter, but suffice to say now that district courts seem somewhat divided over whether the clause prohibits the unattended display of religious symbols in public squares.

PUBLIC PARKS

In common with public schools, parks, and other publicly owned open spaces tend to attract litigation concerning religious speech. About one-third of the religious speech and public forum cases concern parks and open spaces such as state fairgrounds, municipal sidewalks, sports stadiums, and even national forest lands owned by the federal government. Overall, courts protect religious expression in roughly 63 percent of the cases, indicating that district courts often view parks as appropriate places for communicative activity based on a religious message. Yet, some types of activity are more protected than others.

Preaching, for instance, is protected most of the time, as are religious displays. In fact, religious displays receive far more protection when the location for the display is a public park instead of a government building. In one case, a district judge refused to order the removal of a war memorial in a city-owned park that was inscribed with "For God and Country. Dedicated to the memory of men and women whose love for this nation enabled them to make the supreme sacrifice." As the judge noted, the monument has secular attributes—honoring war dead—that outweigh its religious connotations.[40] Likewise, and in contrast to government buildings, courts have allowed the Chabad-Lubavitch to display menorahs in parks, provided that disclaimers are usually included with the display to point out that a government in no way endorses the menorah's message. When courts refuse to protect the placement of religious displays in parks, it is almost always due to the fact that a government refuses displays on a viewpoint neutral basis,[41] or the location is so closely affiliated with government functions that religious displays must go to great lengths to demonstrate that the government in no way endorses the display's underlying religious message.[42] In one unique case, several plaintiffs sought to place aboveground, vertical grave markers in a publicly owned cemetery, in violation of government rules allowing only in-ground markers. The plaintiffs argued that gravestones are symbolic expression, and thus protected by the Free Speech Clause. Their free speech complaint was dismissed, and the district judge noted that cemeteries are not public forums open to the free exchange or public debate of ideas. Thus, the city's restrictions on gravestones were constitutional.[43]

Religious solicitations do not receive the same amount of protection in parks and open spaces as in travel terminals. Many of the park cases concern Krishna attempts to practice *sankirtan* in county and state fairgrounds throughout the United States where they could reach high numbers of people in attendance. Often, government-run fairs would try to confine the Krishnas to a fixed location along with other religious and secular groups. Other speakers generally complied with so-called booth rules that limited them to fixed locations, but for the Krishnas the point of *sankirtan* is that it is ambulatory; Krishna devotees must be able to intermingle with the public, and approach others for solicitations. Many district courts sustained booth rules as allowable "time, place, and manner" regulations that facilitate the orderly flow of fair patrons. The Supreme Court sustained booth rules as well in *Heffron v. International Society for Krishna Consciousness*, where the booth rule at issue only confined Krishnas to a fixed location if they wanted to solicit donations from fair patrons.[44] Otherwise, they could mingle among the crowd and orally propagate their views. For the six-justice majority, the rules drew an appropriate balance between the government's need to regulate the orderly flow of fair patrons, and the Krishnas' right to religious speech.

Worship services are only protected in 43 percent of the cases, unlike with public schools where churches, congregations, or other nonstudent religious groups are often granted access to use school facilities for worship-based activities. In two cases members of the amorphous "Rainbow Family" were prosecuted for staging "Rainbow Family Gatherings" on National Forest lands owned by the federal government. District courts determined in both cases that Forest Service regulations sharply limiting access to the properties in question are reasonable time, place, and manner regulations on speech and expressive conduct.[45]

OTHER TYPES OF FORUMS

Finally, public forums that do not easily fit into more defined categories are not usually open to religious speech by district courts. Table 5.1 points out that other types of forums are considered open to speech in general 40 percent of the time, which is significantly less than with other forum locations. As well, other forums are open to religious speech in 20 percent of the cases. Thus, district courts only protect religious speech in one out of five public spaces that do not fall under more conventional types

of locations such as public parks or schools. Even though district
court policymaking frequently considers other forums open to
speech as a general rule, when the specific religious message is considered in each case, courts alter their policymaking significantly
and shut off access to other types of public places. District courts are
much more deferential to government management of nontraditional forums such as the state vanity license plates case or radio license disputes discussed in chapter 4.[46] Even though the Supreme
Court announced in *Rosenberger v. Rectors of the University of Virginia* that "metaphysical" public forums, such as a university-funded
student publication system, fall under the First Amendment, district
courts are very reluctant to protect religious speech in these types
of public spaces.[47]

THE PARTISAN PUBLIC SQUARE?

Looking at district court policymaking through the lens of judicial partisanship yields some interesting results. Recall from chapter 4 that partisanship did affect how district judges categorized
public spaces under the public forum framework, although partisan
differences were not that sharp and distinct. When defining the
contours of public spaces, Republican and Democratic judges differ slightly in their views. As the charts demonstrate, however,
partisanship does matter when the content of the forum is at issue.

First, using the specific location of the public forum to frame
partisanship and support for religious speech shows that Democratic and Republican judges do not differ dramatically over most
forum types. For example, the partisan difference between judges
on whether religious speech is allowable in public parks, travel terminals, or other forums is slight. Democratic judges support religious speech in parks and travel terminals more so than
Republicans but only by narrow margins. Where partisan dis-

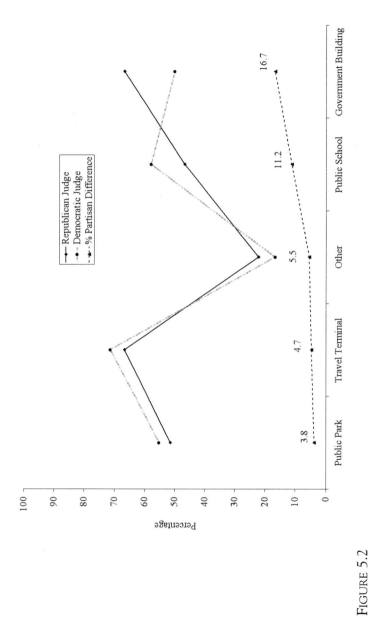

FIGURE 5.2

Partisanship and Pro-Religious Message Decision by Location of Forum. Federal District Courts, 1974–2001.

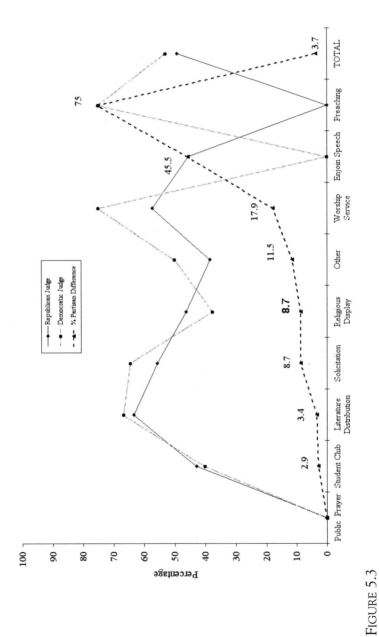

FIGURE 5.3

Partisanship and Pro-Religious Message Decision by Type of Expression. Federal District Courts, 1974–2001.

agreement emerges is with public schools and government buildings. Interestingly, Democrats are more supportive of religious speech in public schools than Republicans. Although Democratic district judges are generally more supportive of civil liberties claims than Republican judges, they might be expected to be less supportive of religious speech in public schools due to long-standing opposition to government support for religion. Rowland and Carp point out in their long-term study of district court policy-making that Democratic judges are by far more supportive of religious liberty, meaning that they tend to protect the free exercise rights of plaintiffs and use the Establishment Clause to cut the ties of government sponsorship of religion. Indeed, Democrats support religious liberty claims 60 percent of the time, and Republicans only support religious liberty claims 36 percent of the time.[48]

A different picture emerges when partisanship is linked with the specific type of expression at issue. Overall, Democratic and Republican judges are only 3.7 percent apart in their support for religious speech, as illustrated in figure 5.3. Democrats support religious speech in the public square in 52.7 percent of the cases, and Republicans support it in 49 percent of the cases. There is no wide difference concerning religious speech cases, unlike other civil liberties issues. Rowland and Carp do demonstrate that with freedom of expression writ large (which includes religious speech cases), Democrats are much more likely to support free speech than Republicans. Yet, with this more nuanced study of religious speech only, the wide gulf between them disappears. However, there are real differences with certain types of expression.

As figure 5.3 points out, partisanship is not a factor with religious expression involving public prayer (Democratic and Republican judges both oppose it), and only slight differences with student religious clubs in schools and the distribution of religious literature in public. More noticeable diversity emerges with cases involving religious solicitation, such as with Krishna *sankirtan* and religious displays in public. Democratic judges are more supportive of religious solicitation, but they flip on the issue of religious displays in public that garners more support from Republicans.

Democrats are more open to allowing worship services in public places than are Republicans, and indeed the 17.9 percent difference is striking. Democratic judges may view worship services fundamentally in terms of the free expression of individuals or groups, and not as a religious exercise per se. Thus they may see allowing worship services in public places less in terms of indirect government support, through the provision of a public space, for a religious exercise, and more as an issue of freedom of expression.

Some cases concern religious speech that is already in the public square, for example having been granted access to a public school or government building by a state or local government agency. Plaintiffs in these disputes ask federal judges to intervene and grant injunctions to order a halt to the religious expression at issue. In these disputes, denial of an injunction is construed as support for religious speech, since denying the order means the speech can remain in the public place. Granting an injunction means the religious speech must be removed. Democratic judges always grant those injunctions; hence as figure 5.3 shows they have no support for religious speech in those types of cases. That is, when asked to order religious speech out of a public space, Democrats always do so, and never rule in favor of the religious speech. Republican judges are almost split, and decide in 54.5 percent of the cases to grant the requested injunction against the religious speech. Conversely, in 45.5 percent of the cases, they support or protect religious speech and deny the injunction. In a real sense, support for speech already in the public square may be due in part to deference on the part of Republican judges to how government agencies, and especially local governments, manage their public properties.

Whither the Establishment Clause?

In some religious speech cases governments deny access to speakers so as not to run afoul of the Establishment Clause. Preventing an establishment of religion, it is argued, is a compelling enough interest to justify restricting the right to free speech. As discussed in chapter 2, the Supreme Court indicates that the Establishment Clause may indeed be a compelling interest to limit speech, but in none of the religious speech cases has the Court affirmed the use of the clause in such a way. In fact, the Court is divided over the circumstances under which speech can be limited by the government's avoidance of accommodating or supporting a religion.

With district court litigation, the Establishment Clause is most frequently an issue in disputes concerning public schools and public parks, and it is invoked in two circumstances. One, a government entity will use the clause to prohibit religious expression in a public space. For this argument, religious expression in government-owned forums is akin to the accommodation of religion, and brings the government close to endorsing and supporting the specific religious message and faith underlying it. Two, the clause is used to drive religious speech out of a public square. In these types of disputes, the government already allows some kind of religious expression on its property, and litigants sue to disallow access to the public forum. In such cases, the government often adopts a "free speech" argument, which means that it must allow religious speech in the public forum so as not to unconstitutionally discriminate against speech in general.

In religious speech disputes the Establishment Clause is at issue most frequently in public schools, as 56.1 percent of the school cases concern both free speech and establishment issues. School authorities will use Establishment Clause barriers to deny access to school property for religious speakers, whether they are students seeking to form a religious club or the Gideons distributing Bibles. For disputes concerning government buildings, the clause is used by public authorities to limit religious speech in almost 44 percent of the cases; with public parks, the clause arises in about 24 percent of the cases. For travel terminal and other location type disputes, the Establishment Clause is almost never an issue.

More telling than the fact that the clause is used most frequently by public schools is how the clause links with specific types of religious expression. One significant trend emerges: the Establishment Clause, as a means of justifying limits on religious speech and expression in the public square, is invoked most often in disputes concerning group-based expression, and not individual expressive activity. Group expression concerns, for example, the student religious group that seeks to use school facilities for its meetings, or a local religious congregation that wants to use a government-owned facility for worship services or other religious activities. In terms of litigation patterns, government authorities charged with policing public squares will rely repeatedly on the Establishment Clause as part of their regulatory framework in disputes concerning group-based expressive activities.

Table 5.3 links the Establishment Clause with the specific type of expression at issue. Notably, the clause is absent from disputes concerning individual types of expression, such as preaching or evangelism, in which the speaker is generally one person who wishes to preach in the public square to others. Likewise, the clause does not occur in litigation concerning religious solicitation, as with the Krishnas, and again in individual expressive activity. Group based expressive activity—student religious clubs and worship services—tend to attract arguments based on the Establishment Clause for limiting speech in the public square. Disputes about religious displays such as nativity scenes and menorahs also raise concerns regarding the Establishment Clause, and to be sure most of the religious display cases are brought by recognized

	Establishment Clause Defense Raised by One Party?		Success Rate of Establishment Clause Claim (%)
	No	Yes	
Preaching	7	1	1
	87.5%	12.5%	100.0%
	4.0%	.6%	
Solicitations	24	0	0
	100.0%		
	13.7%		
Religious club access in school	7	6	5
	53.8%	46.2%	83.3%
	4.0%	3.4%	
Distribution of literature	18	7	2
	72.0%	28.0%	28.6%
	10.3%	4.0%	
Public prayer	3	0	0
	100.0%		
	1.7%		
Enjoin religious speech	4	13	9
	23.5%	76.5%	69.2%
	2.3%	7.4%	
Religious display	12	17	10
	41.4%	58.6%	58.8%
	6.9%	9.7%	
Worship service	24	13	4
	64.9%	35.1%	30.8%
	13.7%	7.4%	
Other	15	4	4
	78.9%	21.1%	100.0%
	8.6%	2.3%	
TOTAL	114	61	35
	65.1%	34.9%	57.4%
	65.1%	34.9%	

TABLE 5.3

Type of Expression Linked with Establishment Clause Defense. Federal District Courts, 1974–2001.

religious groups such as the Chabad-Lubavitch, the Knights of Columbus, or more localized congregations, and should thus be seen as forms of corporate or group religious expression as well.

Does the Establishment Clause actually work to limit religious speech in the public square? For federal trial court policymaking, the results are decidedly mixed. Of all cases in which the clause is used by litigants to justify restrictions on religious speech, district courts ultimately limit that speech and expression 57 percent of the time. That is, the Establishment Clause justifies limits on religious expression in the public square in just over one-half of the cases in which it is at issue. That trial judges rely on the Establishment Clause in just over one-half of the cases indicates to a large degree that there is no consensus among district courts concerning whether and how the clause can be used to limit religious speech. Overall, though, the Establishment Clause exerts a minor impact in district court policymaking since courts rely on it to limit religious speech in just 20 percent of all religious expression and public forum disputes. Thus, courts find other ways of justifying limits on religious speech without delving into Establishment Clause concerns over whether the government is endorsing a religious message, or a religion, by allowing its expression in a public forum.

The most recent Supreme Court decision on religious speech in the public forum, *Good News Club v. Milford Central School*, demonstrates how the Court itself is divided over whether the Establishment Clause limits religious speech in public school. In *Good News*, the Court overturned a school board's refusal to allow a nondenominational evangelical Christian group to conduct religious meetings for elementary school students in school facilities. The board argued that elementary school children are especially impressionistic, thus Establishment Clause concerns are heightened, and the school must go to great lengths to ensure that the children do not think the school is endorsing or supporting one religion. Writing for the five-justice majority, Justice Clarence Thomas argued that "we decline to employ Establishment Clause jurisprudence using a modified heckler's veto, in which a group's religious activity can be proscribed on the basis of what the youngest members of the audience might misperceive." Moreover, "There are countervailing constitutional concerns related to rights of other individuals in the community. In this case, those countervailing concerns are the free speech rights of the Club and its members."[49]

Justice Scalia echoed those sentiments while addressing yet another variant of Establishment Clause doctrine concerning whether the school or others indirectly coerce or pressure students to attend the religious meetings. For Scalia,

> Physical coercion is not at issue here, and so-called "peer pressure," if it can even been considered coercion, is, when it arises from private activities, one of the attendant consequences of a freedom of association that is constitutionally protected. What is at play here is not coercion, but the compulsion of ideas—and the private right to exert and receive that compulsion (or to have one's children receive it) is protected by the Free Speech and Free Exercise Clauses, not banned by the Establishment Clause. A priest has as much liberty to proselytize as a patriot.[50]

Justice Scalia further noted his bright-line view of the conflict between Establishment and religious speech by which religious speech is always protected, provided it is "purely private and . . . occurs in a traditional or designated public forum, publicly announced and open to all on equal terms."[51]

Justice Breyer agreed with the outcome of the case, but wrote a separate opinion to highlight his understanding of what he terms the "critical Establishment Clause question." For Justice Breyer, the issue is "whether a child, participating in the Good News Club's activities, could reasonably perceive the school's permission for the club to use its facilities as an endorsement of religion. . . . The time of day, the age of the children, the nature of the meetings, and other specific circumstances are relevant in helping to determine whether, in fact, the Club so dominates the forum that, in the children's minds, a formal policy of equal access is transformed into a demonstration of approval."[52] The Establishment Clause, for Breyer, is perhaps the most important issue in *Good News* and one that the Court did not fully address. Moreover, in contrast to Justice Scalia's clear rule that private religious speech trumps Establishment Clause concerns, and Justice Thomas's refusal to use the clause as a "heckler's veto," Justice Breyer indicated the importance of delving deeply into the factual context of cases. The timing of the speech, the age of the children, and the type of meetings at issue are all important issues that must be fully addressed in order to determine if the school is endorsing religion or not.

Justice Souter strongly dissented, and, like Breyer, focused on the specific context and factual circumstances surrounding the Good News Club's speech. He noted that "there is a good case that Good News' exercises blur the line between public classroom instruction and private religious indoctrination, leaving a reasonable elementary school pupil unable to appreciate that the former instruction is the business of the school while the latter evangelism is not."[53] Thus, Souter suggested that courts should inquire specifically into the type of speech at issue to determine whether it is akin to religious indoctrination and evangelism; that is, whether the Good News Club seeks to convert others. Indeed, courts should closely inspect why nonschool groups seek to use school facilities anyway. Moreover, "in fact, the temporal and physical continuity of Good News' meetings with the regular school routine seems to be the whole point of using the school.

When meetings were held in a community church, 8 or 10 children attended; after the school became the site, the number went up three-fold."[54] The club's impetus to use school facilities may have more to do with reaching a larger group of students, in Souter's view, than with using publicly available facilities in which to conduct expressive activities. Thus, the issue becomes less a dispute about public forums per se, and more an issue over the strategies of evangelism that religious groups employ. In addition, judges must inquire deeply into the motivation of a religious speaker (or speakers) to use public forums, especially when schools are involved.

Even though the Court consistently protects religious speech as speech under the First Amendment, *Good News* shows the deep divisions among the justices concerning whether the Establishment Clause serves to limit religious speech. For Justices Thomas and Scalia, the Free Speech Clause should prohibit the use of the Establishment Clause to censor religious speech—the so-called heckler's veto—and indeed there should be a bright line between religious speech and establishment of religion that allows speech to trump the separation of church and state. With the bright-line approach to religious speech, detailed factual inquiries become less important. That is, judges do not need to inquire into why a religious group or speaker wants to use an open public forum, and thus do not need to ask whether the speaker's purpose is to discuss issues from a religious perspective, or evangelize and seek converts. As Justice Scalia put it, the free speech rights of priests and patriots are the same.

Justices Souter and Breyer counsel caution. For them, it is important for a judge to know the speaker's motivation, and whether the speaker wants to supply religious information to others or proselytize and seek converts. Although Justices Souter and Breyer do not argue that active proselytism should be prohibited, they suggest that judges should use a heightened awareness of the issues when determining whether the government in charge of a forum violates the Establishment Clause when it allows proselytes into the public square. Courts should undertake a very detailed, searching, factual inquiry when balancing religious speech and Establishment Clause concerns.

To be sure, *Good News* concerns an elementary school as a public forum. In other cases concerning schools such as *Widmar v. Vincent* (public university) and *Lamb's Chapel* (high school) the Court has been less divided over the Establishment Clause. Thus, the principles distilled and debated in *Good News* are not necessarily applicable to other types of religious speech disputes concerning nonschool forums.

In terms of district courts, their policymaking falls somewhere in between Justice Thomas's "heckler's veto" and Justice Souter's searching inquiry: the Establishment Clause is not a constant rule that limits religious speech in most circumstances (the heckler's veto); nor is purely private religious speech presumptively protected from Establishment Clause limitations either. At best, district courts are simply confused over how to reconcile potentially competing Establishment Clause and Free Speech Clause disputes. At worst, some district judges will actively use the Establishment Clause to limit religious speech, whereas other district judges will ignore the separation of church and state altogether.

Linking partisanship to speech and Establishment Clause disputes tends to indicate that, if anything, judges are probably just confused. For example, Republican judges are almost evenly split, with about 50 percent ruling in favor of religious speakers even though the Establishment Clause was at issue, and about 50 percent ruling against the religious speaker (out of a total of forty cases). By contrast, only about 30 percent of Democratic judges rule in favor of the religious speaker (out of a total of twenty cases), indicating that the majority of Democratic judges will use the Establishment Clause to limit religious speech. The even division of Republican judges extends across forum locations too, with judges basically split evenly between protecting or rejecting religious speech in public schools, parks, and government buildings, whenever the Establishment Clause is raised alongside the speech claim.

Partisanship over the importance of the Establishment Clause should not be overstated, for two main reasons. One, slightly more than one-third of religious speech cases also concern the Establishment Clause; the remainder do not. Thus, district courts are less frequently faced with reconciling the rights of religious speakers with the separation of church and state. Two, Republican judges adjudicate two-thirds of those cases that concern the Establishment Clause, which should raise questions about the partisan differences noticed here. Yet, it could well be that the lack of consensus among Republican judges on how to balance religious speech and the separation of church and state is based more on the difficulty that judges have in applying confusing, and divisive, Supreme Court decisions. The high court's inability to clearly articulate whether religious speech trumps Establishment Clause concerns translates down to confusion and lack of policymaking consensus among district court judges, at least as far as Republican judges are concerned. With so few Democratic judges, it is difficult to draw meaningful comparisons.

CONCLUSION

Chapter 4 discusses court policymaking in terms of how public spaces fall under public forum analysis. This chapter, by contrast, focuses on policymaking concerning forum content: when public forums are open to religious speech, and what types of speech and expression are more protected than others. As the prior chapter showed, district courts are generally in agreement about how spe-

cific forum locations should be typed under the traditional, limited
or designated, and nonpublic forum categories. Agreement about
the categorization of forums, however, breaks down when the content of forums is at issue. As this chapter makes clear, district
courts tend to support religious speech claims in about half of the
cases, in real contrast to the Supreme Court's two-decade trend of
indicating that religious speech in public forums is entitled to the
highest constitutional protection.

Determining whether religious speech is allowed into public forums is highly contextual, as the data linking support for religious
speech to specific forum locations indicates. That is, instead of
adopting the Supreme Court's insistent doctrine that elevates religious speech to enjoy the highest protection under the Constitution, courts will more likely determine whether religious speech is
allowable based on the location and usages of each specific forum,
whether it is a public school, park, or travel terminal.

Overall, district courts tend to be most protective of *individual-
ist* types of religious speech, types of expression such as distributing literature or soliciting others for donations, that are normally
engaged in by individuals, and indeed involve a kind of "one on
one" interaction between speaker and listener. Courts are also
more protective of the rights of religious congregations to use public facilities to hold worship services or other types of religious
meetings.

Chapter 4 discussed partisanship and policymaking, and suggests that partisanship (conservative or liberal judges) does have
some impact on how a public space is categorized and open to
speech, although that impact is nominal. In contrast, partisanship
has a more notable effect on the *content* of public forums as that
content links with specific types of expression. Interestingly,
Democratic judges tend to be more supportive of religious speech
claims than Republican judges. Democratic judges are historically
more liberal on civil liberties issues, which also means they tend

to perceive the Establishment Clause as a clearer barrier between government and religion than do Republican judges. Yet, Democratic support for religious speech in public forums shows that at least in the area of religious speech, Democratic judges tend not to see religion in the public square as an issue of the separation of church and state, but more of an issue of free speech. Indeed, support for religious speech, *as free speech*, fits with the traditional liberalism and pro–civil liberties decisions of Democratic judges in general.

The discussion of district court policymaking in cases concerning the Establishment Clause highlights the ambivalence, and perhaps confusion, among lower trial courts over whether the separation of church and state is a powerful enough argument to limit the free speech rights of a religious speaker. The Supreme Court's own division over the role of the Establishment Clause in free speech cases does not offer any real guidance either, which suggests several important points. To start, the inability of lower district courts to reach a consensus on how to balance the Establishment Clause and religious speech indicates that the high court itself needs to clarify its own doctrine first, with clear, definable guidelines that district courts can apply across the board. Yet, few religious speech cases also concern the Establishment Clause, which may indicate that the high court's doctrinal confusion has little impact, and in fact the justices are focusing on a conflict that really does not exist in lower trial courts. Justice Breyer's comment in *Good News* that the Establishment Clause is a "critical" issue is not necessarily born out by lower trial court policymaking. Since disputes hinging upon the clause occur infrequently at the trial level, the criticalness of the Establishment Clause may be overstated by both liberal and conservative justices on the Court.

CHAPTER 6

Conclusion
District Courts, Religious Speech, and the Public Square

THE *GOOD NEWS V. MILFORD Central School* case discussed in chapter 5 reflects the Supreme Court's continuing focus on the free speech and public forum rights of religious speakers. Yet, the Court's division over how and whether the Establishment Clause limits religious speech indicates a lasting disagreement over the constitutional limits on private religious expression in public forums. For this study of district courts and religious speech, Justice Souter's dissenting opinion in *Good News* is especially interesting since he criticizes the majority for addressing the Establishment Clause issue even though it was based on an incomplete factual record developed by the lower district court. For Souter, the Court did not know some very pertinent facts, such as whether the Good News Club held meetings concurrently with school-sponsored activities, or whether other community groups used school facilities immediately after classes end (and as Good News sought to do). Importantly, Souter also identified another issue that the Court ignored: "the extent to which Good News, with 28 students in its membership, may 'dominate the forum' in a way that heightens the perception of official endorsement."[1] "We will never know these facts," he argues, indicating that the justices should be much more cautious in addressing a constitutional issue that is not more fully developed by lower trial and appellate tribunals. By addressing the Establishment Clause dispute without having a full record before it, the Court overstepped its role as an appellate court:

> Respect for our role as a reviewing court rests rather on recognizing that this Court can often learn a good deal from considering how a district court and a court of appeals have worked their way through a difficult issue. It rests on recognizing that an issue as first conceived may come to be seen differently as a case moves through trial and appeal; we are most likely to contribute something of value if we act with the benefit of whatever refinement may come in the course of litigation. And our customary refusal to become a trial court reflects the simple fact that this Court cannot develop a record as well as a trial court can.[2]

Justice Souter emphasizes the importance of trial courts in the initial stages of litigation. Trial courts construe factual situations in specific cases before them and apply the law to those facts. Thus, they "develop a record" that may or may not be appealed up through the appellate hierarchy, and the *Good News* case makes it very clear that the factual record established at the trial level will set the stage for policymaking by higher appellate courts.

To be fair to District Judge Thomas J. McAvoy, who first presided over the *Good News* litigation in 1998, no doubt he thought he construed the facts of the dispute in a fair way and addressed the important constitutional issues that were raised.[3] Justice Souter did not criticize Judge McAvoy's development of the trial record either; he simply highlighted the fact that the constitutional issues under Supreme Court review had changed as the case progressed up the federal judicial ladder. Indeed, the conflict between the Establishment Clause and religious speech only became an issue after the case left District Judge McAvoy's courtroom. Nonetheless, Justice Souter's complaint with the majority in *Good News* demonstrates the importance of district court policymaking.

"Developing the record" is crucial in district court policymaking. A district court's construal of facts not only affects Supreme Court policymaking, as Justice Souter makes abundantly clear; it also affects other trial courts and even prospective litigants. C. K. Rowland and Robert A. Carp note in their long-term study of federal district courts that when trial courts "evaluate evidence and interpret the law, they are formulating policy." That policy further guides "other judges, and, more important, potential litigants."[4] What, then, can potential litigants learn from a study such as this that looks closely at district court policymaking in religious speech cases?

If religious speakers seeking access to public forums rely on religious speech cases decided by the Supreme Court for the past two decades, they might conclude that their speech will be protected under the First Amendment, and they will gain access to government owned spaces. In a series of cases starting with *Widmar v. Vincent* in 1981, and continuing with the *Good News* case in 2001, the high court consistently announced that religious speech should be given the highest protection under the First Amendment. District courts, however, send a decidedly different message to potential litigants.

Recall the dual policymaking role that district courts play. First, courts categorize the public property at issue under public forum doctrine, and determine whether it is a traditional, designated, or nonforum public forum. By so doing, district courts establish whether a government owned property is part of the marketplace of ideas, whether it is open to speech and expression, and if so, how speech in the forum should be regulated. Second, courts determine whether the specific religious speech being litigated can be allowed in the public forum. By looking at the type of forum, the way it is typically used by speakers and regulated by the government, the type of religious expression, and other issues, courts not only define the forum's contour; they also define its content.

District court policymaking communicates to potential litigants that the first hurdle in religious speech litigation—categorizing the public forum at issue—is perhaps the easiest. As chapter 4 illustrates, district courts show a high level of agreement as to how specific locations, such as schools or parks, should be typed under the public forum categories of traditional, limited/designated, or nonpublic forums. For instance, the vast majority of public schools are viewed as limited public forums, and most public parks are considered traditional public forums. Controlling for judicial partisanship, it is clear that courts also agree over the conditions under which forums are open to speech and expression in general. Therefore, religious speakers suing, or contemplating a lawsuit, to gain access to government property should conclude that categorizing the forum involves little controversy. District courts generally agree on the contours of forums, indicating that litigants face few barriers at the initial stages of litigation. The high level of agreement over forum categories, and the fact that the majority of forums litigated are considered already open to speech-related activities, means that litigants should devote more attention to the content of public forums instead. In fact, the content of public forums is the more crucial question for future litigants.

Chapter 5 makes clear that agreement among district courts over how public spaces are categorized under public forum doctrine breaks down with the next policymaking step: that of determining the appropriate content of public forums. In broad terms, courts protect religious speech in about 50 percent of the cases at the trial level, and litigants and potential litigants are by no means assured that a public forum open to speech as a general rule is also open to religious speech. Indeed, district court policymaking unmistakably indicates otherwise. Courts show a willingness to determine whether religious speech is protected based on the location and usage of the forum and also on the specific type of religious expression litigated. For example, distributing religious literature and soliciting donations for a religious cause are both protected in about two-thirds of the cases, as is the right of religious groups to use public properties for worship-related activities. Other types of religious expression are less protected, though, which indicates that at the trial level the specific type of religious speech and expression litigated does matter. Here, district court policymaking seems to counter the Supreme Court's doctrine that the free speech rights of religious speakers are to be protected as any other private expression, meaning that there should really be no distinction between types of religious expression. Preaching, evangelism in general, worship-based expression, or Bible reading by individuals should receive the same protection at the lower trial level. District court policymaking shows otherwise.

DISTRICT COURTS AND THE
HALF-DRESSED PUBLIC SQUARE

Chapter 1 linked religious speech disputes to a larger, national debate over the openness of the public square to religious expression in general. To recall Richard John Neuhaus's argument, the public square is hostile to religious speech and expression, especially in the context of debate over public policy: "the naked public square is the result of political doctrine and practice that would exclude religion and religiously grounded values from the conduct of public business."[5] As he again notes, "the question of religion's access to the public square . . . is first of all a question of understanding the theory and practice of democratic governance. Citi-

zens are the bearers of opinion, including opinion shaped by or es-
pousing religious belief."⁶ Religious expression is, for Neuhaus,
simply one aspect of public expression and debate in general, and
should be accorded as much prominence as any other type of
speech on public issues.

Neuhaus's view of the public square fits standard views of public forum doctrine as defined by the Supreme Court. Justice
Kennedy neatly underscores the relationship of public forum doctrine and open democratic debate in *International Society for
Krishna Consciousness v. Lee*, where he argues that the public
forum is premised on the "principle that in a free nation citizens
must have the right to gather and speak with other persons in public places. The recognition that certain government-owned property is a public forum provides open notice to citizens that their
freedoms may be exercised there without fear of a censorial government, adding tangible reinforcement to the idea that we are a
free people."⁷

By placing the public square into an empirical framework,
David Yamane discovered that religious speech and expression are
not absent from the public square at all. In his study of state legislative hearings, Yamane concludes that religious speakers are
very active in presenting religious viewpoints to legislators, thus
the public square—in the form of legislative hearings—is by no
means devoid of religious content.⁸

As with Yamane's empirical study of the public square in state
legislative hearings, so too can district courts serve to empirically
ground the debate over religious speech in the square. Public
forum disputes concern the ability of speakers to access government owned and maintained property to present a point of view.
The ready availability of government property makes it, broadly, a
public square open to all. "The right to use government property
for one's private expression," as Justice Scalia indicates in *Capitol
Square Review & Advisory Board v. Pinette*, "depends upon whether

the property has by law or tradition been given the status of a public forum."[9] Indeed, for Justice Scalia and others on the Supreme Court, the public forum should almost always be open to religious speech, since Court precedent "establishes that private religious speech, far from being a First Amendment orphan, is as fully protected under the Free Speech Clause as secular private expression."[10]

District court policymaking on religious speech and public forums helps frame the ongoing debate over religion in the public square and adds empirical depth to the ongoing argument over religion in the public square. Trial courts concur that government-owned properties—the public square—are usually open to some type of speech and expression. Yet, they disagree over the conditions under which religious speech can access the public square. Importantly, this is not to argue that district courts treat religious speech differently than secular speech, and that religious speakers do not enjoy as much access to the public forum as nonreligious speakers. Thus, whether trial courts agree with Justice Scalia's dictum that the First Amendment treats secular and religious speech the same is not known. What is known and observed, however, is that trial courts tend to distinguish between types of religious speech for purposes of access to the public square. The consequence of district court policymaking for religious speech in the public square is simply that some types of religious speech are allowed into the square, and others are not. Recall from chapter 5 that trial courts protect religious speech in about half of the cases, and courts have a propensity to protect certain types of religious expression over others. In terms of the public square, some religious speech is allowed in by trial courts and some is not. Trial courts favor some types of religious expression over others. The overall impact of district court policymaking then is that the public square is not quite naked and devoid of religious content; but it is not fully clothed either. Indeed, at least in terms of trial court policymaking, the presence of religious expression in the public square is not necessarily based on the message per se, but on the manner of expression.

Litigation at the district court level also presents an overall picture of the marketplace of public forum and religious speech policymaking. Constitutional law scholars often focus exclusively on the Supreme Court's policymaking, and here the Court's review of public forum and religious speech disputes covers a wide range of forums, from public universities in *Widmar v. Vincent* and elementary schools in *Good News*, to state fairgrounds and airports in *Heffron v. ISKCON* and *ISKCON v. Lee*. Studying district court litigation places that range of public forums in a broader framework, which leads to a deeper understanding of the locations for religious speech in general. For instance, litigation symmetries at the district court level show that three-fourths of religious speech cases concern two types of forums: public schools and public parks. Other forum locations, from travel terminals to government buildings, are not as numerous. Not only do litigant symmetries show where trial court policymaking is concentrated; they also show where religious speakers most want to place their message. To be sure, religious speech litigation may not be representative of all disputes over religious speech and public forums, since litigation only includes those speakers who opt to sue over forum access. Therefore, generalizing from observed litigation in federal courts to all disagreements over religious speech in public forums is not warranted. Nonetheless, district court litigation can at least provide important clues as to the types of public spaces that religious speakers seek, and indeed litigation can at least suggest a baseline that can then be compared to religious speech in all public spaces outside of the context of lawsuits and trial court policymaking.

As mentioned above, district court policymaking most often concerns two types of public forums: schools and parks. Thus, at least at the trial court level, public forum and religious speech doctrine develops primarily in the context of two types of public spaces. As well, litigation symmetries also show that three-fourths of the defendants at the trial court level are local government entities charged with regulating access to local public forums. Not only are district courts focusing on few specific types of public forums, but they are also bound up in local political conflicts over how local forums are to be managed. The local nature of religious speech and public forum disputes suggests that they are frequently part of ongoing conflicts between local governments and local public opinion, and indeed are part of the larger debate over accommodation of religious belief at the local level. As Ted Jelen highlights, local governments must often respond to local public opinion that generally supports government accommodation of religion, whether in the form of prayer at local government meetings or religious exercises in government-maintained forums. Indeed, as Jelen argues, "local policymaking in most areas of the United States is likely to take on a Christian preferentialist cast," meaning that local policies will subtly reflect, or prefer, the wishes of a local Christian majority. Jelen does not argue that all local governments accommodate Christian religions, nor does he view this type of local policymaking as inevitable. He simply links local politics to the fact that American public opinion tends to support the blending of politics and religion at the most local level.[11]

District court policymaking reflects Jelen's point that disputes over religion and politics are often local in nature. Religious speech and public forum cases show that these disputes often involve local clashes of ideas, policies, and principles. One difference, though, is that in Jelen's typology local governments tend to be more supportive of accommodating religion than lawsuits over religious speech would indicate. District courts are different, in that they may tend to be less supportive than local political processes in protecting religious expression in public places.

If Jelen's point about the "Christian preferentialist" cast of local governments and local public opinion is correct, then this analysis of district court policymaking and religious speech suggests two interesting avenues for further study. First, district court litigation may result when disputes between local governments and religious speakers over access to a forum are unresolved. That is, district courts may only get involved in religious speech cases after the local political process has failed to accommodate the speaker(s). More detailed case studies are necessary to accurately link district court policymaking to local government policymaking, and this study does not do that. Yet, the data presented in the above chapters suggests that there is a detailed and subtler relationship between district courts and local governments that needs investigation.[12]

Second, Jelen's analysis suggests that local governments may be predisposed to grant religious speakers access to local public forums, which indicates perhaps that litigants who do use district courts to try to gain access to a forum may be better advised to use the local political process instead. That is, perhaps litigants are too quick to sue, and they have not explored all the local political and policymaking angles available to them. Again, more detailed case studies are needed here to determine the point at which litigants turn away from using a local political process to gain access to a forum, and turn to a federal court.

WHOSE VOICE? WHOSE DOCTRINE?

The American Center of Law and Justice is affiliated with and funded by the Christian Coalition, and is considered by many to be one of the primary litigation arms of the Christian Right.[13] Its lead counsel, Jay Alan Sekulow, actively works to protect the free speech rights of religious speakers. In his words,

We deal with problems concerning access to parks, school
campuses at every level, malls, street corners and, of course,
airports. . . . There were already aggressive, effective Christian organizations that specialized in litigating religious freedom issues—The National Legal Foundation and the
Rutherford Institute, for example—but I saw a growing need
to challenge the state's infringement upon the right of Christians to proclaim the gospel.[14]

Sekulow highlights an important strategy of some Christian Right
litigators: many religious liberty disputes over religious conduct in
public places such as parks and schools can be recast as disputes
over religious speech. To be sure, the ACLJ has taken steps to actively protect the free speech rights of religious speakers.[15] Their
strategy entails sending informational letters to public school districts throughout the United States outlining, among other things,
the free speech rights of students to engage in individual prayer or
Bible reading in school. It is a strategy of "prelitigation," as Steven
Brown explains, by which threats to litigate a religious speech
issue give the public forum a stark choice: change access policies
to allow religious speech into a forum, or run the risk of expensive
and time-consuming litigation.[16] The ACLJ is most active at the
appellate stage of litigation, although it does sponsor or assist a few
trial cases too. Recall from chapter 3, however, that very few religious speech and public forum cases at the trial level are initiated
with interest group backing; most are prosecuted by individuals or
religious groups acting on their own accord.

For the public square, however, Sekulow's point about protecting the right of Christians to proclaim the Gospel links with litigation concerning religious speech. Chapter 3 compared religious
liberty and religious speech litigants and noted that there is a
greater diversity of faiths and religions litigating under the Free
Exercise Clause in the First Amendment than under the Free

Speech Clause. Whereas Christian litigants file about half of the free exercise disputes in federal district courts, with the other filed by a plethora of faiths such as the Native American church, Muslims, Jews, and new age religions, Christian litigants initiate three-fourths of the religious speech and public forum disputes. In terms of religious speech disputes, Christians wishing to "proclaim the gospel," in Sekulow's words, dominate district court litigation.

Diana Eck's view of the public square places Christian proclamation of the gospel into further relief. For Eck, "the American public square is scarcely 'naked,' but filled with religious voices on all sides of the issues—from abortion to capital punishment. And it is not Christian, nor Judeo-Christian, nor Judeo-Christian-Islamic, but increasingly multireligious. Diverse religious communities are visible . . . and diverse voices contribute to the public discussion."[17] That may well be true for the public square at large, which would include all outlets for religious speech, from the media and legislative hearings to government owned forums, but at the more minute level of litigation in federal district courts, disputes over the public square clearly do not concern a diversity of messages and faiths at all. The public square writ large may be multireligious, but at the level of trial court policymaking it most certainly is not. The main, indeed almost exclusive, message seeking access via federal trial courts is evangelical Christianity.

What might be the attendant effects of religious speech litigation dominated by Christian speakers "seeking to proclaim the Gospel"? The larger picture of evangelical Christianity in the United States must preface that question. Recall that most of the Christian speakers, discussed in chapter 3, are either individuals acting upon their own basic religious need to proselytize, and many come from nondenominational churches or religious organizations that are primarily local in character. Few "seeking to proclaim the Gospel" come from traditional, conventional religious denominations with national organizations and hierarchies.

Speakers do not come from what religion scholars refer to as the mainline Protestant denominations such as the Episcopal, Methodist, and Presbyterian churches, or the Catholic church. Nor do they come from the national evangelical denominations such as the Southern Baptist Convention or the Assemblies of God. Christian litigants in the public forum reflect a larger trend in American religious society: that of the growth of nondenominational, evangelical churches, described by Richard Ostling:

> Since World War II, the sprawling and loosely organized conservative Evangelical movement has become the new establishment, the largest single religious faction in the United States. The Evangelicals are the innovators of American religion—in radio, television, religious movies, advertising, publishing, Christian pop and rock music, foreign mission work, seminary education, and cyberspace.[18]

The National Congregations Study conducted by Mark Chaves and others shows the growth of nondenominational evangelical Christianity. The NCS surveyed American religious congregations in 1998, and among other things concluded that approximately 19 percent of all religious congregations are nondenominational Christian organizations: "If these congregations were all in one denomination, they would constitute the third largest denomination in number of participants and the largest in number of congregations."[19] In a real sense, then, the nondenominational Christian speech litigated in district courts stems from an evangelical movement that may be "loosely organized" in Ostling's terms yet accounts for the sizable population of one-fifth of religious congregations in America.

The evangelical Christian voice has purchase in the public square due to its domination of religious speech litigation. To be sure, evangelical speakers win approximately 50 percent of their cases, as chapter 5 notes, so by no means are trial courts strongly supportive of their speech (just as trial courts are not dismissive of their speech, either). Yet, just the ability to dominate litigation—literally, to file most of the cases at the trial level—means that, independent of court outcomes, Christian litigants are able to influence the development of the law to a large degree.

Does the dominance of Christian speakers in forum litigation mean, to paraphrase Justice Scalia's dictum in *Pinette*, that private religious [i.e., Christian] expression "is as fully protected under the Free Speech Clause as secular private expression?" Most of the Supreme Court cases protecting religious speech in recent memory concern Christian-based speech, and the development of religious speech and public forum jurisprudence occurs almost exclusively in the context of such speech.[20] Moreover, with the growing number of evangelical congregations—and by implication, evangelical speakers—the religious speech litigated is not the speech of small, marginal religions. It is the speech of a rapidly growing segment of American religious life.

An interesting contrast can be made between litigation concerning disputes between religious speech in the public forum and the free exercise of religion. Ted Jelen notes that under the Free Exercise Clause, the Supreme Court is "willing to protect the prerogatives of unconventional groups."[21] Unconventional groups include religious minorities such as the Jehovah's Witnesses, Santerians, the Amish, Native Americans, and the Seventh Day Adventists, groups that frequently bear the brunt of majoritarian attempts to regulate religious practices. Such groups are "unconventional" because their religious beliefs and practices do not mesh with the beliefs and practices of mainline Protestant and Catholic churches. Free Exercise jurisprudence developed in the context of what Barbara Burt and Frank Way term "marginal religions," or those groups "whose rituals or religious prescriptions and proscriptions have placed them at some distance from the mainstream of Judaeo-Christian America."[22] As Burt and Way further point out, marginal religions "are more likely to experience conflict with secular laws than members of the Roman Catholic faith or . . . mainline Protestant churches, and consequently they become involved in free exercise litigation."[23] Although marginal groups do not win all their cases, they nonetheless dominate and file more free exercise claims than mainstream religions. Thus, the underlying context of free exercise litigation is the protection of the constitutional rights to religious minorities to practice their religion.

The context of religious speech litigation differs markedly from that of free exercise litigation, as it is not dominated by religious minorities. To be sure, evangelical Christians seeking to "proclaim the Gospel" may consider themselves to be religious minorities, in that they are not part of the more traditional mainline Protestant, Catholic, or other churches that typically comprise the American Christian tradition. Indeed, some evangelicals may perceive hostility against them on the part of mainline Protestants, Catholics, and even secular Americans. Yet, to compare evangelical Christians, who comprise a considerable number of American Christians, to Native American religionists, who are significantly fewer in number, indicates that "religious minority" can of course have different connotations and meanings. Evangelical Christians might not be part of the religious "mainstream" in American religious life, but given their numbers—which are increasing—they are by no means part of the religious minority in American religious life either.

A CONSTITUTIONAL DIALOGUE?

A recent addition to the growing literature on law and religion in the United States suggests that too many scholars focus on the role of courts in enunciating legal doctrine, and overlook how the political process—legislatures, executives, and interest groups—significantly affects law and religion. Louis Fisher argues that "though it may seem counterintuitive, the regular political process has safeguarded the religious freedom of minorities as well as—and often better than—the courts."[24] For Fisher, a "powerful dialogue operates between judicial and nonjudicial bodies" in which individual rights are defined and protected by courts and other component parts of the political system.[25] Thus, "the regular political process is called upon to protect religious liberty, and not merely for powerful religious groups but small ones as well. . . . [C]ourts find themselves engaged in a 'continuing colloquy' with political institutions and society at large, a process in which constitutional principles are 'evolved conversationally not perfected unilaterally.'"[26]

Fisher applies his "constitutional dialogue" argument to the issue of religious speech and expression in public schools. He notes that several religious groups spanning diverse religious traditions in the United States, along with the secular ACLU and the National Educational Association, lobbied Congress for the Equal Access Act in 1984. The federal statute stipulates that public schools receiving federal funds cannot deny access to student groups that wish to conduct meetings on school property due to the group's religious, philosophical, or political content of its speech. The act instructs, essentially, that as long as a public school allows some student groups to use its facilities for meetings before or after school hours, it is a limited open forum and cannot discriminate against student groups due to the content of their speech or message. To be sure, the wide array of groups supporting the Equal Access Act had different reasons to justify their support. The ACLU and NEA saw that statute as protecting the free speech rights of all student groups. Evangelical Christian groups saw the act as protecting the religious speech rights of their students, and indeed as one way of circumventing the Supreme Court's restrictions on school prayer and Bible reading announced in *Engel v. Vitale* in 1962 and *Abington School District v. Schempp* in 1963.[27] Regardless of the motivations of groups and legislators supporting it, the Equal Access Act did institute an ongoing dialogue among courts, Congress, and presidents about the appropriate (and constitutional) role of religious speech in public schools. Notable is the involvement of Presidents Bill Clinton and George W. Bush in furthering that dialogue.

President Clinton instructed his Secretary of Education, Richard Riley, to issue a memorandum to all public school districts in the United States that outlined the rights of students under the Free Speech and Free Exercise Clauses of the First Amendment. As Fisher notes, "the memo was designed to take some of the steam out of a proposed school prayer amendment. In this memo, Clinton said nothing in the First Amendment 'converts our public schools into religion-free zones, or requires all religious expression to be left behind at the schoolhouse door.'"[28]

Between 1995, with the federal guidelines' initial release, and 1998, when they were released again, Secretary of Education Richard Riley held three "religious-education summits" to "inform faith communities and educators about the guidelines and to encourage continued dialogue and cooperation."[29] Secretary Riley noted that the guidelines on student religious expression "allow school districts to avoid contentious disputes by developing a common understanding among students, teachers, parents, and the broader community that the First Amendment does in fact provide ample room for religious expression by students . . . these guidelines are part of an ongoing and growing effort by educators and America's religious community to find a new common ground."

The constitutional dialogue over student religious expression continues with President George W. Bush. In 2001, the Bush

administration and Congress agreed upon sweeping reforms in
American elementary and secondary education, implemented in
the No Child Left Behind Act of 2001 (NCLB), which amends
the 1965 Elementary and Secondary Education Act (ESEA). The
NCLB requires the Secretary of Education to issue guidelines on
constitutionally protected prayer in public elementary and secondary schools. Moreover, the statute also requires that as a con-
dition of receiving federal funds under the Elementary and
Secondary Education Act, a local educational agency (LEA) must
certify in writing to its state educational agency (SEA) that its
policies on student expression do not prevent or deny participation in constitutionally protected prayer in public schools. Pursuant to the statute, Secretary of Education Rod Paige issued the
required guidelines to public schools, and as Secretary Paige's letter to schools puts it, "public schools should not be hostile to the
religious rights of their students and their families."[30] The federal
guidelines are quite detailed and are based upon the Supreme
Court's First Amendment jurisprudence stretching from *Cantwell
v. Connecticut* in 1940 to the more recent *Santa Fe Independent
School District v. Doe* case in 2000 that concerns prayer at a public
high school football game in Texas. The rules touch upon a broad
range of topics, and include individual student prayer during noninstructional time at school, organized prayer groups, moments of
silence, student religious expression and prayer in classroom as-
signments such as artwork, written reports, and the like, and the
selection of student religious speakers on "genuinely neutral, evenhanded criteria."

State educational agencies must annually (by November 1) certify to the federal Department of Education that no LEAs within
their jurisdiction have policies that prevent or otherwise deny participation in constitutionally protected prayer and religious expression.[31] Evidently the threat of losing federal monies under the
ESEA is taken seriously by school districts nationwide. The First

Amendment Center notes that the first round of initial responses under NCLB, which were due on April 15, 2003, shows that most of the approximately fifteen thousand school districts in the United States comply with the federal school prayer guidelines.[32] The nature of this new reporting requirement probably prevented some districts from reporting on time to their SEAs, and reporting indicators point to confusion about the guidelines, or reporting requirements, as the main reason some districts had not certified their compliance with the federal rules. Federal Education Department spokesperson Susan Aspey, quoted in the First Amendment Center's report, states that in mid-2003 the Education Department is "not at the point where we're talking about taking money away from schools or states." Aspey notes that there are glitches in how states report school prayer compliance under NCLB: "this is the first time for everyone [and] there are going to be some growing pains."

Political and legal fights over the NCLB school prayer guidelines are no doubt brewing. Matthew Staver, president of the Christian Right legal advocacy group Liberty Counsel, cautions that the accuracy of school district compliance is a real concern. The guidelines indicate that schools must comply in good faith, but as Staver suggests, "some of these schools have probably represented they're in compliance when they're not."[33] Americans United for the Separation of Church and State note other concerns, though, and point out that the guidelines may not be based on a proper, and accurate, reading of Supreme Court jurisprudence. For example, the federal guidelines state that students may offer religious prayers at graduation ceremonies, as long as those students are selected on the basis of "neutral, evenhanded criteria and retain primary control over the content of their expression." Yet, as Americans United makes clear, the high court's decisions on school prayer at ceremonial events, coupled with confusion in lower federal courts about the issue, show that the federal govern-

ment "overstates the case when it asserts that the law *mandates*
that prayers must be permitted at school events under certain circumstances."[34] Americans United therefore charges "it is an un-
precedented effort to coerce school districts, through the threat of
the withholding of federal funds, to comply with a selective and
inaccurate interpretation of constitutional law." It may overstate
the case somewhat, but Americans United does raise a valid point:
there might be a disconnection between how the Supreme Court,
and lower federal courts, view student religious expression, and
how federal court cases are interpreted and applied by the Department of Education. Thus, two significant fights over the religious
speech guidelines under the NCLB Act are fermenting among interest groups monitoring religious speech and religious liberty. For
many evangelicals and the Christian Right, the "good faith" compliance of school districts is of fundamental importance. That is,
schools may well certify that they comply with federal guidelines,
when in reality they maintain subtly discriminatory policies that
deny religious speakers—especially Christian speakers—the opportunity to engage in religious expression. For groups devoted to
the strict separation of church and state, the federal guidelines
misstate First Amendment law covering religious speech, and may
in fact interpret that law too broadly so that religious speakers find
their expressive rights enlarged through administrative fiat instead
of careful, meticulous, judicial interpretation of the Free Speech
Clause itself.

The constitutional dialogue concerning student religious expression in public schools has meandered from early federal court
cases concerning school prayer and student religious expression in
the 1960s and 1970s through the Equal Access Act in 1984 to the
No Child Left Behind Act of 2001. The debate has been "dia-
logued" in a bipartisan manner, by both Democratic and Republican presidential administrations, and by Democratic and
Republican controlled Congresses. Thus, the constitutional collo-

quy, at least in the political branches, is premised on a common understanding that students should and do have rights of religious expression in public school.

Importantly, there are notable differences between the Equal Access Act and the No Child Left Behind Act. Whereas the Equal Access Act grants a federal statutory right to public school students to engage in religious and other types of expression in schools, the NCLB Act eschews a federally defined right to pray, and instead favors the economic incentive of federal grants to public schools by conditioning the receipt of federal monies on a school's written certification that it does not interfere with constitutionally protected prayer in public schools. The Equal Access Act refers to student expression generally, and considers that religious speech is as protected as philosophical or political speech. Under the act, religious speech is one of many types of student expression that are protected. The No Child Left Behind Act specifically focuses on school prayer, and Secretary Paige's guidelines for public schools only outline the kinds of prayer activities that are constitutionally protected under the First Amendment. Thus, student prayer is singled out of the corpus of student expression for special protection under federal law.

Where do federal district courts fit into this ongoing constitutional dialogue? Fisher's "powerful dialogue" over religious liberty and religious expression mainly includes the Supreme Court, Congress, and the executive branch. The Court's jurisprudence on religious liberty and expression prompts congressional action, for instance in the form of the EAA and NCLB, which in turn prompts executive action in the form of federal guidelines issued by the Secretary of Education. District courts do not directly participate in this constitutional dialogue, which is not surprising given that they often operate outside of the public spotlight and can be overturned by higher appellate courts. Thus, legislators and executives will probably reserve scarce political capital for high-profile constitutional dialogues prompted by the Supreme Court. Although district courts do not directly participate in this constitutional colloquy, they are certainly affected by it.

Recall the discussion in chapter 4 of court policymaking concerning the locations and contours of public forums. Litigation concerning public school forums increased significantly up to the mid-1990s. Between 1995 and the end of this study in 2001, the number of district court cases concerning public school forums distinctly declined. The hearings of the United States Commission on Civil Rights investigating religious speech in public schools concluded that the downturn in litigation over religious speech in public school forums was based to a large extent on the Equal Access Act passed in 1984, and the Department of Education's guidelines from the 1990s. Several groups testifying before the commission indicated that schools use the act and federal guidelines as touchstones for their own policies on student religious expression, with the result that many, if not most, conflicts between schools and students are now resolved outside of the courthouse, without resort to litigation. Indeed, most groups testifying before the commission agreed that congressional legislation, coupled with federal guidelines, had helped schools clarify their policies on student religious speech, with the result that litigation over religious speech in schools decreased significantly.

Thus, even though district courts are not directly engaged in the ongoing dialogue over student religious speech, they are affected by it. The constitutional discussion between the Supreme Court, Congress, and the executive branch on religious speech in schools, and the process of clarifying the law, ultimately leads to fewer cases at the district court level. Through the interaction of the Court, Congress, the executive branch, and public schools, the rights of student religious speakers are clarified, and codified into local policies that allow for the resolution of conflicts over religious expression in public schools without resort to litigation.

The impact of the ongoing discussion over student religious speech not only leads to more stringent protections for their speech; it also decreases litigation in district courts.

The federal government's focus on public school forums is politically intriguing. Recollect from chapter 4 that public school forums comprise almost 38 percent of district court cases concerning religious speech. Although public school forums are the most numerous, in total they comprise slightly more than one-third of all district cases dealing with religious speech. There are other types of public forums litigated, such as travel terminals, public parks and open spaces such as fairgrounds, and other public places that are not easily categorized. Why, then, are public school forums the focus of an ongoing constitutional dialogue, whereas other types of forums are not? Why are federal policy guidelines in place that affect religious speech in public schools—and note that those guidelines are now linked to the receipt of federal funds—whereas religious speech in other local forums such as public parks are not affected by federal policymaking at all, other than through district courts?

A definitive answer is beyond the scope of this work, and indeed the questions bear no strong link to the subject of this study on federal district court policymaking. Yet, it seems as if the attention given by the political process to religious speech in public schools has ramifications for district court dockets. As Congress and the executive branch have clarified the conditions under which religious speech is to be tolerated in schools and have linked religious speech in schools to federal funding, perhaps fewer religious speech disputes end up in litigation. As Congress and the executive branch simplify constitutional doctrine and public policy concerning religious expression, district courts are less engaged in the policymaking process.

THE CONTINUING DEBATE OVER RELIGIOUS
SPEECH IN PUBLIC SQUARES

Legal disputes over religious speech in public forums are here to stay. Not only are many different types of expression implicated in lawsuits, but also diverse types of forums, from public schools at all levels to public parks and government buildings. Public forum doctrine is seemingly settled, although arguably difficult for judges to apply. The traditional, designated, and nonforum categories for public spaces created by the Supreme Court are a workable framework for addressing free speech disputes in government-owned spaces and are adaptable to diverse types of expression and content such as political speech and of course religious speech.

Religious speech and public forum disputes present district courts with an ever-changing pattern of litigation involving different types of expression, and different and even unusual types of forums. It is fitting, then, to conclude with two pending disputes about religious speech in public forums that perhaps challenge the First Amendment and district court policymaking in new and unique ways. One dispute concerns bricks purchased by individuals through a school fundraising scheme and embedded in a public school walkway. The bricks at issue have religious messages written on them. The second dispute concerns religious speech of a very vitriolic and hateful kind, and the extent to which it can be kept out of the public square.

IF ONLY BRICKS COULD SPEAK . . .

In March 2003, several families sued the Loudon County, Virginia, school district for allegedly depriving them of their First Amendment free speech rights when school officials removed bricks they had sponsored from a school walkway.[35] The families bought the bricks during a fundraiser for a high school in the

Loudon system and had them engraved with their children's names and Christian crosses. The bricks were then used for part of the walkway for a new school. School administrators received a complaint about the crosses on the bricks, and subsequently removed the bricks from the walkway after the school district's counsel warned that it would violate the Establishment Clause for them to remain as part of the school's permanent infrastructure.

One school board member opined "the school is in a sense endorsing what it puts on the walkway. It's a part of the school structure, and those bricks are owned by Loudon County Public Schools once they're donated." A parent who bought one of the cross bricks countered that "we've turned intolerance around. It's no longer about the rights of the many. It's about the rights of the few." Never mind, of course, that the parents who bought the bricks with crosses were a distinct minority, and therefore "the few." The case poses some interesting problems for the federal district court in Alexandria, Virginia, that is to decide the case.

To start, the court must determine if sponsorship of bricks with messages on them is, in and of itself, a type of expression protected by the First Amendment. Linked with that policymaking decision is whether the parents buying the bricks retain their free speech rights even after they donate the bricks to the school system. Public forum doctrine also applies, and here the court must decide how the public school walkway should be categorized under public forum doctrine. Prior district court cases indicate, by the way, that public school walkways are usually designated public forums, open to speech and expression at the school's indication. But, earlier cases concerning school walkways focus on the rights of individual speakers to use those walkways for expressive activities, such as distributing literature and oral speaking. The Loudon County case does not involve individual speech per se, but a kind of symbolic speech through messages on sidewalk bricks. The bricks themselves link with the public property and become the message bearer, in this case an explicitly religious message of a Christian cross. As one school board member concluded, the school district is in a real Catch-22: removing the bricks may violate the free speech rights of the brick donors; replacing the bricks may violate the Establishment Clause due the school's perceived endorsement of a religious message. "We're going to get sued either way," the school board member put it. "There's no doubt in my mind."

THE DARK SIDE OF THE SQUARE: CASPER, WYOMING'S "MONUMENT FROM HELL"

The inevitability of litigation over school bricks may strike one as an inefficient waste of legal resources and court time for a minor goal: the display of a religious message on a small brick, which most passersby will most likely not even notice. But, disputes over bricks pale in comparison to the ugly turn of religious speech disputes that Casper, Wyoming, witnessed in late 2003. Reverend Fred Phelps, a nationally prominent anti-gay activist based at Westboro Baptist Church in Topeka, Kansas, recently announced his intention to place a privately funded anti-gay memorial in Casper's Central Park, to remind passersby of Matthew Shepard, the gay University of Wyoming student murdered in October 1998 because of his homosexuality. Phelps's monument will be approximately six feet high, three feet wide, of granite or marble, with a plaque that reads: "Matthew Shepard Entered Hell October 12, 1998, at age 21 in Defiance of God's Warning: "Thou shalt not lie with mankind as with womankind; it is abomination." Leviticus 18:22."[36] What complicates Phelps's anti-gay, yet religious expression, is the fact that Casper allowed a display of the Ten Commandments to be donated to the city and placed in Central Park by the Fraternal Order of the Eagles in 1965, a monument that remained in place until Phelps's request for his own monument in 2003. That Casper could allow one type and content of religious expression in the public square, such as the Ten Commandments, but not the other, such as Phelps's religiously motivated anti-gay monument, raises the specter of the Casper city government regulating the content of the public square as well as the religious speaker's viewpoint. The Casper City Council unanimously rejected Phelps's request and immediately after voted 5:4 to move the Ten Commandments monument to a plaza dedicated to a variety of historical documents. The creation of the plaza, though, raised the ire of the Freedom From Religion Foundation of Madison, Wisconsin, which threatened to sue the city if it created a specific plaza to house the Ten Commandments. Dan Barker from the foundation opined that the city's plaza plan "looks like a ruse; it looks like a trick for them to keep it. It would probably be unconstitutional because the intention of the city is to maintain a religious document."[37] Writing for the on-line magazine *Slate*, Emily Bazelon states that "Casper is just scrambling after the fact to preserve the religious message it likes and scrap the one it doesn't. . . . the First Amendment doesn't allow the government to fight hate speech by building a new public square in which all speech save for hate speech is welcome."[38]

The dispute over Phelps's anti-gay memorial highlights one of the worrisome dilemmas of religious speech in the public square: should the public square contain religious invective that is harmful, threatening, and spiteful? The First Amendment protects the right of the religious speaker to access the public square to engage in religious expression. Recall Justice Scalia's dictum in *Capitol Square Review & Advisory Board v. Pinette*: "Our precedent establishes that private religious speech, far from being a First Amendment orphan, is as fully protected under the Free Speech Clause as secular private expression."[39] To accept religious speech as the equivalent of private, secular speech also means that the government cannot generally regulate the content of that religious speech, or the viewpoint of the religious speaker. In *Pinette* Justice Scalia further explains that with public forums opened to expressive activity, "a State's right to limit protected expressive activity is sharply circumscribed: it may impose reasonable, content-neutral time, place and manner restrictions. . . . *but it may regulate expressive content only if such a restriction is necessary, and narrowly drawn, to serve a compelling state interest.*"[40] Although Phelps's request for the Matthew Shepard memorial was denied, no federal court has visited the issue as to whether Casper might have a compelling interest to regulate the expressive content of the memorial. But, under the Supreme Court's hate speech jurisprudence, most prominently *R. A. V. v. City of St. Paul*, regulating the content of a speaker's expression because it targets minority individuals or groups historically disfavored by the majority violates the First Amendment. The Free Speech Clause "does not permit [the government] to impose special prohibitions on those speakers who express views on disfavored subjects."[41] Thus, if Casper, Wyoming, has a public square open to the display of the Ten Commandments, all religious speakers can expect to use the public square for expressive purposes. Casper cannot pick and choose which religious messages can access the square, and which cannot. It cannot regulate the square by disfavoring some religious speech, such as Phelps's anti-gay speech, while favoring the Ten Commandments. Consequently, the religious speech in the public square debate has a very ugly side to it, and takes on an "all-or-nothing" cast. Either all religious messages are in the public square, or none. Allowing religious speech may well lighten up the public square, but it may well darken it too.

NOTES

PREFACE

1. The case population was compiled through several LEXIS searches, the most notable of which used the search term "relig!" limited by "public forum" in the federal district court file for all available dates. That specific search returned 446 cases, ranging in dates from February 1973 to May 2001. The cases were reviewed, and two types of cases were chosen for analysis: those in which litigants sought to place their religious speech *in* the public forum, and those cases in which litigants sought to keep religious speech *out* of the public forum.

2. *Travis v. Owego-Apalachin School,* 1990 U.S. Dist. LEXIS 8492, at *21 (N.D. New York, 1990).

3. Joel B. Grossman, Herbert M. Kritzer, Kristin Bumiller, Austin Sarat, and Stephen McDougal, "Dimensions of Institutional Participation: Who Uses the Courts, and How?" *The Journal of Politics* 44 (February 1982): 86–114.

4. Ibid., 87.

5. Ibid., 89.

6. Richard E. Morgan, *The Politics of Religious Conflict: Church and State in America* (New York: Pegasus, 1968), 19.

7. See also Allen Hertzke, *Representing God in Washington: The Role of Religious Lobbies in the American Polity* (Knoxville: University of Tennessee Press, 1988).

8. For a good discussion of political science literature on this point, see Geoffrey C. Layman and Edward G. Carmines, "Cultural Conflict in American Politics: Religious Traditionalism, Post-

materialism, and U.S. Political Behavior," *The Journal of Politics* 59 (August 1997): 751–77.

9. Gregg Ivers, "Organized Religion and the Supreme Court," *Journal of Church and State* 32 (Autumn 1990): 775–94.

10. Frank Way and Barbara Burt, "Religious Marginality and the Free Exercise Clause," American *Political Science Review* 77 (1983): 652–65.

11. *Grayned v. City of Rockford*, 408 U.S. 124 (1972).

12. See notably J. Woodford Howard, *Courts of Appeals in the Federal Judicial System: A Study of the Second, Fifth, and District of Columbia Circuits* (Princeton, N.J.: Princeton University Press, 1981). See also C. K. Rowland and Robert A. Carp, *Politics and Judgment in Federal District Courts* (Lawrence: University Press of Kansas, 1996), 58–87.

13. See John C. Blakeman and Don M. Greco, "Federal District Court Decision Making in Public Forum and Religious Speech Cases, 1973–2001," *Journal For the Scientific Study of Religion* 43, no. 3 (2004): 437–47.

CHAPTER 1

1. The U.S. Census by law cannot collect information on religious membership or denominational affiliation. However, the Glenmary Research Center does maintain a religious census. See Dale E. Jones, Sherry Doty, James E. Horsch, Richard Houseal, Mac Lynn, John P. Marcum, Kenneth M. Sanchagrin, and Richard Taylor, *Religious Congregations and Membership in the United States 2000: An Enumeration by Region, State, and County Based on Data Reported by 149 Religious Bodies* (Nashville, Tenn.: Glenmary Research Center, 2002). The figures for Wood County, Wisconsin, are from page 513 of the bound volume. It is also important to note that Marshfield straddles both Wood County and Marathon

County. Approximately eighteen thousand of Marshfield's residents live in Wood County, and eight hundred live in Marathon County.

2. *Freedom From Religion Foundation, Inc. and Clarence Reinders v. City of Marshfield and Henry Praschak Memorial Fund, Inc.*, 203 F.3d 487 (7th Circ. 2000), 489–90.

3. Ibid., 495, emphasis added.

4. Ibid., 497.

5. Quoted in Jonathan Gneiser, "Religious Debates Stir: Public Grounds No Place for Church Items, Say Critics," *Central Wisconsin Sunday*, Sunday, November 2, 2003.

6. 515 U.S. 753, 760 (1995).

7. 505 672, 696 (1992).

8. *Trinity United Methodist Parish et al. v. Board of Education of the City School District of the City of Newburgh*, 907 F. Supp. 707, 711 (S.D. New York, 1995).

9. *Sister Mary Reilly et al. v. Noel*, 384 F. Supp. 741 (1974).

10. *Hague v. CIO*, 307 U.S. 496 (1939).

11. *ISKCON v. Evans*, 440 F. Supp. 414 (1977); *ISKCON v. Bowen*, 456 F. Supp. 437 (1978).

12. *ISKCON v. Wolke*, 453 F. Supp. 869 (1978); *Fernandes v. Limmer* 465 F. Supp. 493 (1979).

13. See *ISKCON v. Lee*, 505 U.S. 682 (1992) and *Heffron v. ISKCON*, 452 U.S. 640 (1981).

14. *C. H. v. Oliva et al., Medford Township Board of Education; New Jersey Department of Education*, 990 F. Supp. 341 (1997).

15. Gilbert A. Holmes, "Student Religious Expression in School: Is It Religion or Speech, and Does It Matter?" *University of Miami Law Review* (Winter 1994): 378–79.

16. Martha McCarthy, "Religion and Education: Whither the Establishment Clause?" *Indiana Law Journal* (Winter 2000): 131.

17. John C. Blakeman, "Federal District Courts, Religious Speech, and the Public Forum: An Analysis of Litigation Patterns and

Outcomes," *Journal of Church and State* 44 (Winter 2002): 93–115.

18. Ibid.

19. Richard John Neuhaus, *The Naked Public Square* (Grand Rapids, Mich.: Eerdmans Publishing, 1984), vii.

20. Ibid., 25.

21. Richard John Neuhaus, "A New Order of Religious Freedom," in Stephen M. Feldman, ed., *Law and Religion: A Critical Anthology* (New York: New York University Press, 2000), 89.

22. Ibid., 92.

23. Stephen L. Carter, *The Culture of Disbelief: How American Law and Politics Trivialize Religion* (New York: Anchor Books, 1994), 54.

24. Ibid., 101.

25. Jeff Spinner-Halev, *Surviving Diversity: Religion and Democratic Citizenship* (Baltimore: The Johns Hopkins University Press, 2000), 143–44.

26. Robert Audi and Nicholas Wolterstorff, *Religion in the Public Square: the Place of Religious Convictions in Political Debate* (New York: Rowman and Littlefield, 1997), 53.

27. Ibid., 54.

28. Patrick Glynn, "Conscience and the Public Square: Heeding the Still, Small Voice," in E. J. Dionne Jr. and John J. DiIulio Jr., eds., *What's God Got to Do with the American Experiment?* (Washington, D.C.: Brookings Institution Press, 2000), 83.

29. Spinner-Halev, supra note 25, 151–52.

30. Diana L. Eck, "The Multireligious Public Square," in Marjorie Garber and Rebecca L. Walkowitz, eds., *One Nation Under God? Religion and American Culture* (New York: Routledge, 1999), 17.

31. Ibid., 9–17.

32. David Yamane, "Naked Public Square or Crumbling Wall of Separation? Evidence from Legislative Hearings in Wisconsin," *Review of Religious Research* 42, no. 2 (2000): 176.

33. Ibid., 189.
34. Spinner-Halev, supra note 25, 163–65.
35. Eck, supra note 30, 12.
36. *Travis v. Owego-Apalachin School*, 1990 U.S. Dist. LEXIS 8492, at *21 (N.D. New York, 1990).
37. *Trinity United Methodist Parish et al. v. Board of Education of the City School District of the City of Newburgh*, 907 F. Supp. 707, 711 (S.D. New York, 1995).
38. *Niemotko v. Maryland*, 340 U.S. 263, 282–83 (1951), Frankfurter, J., concurring.
39. 460 U.S. 37 (1982).
40. *Perry Education Association v. Perry Local Educators' Association*, 460 U.S. 37 (1983), 45. *Perry* does not concern religious speech, but does offer a concise synopsis of public forum doctrine.
41. Ibid., 45–46.
42. Ibid.
43. Ibid., 47.
44. 505 U.S. 672, 695 (1992), Kennedy, J., concurring.
45. Ibid., 696.
46. Howard O. Hunter and Polly J. Price, "Regulation of Religious Proselytism in the United States," *B.Y.U. Law Review* (2001): 537, 538.
47. 408 U.S. 104, 115–17 (1972).
48. Ibid., 117.
49. *Carey v. Brown*, 447 U.S. 455, 461 (1980).
50. 408 U.S. 92, 96 (1972).
51. Ibid., 45–46.
52. Ibid.
53. Ibid., 46.
54. Jack W. Peltason, *58 Lonely Men: Southern Federal Judges and School Desegregation* (Urbana: University of Illinois Press, 1971).
55. Ibid., 29.
56. Ibid., 21.

57. Robert A. Carp and C. K. Rowland, *Policymaking and Politics in the Federal District Courts* (Knoxville: University of Tennessee Press, 1983), 8.

58. For an illuminating case study of the pressures generated by the local and national roles played by district courts, consult Phillip J. Cooper, *Hard Judicial Choices* (Oxford: Oxford University Press, 1988).

59. C. K. Rowland and Robert A. Carp, *Politics and Judgment in Federal District Courts* (Lawrence: University Press of Kansas, 1996), 9.

60. Ibid.

61. See generally Bradley C. Canon and Charles A. Johnson, *Judicial Policies: Implementation and Impact*, 2nd ed. (Washington, D.C.: Congressional Quarterly Press, 1999), 1–28.

62. Ibid., 27, quoting Robert A. Carp and C. K. Rowland, *Policymaking and Politics in the Federal District Courts* (Knoxville: University of Tennessee Press, 1983), 3.

63. See Carp and Rowland, supra note 57, 10.

64. Kevin L. Lyles, *The Gatekeepers: Federal District Courts in the Political Process* (Westport, Conn.: Praeger, 1997), 3.

65. Rowland and Carp, supra note 59, 4.

66. See, e.g., *Heffron v. ISKCON*, 452 U.S. 640 (1981), *Widmar v. Vincent*, 454 U.S. 263 (1981), *ISKCON v. Lee*, 505 U.S. 830 (1992), *Lamb's Chapel v. Center Moriches Union Free School District*, 508 U.S. 384 (1993), *Rosenberger v. University of Virginia*, 515 U.S. 819 (1995), and *Good News Club v. Milford Central School District*, 121 S. Ct. 2093 (2001).

67. Lynn Mather, "The Fired Football Coach," in Lee Epstein, ed., *Contemplating Courts* (Washington, D.C.: Congressional Quarterly Press, 1995), 173.

CHAPTER 2

1. *Capitol Square Review & Advisory Bd. v. Pinette*, 515 U.S. 753, 760 (1995).
2. 460 U.S. 37, 44–46 (1983).
3. *ISKCON v. Lee*, 505 U.S. 672, 694 (1992).
4. Ibid.
5. 307 U.S. 496, 515–16 (1939).
6. 460 U.S. 37, 44–46 (1983).
7. 505 U.S. 672 (1992).
8. Ibid., 680–81.
9. Ibid., 682.
10. Ibid., 694.
11. Ibid., 697–98.
12. Interestingly, Justice Kennedy wrote the majority opinion in *Rosenberger v. University of Virginia*, where he argued that the university created a "metaphysical" forum by using mandatory student activity fees to fund student publications such as newspapers and magazines. In his analysis, the funding system created the forum. Notably, it was not a forum in a physical or a spatial sense, and thus Justice Kennedy demonstrates that the Court's forum jurisprudence may not be as rigid and narrow as he indicates in *Lee*. *Rosenberger* is discussed presently.
13. 316 U.S. 584 (1942).
14. *Jones v. Opelika*, 316 U.S. 584, 595 (1942).
15. Ibid., 597.
16. For an engaging discussion, see Merlin Owen Newton, *Armed with the Constitution: Jehovah's Witnesses in Alabama and the U.S. Supreme Court* (Tuscaloosa: University of Alabama Press, 1995).
17. 308 U.S. 147 (1938), 160–61.
18. *Schneider v. State*, 308 U.S. 147 (1939), 164.
19. Ibid.
20. 303 U.S. 444 (1938), 448.

21. Ibid., 452.
22. 312 U.S. 569 (1941).
23. 315 U.S. 568 (1942).
24. 321 U.S. 158 (1944).
25. 319 U.S. 105 (1943).
26. Ibid., 108–9.
27. 340 U.S. 268 (1951), 272.
28. Ibid., 282.
29. 319 U.S. 105 (1943), 115.
30. Ibid., 127.
31. Ibid., 127–28.
32. Ibid., 129.
33. Ibid., 134.
34. Ibid., 131.
35. Ibid., 140.
36. *Douglas v. City of Jeanette*, 319 U.S. 157, 181 (1943).
37. 321 U.S. 573 (1944).
38. Ibid., 580–81.
39. Ibid., 282–83.
40. 340 U.S. 290, 294 (1951).
41. 454 U.S. 263 (1981), 269.
42. Ibid., 273.
43. Ibid., 276–77.
44. *Board of Education of Westside Community Schools v. Mergens By and Through Mergens*, 496 U.S. 226 (1990).
45. 20 U.S.C. §§ 4071(a) and (b). Specifically, the act provides: "It shall be unlawful for any public secondary school which receives Federal financial assistance and which has a limited open forum to deny equal access or a fair opportunity to, or discriminate against, any students who wish to conduct a meeting within that limited open forum on the basis of the religious, political, philosophical, or other content of the speech at such meetings."
46. *Mergens*, supra note 44, 246–47.

47. Ibid., 250.
48. Ibid., 265–66, Marshall, J., concurring.
49. Ibid., 267.
50. 515 U.S. 819 (1995), 830.
51. Ibid., 845–46.
52. Ibid., 858.
53. 515 U.S. 753 (1995), 760.
54. Ibid., 762.
55. Ibid., 763.
56. Ibid., 770.
57. *Good News Club v. Milford Central School*, 533 U.S. 98, 112 (2001).
58. Ibid., 138–39, Justice Souter, dissenting.
59. Ibid., 130, Justice Stevens, dissenting.
60. Ibid., 132, Justice Stevens, dissenting.
61. Ibid., 111, per Justice Thomas, majority opinion.
62. Richard John Neuhaus, "A New Order of Religious Freedom," in Stephen M. Feldman, ed., *Law and Religion: A Critical Anthology* (New York: New York University Press, 2000), 89.
63. Steven G. Gey, "The No Religion Zone: Constitutional Limitations on Religious Association in the Public Sphere," 85 *Minnesota Law Review* 1885, 1896 (2001).
64. Ibid.

CHAPTER 3

1. John T. Noonan Jr. and Edward McGlynn Gaffney Jr., *Religious Freedom: History, Cases, and Other Materials on the Interaction of Religion and Government* (New York: Foundation Press, 2001), 375. See also Julia Mitchell Corbett, *Religion in America*, 4th ed. (Upper Saddle River, N.J.: Prentice Hall, 2000), 257–59.
2. Philip Kenneson, "Sixteen Contentious Words," *Reviews in Reli-*

gion and Theology 7, no. 3 (June 2000): 343. See also Martha M. McCarthy, "People of Faith as Political Activists in Public Schools," *Education and Urban Society* 28, no. 3 (May 1996): 308–26.

3. Joel B. Grossman, Herbert Kritzer, et al., "Dimensions of Institutional Participation: Who Uses the Courts, and How?" *The Journal of Politics* 44, no. 1 (February 1982): 87.

4. Frank Zemans, "Legal Mobilization: The Neglected Role of the Law in the Political System," *American Political Science Review* 77 (1983): 692.

5. Associated Press report, July 13, 1999.

6. "Supreme Court Says Mohammed Won't Be Removed from Frieze," *Church and State*, April 1997, 18.

7. "Waxahachie Superintendent Allows Wiccan Necklace," *Waco Tribune Herald*, Friday, September 13, 2002, 4c.

8. Grossman, et al., supra note 4, 91.

9. *U.S. v. Silberman*, 464 F. Supp. 866 (1979).

10. Mary Ann Glendon, *Rights Talk: The Impoverishment of Political Discourse* (New York: Free Press, 1991). Glendon's book offers an important critique of how the "simplistic" view of constitutional rights in the American constitutional system often distorts and prevents meaningful political discussion. Among the many points that Glendon makes is that Americans often view their rights as absolutes. Linked with that is the conception of the possessor of rights as a "self-determining, unencumbered, individual, a being connected to others only by choice." *Rights Talk*, 48.

11. 1992 U.S. Dist. LEXIS 11352. "JN 3:16" refers to the Gospel of John in the New Testament, chapter 3, verse 16, which reads: "For God so loved the world that he gave his one and only Son, that whoever believes in him shall not perish but have eternal life." John 3:16 signs are a ubiquitous feature at many public events in the United States, especially sporting events, most likely due to the evangelical context of the verse. As the district

court in the *Francis* case noted, other signs were displayed at the Washington, D.C., Armory that day too, including John 3:16, John 3:7, Madden 3:16, and Rev. 3:20.

12. Joseph F. Kobylka, *The Politics of Obscenity: Group Litigation in a Time of Legal Change* (Westport, Conn.: Greenwood Press, 1991), 13.

13. See generally *U.S. v. Silberman*, 464 F. Supp. 866 (M.D. Florida, Jacksonville Division, 1979).

14. For state fairs, see *ISKCON v. Evans*, 440 F. Supp. 414 (S.D. Ohio, Eastern Division, 1977). For solicitations at airports, see *Fernandes v. Limmer*, 465 F. Supp. 493 (N.D. Texas, Dallas Division, 1979), and for ISKCON *sankirtan* at the U.N. Visitor's Gate, see *ISKCON v. City of New York*, 484 F. Supp. 966 (S.D. New York, 1979). Finally, for solicitations within a municipality in general, see *ISKCON of Berkeley v. Kearnes*, 454 F. Supp. 116 (E.D. California, 1978).

15. 452 U.S. 640 (1981).

16. Barbara J. Redman, "Strange Bedfellows: Lubavitcher Hasidim and Conservative Christians," *Journal of Church and State* 34, no. 3 (Summer 1992): 523.

17. See, e.g., *Chabad-Lubavitch of Georgia v. Harris, Governor of Georgia* 752 F. Supp. 1063 (N.D. Georgia, 1990).

18. *Wallace and Northgate Community Church v. Washoe County School District*, 701 F. Supp. 187 (D. Nevada, 1988).

19. See, e.g., *Warren v. Fairfax County, Virginia*, 988 F. Supp. 957 (E.D. Virginia, Alexandria Div., 1997); *Knights of Columbus v. Town of Lexington*, 124 F. Supp. 2d 119 (D. Massachusetts, 2000).

20. See, e.g., *Cady v. City of Chicago*, 855 F. Supp. 922 (N.D. Illinois, 1993).

21. See, e.g., *ISKCON v. Evans*, 440 F. Supp. 414 (S.D. Ohio, Eastern Div., 1977); *ISKCON v. Bowen, Governor of Indiana*, 456 F. Supp. 437 (S.D. Indiana, Indianapolis Div., 1978).

22. *Paulsen v. Lehman*, 839 F. Supp. 147 (E.D. New York, 1993).

23. *Pruitt v. Wilder* 840 F. Supp. 414 (E.D. Virginia, 1994). The district judge decided that an automobile vanity license plate issued by the Commonwealth of Virginia is not a metaphysical public forum.

24. *ISKCON of Potomac v. Ridenour*, 830 F. Supp. 1 (D. District of Columbia, 1993).

25. Jeff Spinner-Halev, *Surviving Diversity: Religion and Democratic Citizenship* (Baltimore: The Johns Hopkins University Press, 2000), 151–52.

26. Richard E. Morgan, *The Politics of Religious Conflict: Church and State in America* (New York: Pegasus, 1968), 94–95.

27. See for instance, Donald Reich, "The Impact of Judicial Decisionmaking: The School Prayer Cases," in David R. Manwaring et al., *The Supreme Court as Policymaker: Three Studies on the Impact of Judicial Decisions* (Carbondale: Public Affairs Research Bureau, 1972), 44–82; Frank Way, "Stability and Change in Constitutional Litigation: The Public Piety Cases," *The Journal of Politics* 47, no. 3 (August 1985): 910–25.

28. Ted G. Jelen, *To Serve God and Mammon: Church-State Relations in American Politics* (Boulder, Colo.: Westview Press, 2000), 64.

29. Ted G. Jelen, "Political Culture, Political Structure, and Political Conflict: The Persistence of Church-State Conflict in the United States," in Mary C. Segers, ed., *Piety, Politics, and Pluralism: Religion, the Courts, and the 2000 Election* (Lanham, Md. Rowman and Littlefield, 2002), 212.

30. Lillian R. BeVier, "Religion in Congress and the Courts: Issues of Institutional Competence," *Harvard Journal of Law and Public Policy* 22 (Fall 1998): 65.

31. Morgan, supra note 26, 19.

32. See also Allen Hertzke, *Representing God in Washington: The Role of Religious Lobbies in the American Polity* (Knoxville, Tenn.: University of Tennessee Press, 1988).

33. See, for example, Lyman A. Kellstedt and John C. Green,

"Knowing God's Many People: Denominational Preference and Political Behavior," in David C. Leege and Lyman A. Kellstedt, eds., *Rediscovering the Religious Factor in American Politics* (Armonk, N.Y.: M. E. Sharpe, 1993), 53–72.

34. For a good discussion of political science literature on this point, see Geoffrey C. Layman and Edward G. Carmines, "Cultural Conflict in American Politics: Religious Traditionalism, Postmaterialism, and U.S. Political Behavior," *The Journal of Politics* 59 (August 1997): 751–77.

35. Gregg Ivers, "Organized Religion and the Supreme Court," *Journal of Church and State* 32 (Autumn 1990): 775–94.

36. Frank Way and Barbara Burt, "Religious Marginality and the Free Exercise Clause," *American Political Science Review* 77 (1983): 652–65.

37. Categorizing litigants based on the broad-based, underlying religious message demonstrates important litigation trends. There are, though, important methodological difficulties associated with this. The data are collected from district court cases in the *LEXIS* database. Although *LEXIS* contains almost all federal district court opinions, published and unpublished, and thus provides a thorough record, courts generally discuss the religion of litigants in broad terms only. Thus, it is often difficult to determine the specific denomination involved in the litigation. Unlike briefs filed by organized interest groups in the circuit courts and the Supreme Court, which will detail the religious affiliation of parties in the litigation, the federal district record is often sparse as to the precise religious affiliation of the litigants. This leads to a methodological choice made for this study, which was to simply type the speech or expression at issue according to the broad religious background of the message. To do otherwise would involve conjecture and guesswork. Thus, limitations within the data source itself prohibit a more detailed look at the specific *denominational* affiliation of each litigant. To be sure,

studying political behavior in the context of specific denominations—a set of religious institutions that are formally linked to
each other and share common beliefs and practices—allows
scholars to delve into the links between religion and politics in a
highly detailed manner. However, the data for studying religious
speech simply do not support categorizing speech on denominational lines, simply because of the paucity of court records.

38. See, e.g., *Lubavitch of Iowa v. Walters*, 684 F. Supp. 610 (S.D.
Iowa, 1988) and *Lubavitch v. Public Building Commission of Chicago*,
700 F. Supp. 1497 (N.D. Illinois, 1988).

39. See, e.g., *Jews for Jesus v. Board of Airport Commissioners of the
City of Los Angeles*, 661 F. Supp. 1223 (C.D. California, 1985). To
be sure, it is arguable whether the Jews for Jesus group seeks to
disseminate a faith-based message grounded in the Jewish, or
Christian, faith.

40. Kathleen M. Moore, *Al Mughtaribum: American Law and the
Transformation of Muslim Life in the United States* (Albany: State
University of New York Press, 1995), 69–102.

41. *Mehdi and Khankan v. USPS*, 988 F. Supp. 721 (S.D. New York,
1997).

42. See Way and Burt, supra note 36. Christian-based groups include
Mainline Protestant churches, the Roman Catholic Church,
sects such as the Amish, Quakers, Jehovah's Witnesses, Seventh
Day Adventists, Holiness Pentecostals, and other fundamentalist
Protestants. Unfortunately, the district court records in religious
speech and public forum cases *do not* allow for this level of precision in categorizing religious groups. Generally, district courts in
religious speech cases, for whatever reasons, do not indicate the
specific denomination involved, which raises a very interesting
question: in Way and Burt's analysis, trial courts *do* often indicate
the specific denomination in the case. Why, then, are district
courts less inclined to do so in religious speech disputes?

43. John Wybraniec and Roger Finke, "Religious Regulation and the

Courts: The Judiciary's Changing Role in Protecting Minority Religions from Majority Rule," *Journal for the Scientific Study of Religion* 40, no. 3 (2001): 434. Wybraniec and Finke divide Christian litigants into several different denominations, such as Baptist, mainline Protestant, and Catholic. This author has simply collapsed all of the Christian categories into one overall percentage of cases.

44. *One World Family Now v. City of Miami Beach*, 990 F. Supp. 1427, 1440 (S.D. Florida, 1997).

45. *ISKCON v. Engelhardt*, 425 F. Supp. 176 (W.D. Missouri, 1976).

46. For state fairs, see *ISKCON v. Evans*, 440 F. Supp. 414 (S.D. Ohio, Eastern Division, 1977). For solicitations at airports, see *Fernandes v. Limmer*, 465 F. Supp. 493 (N.D. Texas, Dallas Division, 1979), and for ISKCON *sankirtan* at the U.N. Visitor's Gate, see *ISKCON v. City of New York*, 484 F. Supp. 966 (S.D. New York, 1979). Finally, for solicitations within a municipality in general, see *ISKCON of Berkeley v. Kearnes*, 454 F. Supp. 116 (E.D. California, 1978).

47. E. Burke Rochford Jr., "Demons, Karmies, and Non-Devotees: Culture, Group Boundaries, and the Development of Hare Krishna in North America and Europe," *Social Compass* 47, no. 2 (2000): 173.

48. Ibid., 174.

49. See generally E. Burke Rochford Jr., "Factionalism, Group Defection, and Schism in the Hare Krishna Movement," *Journal for the Scientific Study of Religion* 28, no. 2 (1989): 162–79.

50. Suzanna Sherry, "Religion and the Public Square: Making Democracy Safe for Religious Minorities," *DePaul Law Review* 47 (Spring 1998): 503.

51. Gregg Ivers, *To Build a Wall: American Jews and the Separation of Church and State* (Charlottesville: University Press of Virginia, 1995), 5.

52. See Barbara J. Redman, supra note 16, 525.

53. Rabbi Irving Greenberg, "Jewish Denominationalism Meets the Open Society," in Marjorie Garber and Rebecca L. Walkowitz, *One Nation Under God? Religion and American Culture* (New York: Routledge, 1999), 47.

54. Ibid.

55. *Kaplan v. City of Burlington*, 700 F. Supp. 1315 (D. Vermont, 1988).

56. Michael J. Broyde, "Proselytism and Jewish Law: Inreach, Outreach, and the Jewish Tradition," in John Witte Jr. and Richard C. Martin, eds., *Sharing the Book: Religious Perspectives on the Rights and Wrongs of Proselytism* (Maryknoll, N.Y.: Orbis Books, 1999), 59.

57. *Tenafly Eruv Association et al. v. The Borough of Tenafly et al.*, 155 F. Supp. 2d. 142, 146 (D. New Jersey, 2001).

58. Ibid., 87.

59. Ibid.

60. Robert Booth Fowler, Allen D. Hetzke, and Laura R. Olson, *Religion and Politics in America: Faith, Culture, and Strategic Choices* (Boulder, Colo.: Westview Press, 2000), 199; Moore, supra note 40, 7.

61. Moore, supra note 40, 11.

62. Ibid., 69–102.

63. Ibid.

64. See Tim Stafford, "Move Over ACLU," *Christianity Today*, October 25, 1993, p. 20.

65. "Unlikely Crusaders: Jay Sekulow, Messianic Jew of the Christian Right," *Washington Post*, October 21, 1997, p. D01.

66. Steven P. Brown, *Trumping Religion: The New Christian Right, the Free Speech Clause, and the Courts* (Tuscaloosa: University of Alabama Press, 2002), 47–61.

67. Ibid., 141.

68. *Clergy and Laity Concerned v. Chicago Board of Education*, 586 F. Supp. 1408 (N.D. Illinois, 1984).

69. *Gregoire v. Centennial School District*, 674 F. Supp. 172 (E.D. Pennsylvania, 1987).

70. *Wallace and Northgate Community Church v. Washoe County School District*, 701 F. Supp. 187 (D. Nevada, 1988).

71. *Youth Opportunities Unlimited, Inc., v. Board of Public Education of Pittsburgh*, 769 F. Supp. 1346 (W.D. Pennsylvania, 1991).

72. *Lamb's Chapel v. Center Moriches Union Free School District*, 770 F. Supp. 91 (E.D. New York, 1991).

73. *Wallace*, supra note 70.

74. *Lamb's Chapel v. Center Moriches Union Free School District*, 508 U.S. 384, 395 (1993).

75. *Good News Club et al. v. Milford Central School*, 21 F. Supp. 2d 147 (N.D. New York, 1998).

76. Quoted in Rob Boston, "Evangelism, Public Schools and the Supreme Court," *Church & State* (January 2001): 8.

77. *Good News Club v. Milford Central School*, 99-2036 (2001).

78. Fuller discussion of the rise and fall of religious sects and denominations is beyond this work. However, see generally Roger Finke and Rodney Stark, *The Churching of America, 1776–1990: Winners and Losers in Our Religious Economy* (New Brunswick: Rutgers University Press, 1992), 237–77; Barry A. Kosmin and Seymour P. Lachman, *One Nation Under God: Religion in Contemporary American Society* (New York: Harmony Books, 1993), 251–78; and Andrew Kohut, John C. Green, Scott Keeter, and Robert C. Toth, *The Diminishing Divide: Religion's Changing Role in American Politics* (Washington, D.C: Brookings Institution Press, 2000), 16–34.

79. Robert Booth Fowler, Allen D. Hertzke, and Laura R. Olson, *Religion and Politics in America: Faith, Culture, and Strategic Choices* (Boulder, Colo.: Westview Press, 1999), 43.

80. Quoted in Boston, supra note 76, 8.

81. Ibid.

82. *Gilles v. Torgersen*, 1995 U.S. Dist. LEXIS 8502, January 31, 1995

(W.D. Virginia, 1995). Vacated and remanded, 71 F.3d 497 (4th Cir. Virginia, 1995).

83. *DeNooyer v. Livonia Public Schools*, 779 F. Supp. 744 (E.D. Michigan, 1992).

84. See *Holy Spirit Association for the Unification of World Christianity v. Hodge*, 582 F. Supp. 592 (N.D. Texas, 1984) and *Westfall v. Board of Commissioners of Clayton County, Georgia*, 477 F. Supp. 862 (N.D. Georgia, 1979).

85. *City of Angels Mission Church v. City of Houston*, 716 F. Supp. 982 (S.D. Texas, 1989), and *Church of the Soldiers of the Cross of Christ v. City of Riverside*, 886 F. Supp. 721 (C.D. California, 1995).

86. *Bacon v. Bradley-Bourbonnais High School District No. 307*, 707 F. Supp. 1005 (C.D. Illinois, 1989).

87. Quoted in Robert S. Alley, *Without a Prayer: Religious Expression in Public Schools* (Amherst, N.Y.: Prometheus Books, 1996), 120.

88. 411 U.S. 192 (1973).

89. See 62 F. 3d 1040, 1046 (8th Circ. Nebraska, 1995).

90. *Peck v. Upshur County Board of Education*, 941 F. Supp. 1465 (N.D. West Virginia, 1996).

91. *Thompson v. Waynesboro Area School District*, 673 F. Supp. 1379 (M.D. Pennsylvania, 1987).

92. *Hedges v. Wauconda Community Unit School District No. 118*, 807 F. Supp. 444 (N.D. Illinois, 1992).

93. *Henry v. School Board of Colorado Springs School District No. 11*, 760 F. Supp. 856 (D. Colorado, 1991).

94. 454 U.S. 263 (1981).

95. 496 U.S. 226 (1990).

96. Dena S. Davis, "Religious Clubs in the Public Schools: What Happened After Mergens?" *Albany Law Review* 64 (2000): 237.

97. Ibid., 238.

98. "First Priority Clubs Target Public School Kids for Religious Conversion," *Church & State* (January 1997): p. 18.

99. Martha M. McCarthy, "People of Faith as Political Activists in

Public Schools," *Education and Urban Society* 28, no. 3 (May 1996): 308–26.

100. *Daniel Donnelly et al. v. Dennis Lynch et al.*, 525 F. Supp. 1150, 1180 (D. Rhode Island, 1981).

101. *McCreary v. Village of Scarsdale*, 575 F. Supp. 1112, 1130 (S.D. New York, 1983).

102. *Doe v. Small*, 726 F. Supp. 713, 717 (N.D. Illinois, 1989).

103. Ibid., 724.

104. More specifically, the court concluded that the sign display violated all three tenets of the *Lemon* test from *Lemon v. Kurtzman*, 403 U.S. 602 (1971). Thus, the display had no secular purpose, had the primary effect of advancing religion, and also fostered excessive entanglement between government and religion. See *Doe v. County of Montgomery*, 915 F. Supp. 32 (1996), 34–39.

CHAPTER 4

1. *Cornelius v. NAACP Legal Defense and Educational Fund, Inc.*, 473 U.S. 788, 800 (1985).

2. *Niemotko v. Maryland*, 340 U.S. 263, 282–83 (1951), Frankfurter, J., concurring.

3. *Grayned v. City of Rockford*, 408 U.S. 102, 116 (1972).

4. *Travis v. Owego-Apalachin School District*, 1990 U.S. Dist. LEXIS 8492 (N.D. New York, 1990), 6–7; quoting N.Y. Educ. L. § 414.

5. Ibid., 24.

6. Ibid., 17.

7. *Perry Education Association v. Perry Local Educators' Association*, 460 U.S. 3, 45–47 (1983).

8. Public parks and other open spaces are consolidated into one category for the purposes of this analysis. A public park is quite obvious; less so are other open spaces such as pedestrian malls, state fairgrounds, the grounds inside a circular driveway, or plazas sur-

rounding local courthouses or state capitol buildings. In general, if the location of the public space in question is open, and not enclosed by a building, it is typed as a public park for the purposes of this study.

9. *ISKCON v. Engelhardt*, 425 F. Supp. 176 (W.D. Missouri, 1976).

10. *Community for Creative Non-Violence v. Turner*, 714 F. Supp. 29 (D.District of Columbia, 1989); *Jews for Jesus v. Massachusetts Bay Transportation Authority*, 783 F. Supp. 1500 (D. Massachusetts, 1991).

11. *U.S. v. Boeswetter*, 463 F. Supp. 370 (D.District of Columbia, 1978).

12. *Shea v. Brister*, 26 F. Supp. 2d 943, 944 (S.D. Texas, 1998).

13. *Martin DeBoer v. Village of Oak Park*, 53 F. Supp. 2d 982 (N.D. Illinois, 1999).

14. *U.S. v. Any and All Radio Station Equipment*, 93 F. Supp. 2d. 414 (S.D. New York, 2000). See also *Fordham University v. Brown*, 856 F. Supp. 684 (D.District of Columbia, 1994).

15. *Pruitt v. Wilder*, 840 F. Supp. 414 (E.D. Virginia, 1994).

16. Clyde Wilcox, *Onward Christian Soldiers? The Religious Right in American Politics*, 2nd ed. (Boulder, Colo.: Westview Press, 2001), 118.

17. See in general *Curriculum, Religion, and Public Education: Conversations for an Enlarging Public Square* (New York: Teachers College Press, Columbia University, 1998).

18. 887 F. Supp. 902 (N.D. Mississippi, 1995).

19. 484 U.S. 260, 268 (1988).

20. See *Widmar v. Vincent*, 454 U.S. 263 (1981), and *Rosenberger v. University of Virginia*, 515 U.S. 819 (1995).

21. See *Lamb's Chapel v. Center Moriches Union Free School District*, 508 U.S. 384 (1993), and *Good News Club v. Milford Central School*, 533 U.S. 98 (2001).

22. 615 F. Supp. 761, 765 (S.D. Indiana, 1985).

23. 990 F. Supp. 341 (D. New Jersey, 1997).

268   *Notes*

24. *Good News Club v. Milford Central School*, 533 U.S. 98, 107 (2001).
25. 20 U.S.C. §§ 4071–74.
26. *Board of Education of Westside Community Schools v. Mergens By and Through Mergens*, 496 U.S. 226 (1990).
27. Note the disagreement between Richard T. Foltin of the American Jewish Congress and Jay Alan Sekulow of the American Center for Law and Justice in "This Way? Religious Expression in Public Schools," *Civil Rights Journal*, U.S. Commission on Civil Rights (Fall 1998): 36–41.
28. Dena S. Davis, "Religious Clubs in the Public Schools: What Happened After Mergens?" *Albany Law Review* 64 (2000): 225–39.
29. Letter from U.S. Secretary of Education Richard W. Riley to American Educators, 1998. Available from http://www.ed.gov/Speeches/98-1995/religion.html. In 2001, Congress amended the federal Elementary and Secondary Education Act with the No Child Left Behind Act that mandated sweeping reforms in public education. Pursuant to the new law, local educational authorities must certify that they have no policies that discriminate against student religious expression. In 2003, pursuant to the federal mandate, Secretary of Education Ron Page released guidelines on religious expression in public schools. Those guidelines, and the No Child Left Behind Act, are discussed in detail in chapter 6.
30. See testimony of Marc Stern before the U.S. Commission on Civil Rights, Washington, D.C., May 20, 1998. See *Schools and Religion: Executive Summary and Transcript of Proceedings Held in Washington, D.C., New York City, and Seattle, Wash., Spring/Summer 1998* (December 1999).
31. See testimony of Julie Underwood, counsel to the National School Boards Association, quoted in ibid., 87.
32. Ibid.

33. *STORTI v. Southeastern Transportation Authority*, 1999 U.S. Dist. LEXIS 14515 (E.D. Pennsylvania, 1999).
34. *ISKCON v. Lee*, 721 F. Supp. 572 (S.D. New York, 1989).
35. *Jews for Jesus v. Massachusetts Bay Transportation Authority*, 783 F. Supp. 1500 (D. Massachusetts, 1991).
36. 505 U.S. 672, 680–81 (1972).
37. 966 F. Supp. 956, 963–64 (C.D. California, 1997).
38. Ibid., 969–70.
39. However, the district court's decision was vacated and remanded by the Ninth Circuit in *International Society for Krishna Consciousness of California v. City of Los Angeles*, 2000 U.S. App. LEXIS 38622, June 28, 2000, for further proceedings consistent with *Los Angeles Alliance for Survival v. City of Los Angeles*, 22 Cal. 4th 352, 993 P.2d 334 (2000), in which the Supreme Court of California sustained a Los Angeles ordinance banning the aggressive solicitation for immediate funds. The Ninth Circuit vacate/remand order does not overturn the district court, but instead asks the lower court to reconsider in light of developing California Constitutional law.
40. *Bynum v. U.S. Capitol Police Board*, 93 F. Supp. 2d 50 (D. District of Columbia, 2000).
41. *Pfeifer v. City of West Allis*, 91 F. Supp. 2d 1253 (E.D. Wisconsin, 2000).
42. 473 U.S. 788, 803 (1983).
43. 79 F. Supp. 2d 979 (N.D. Indiana, 1999).
44. As District Judge Allen Sharp notes in his opinion, the FOE program was started by a Minnesota juvenile court judge concerned that juvenile offenders "have some code of conduct or standards by which to govern their actions." Thus, he considered that "they could benefit from exposure to one of mankind's earliest codes of conduct, the Ten Commandments." Evidently his idea received national recognition when it was endorsed by movie producer

and director Cecille B. DeMille, who produced the 1950s movie *The Ten Commandments*. See ibid., 983.

45. Notably, the Seventh Circuit Court of Appeals reversed the district court's decision on the grounds that the display of the Ten Commandments violated the Establishment Clause of the First Amendment. See *Books v. City of Elkhart, Indiana*, 235 F.3d 292 (7th Circ. 2000); Certiorari Denied May 29, 2001, Reported at: 2001 U.S. LEXIS 4120.

46. 308 U.S. 496, 515 (1939).

47. 2001 U.S. Dist. LEXIS 2438 (N.D. New York, 2001).

48. 35 F. Supp. 2d 1358, 1359 (M.D. Florida, 1999).

49. See generally *Mary Angeline v. Mahoning County Agricultural Society*, 993 F. Supp. 627 (N.D. Ohio, 1998).

50. 752 F. Supp. 1063, 1066 (N.D. Georgia, 1990).

51. 515 U.S. 753 (1995).

52. 988 F. Supp. 957, 962 (E.D. Virginia, 1997).

53. 484 U.S. F. Supp. 966, 970 (S.D. New York, 1979).

54. Ibid., 971.

55. 515 U.S. 819, 830 (1995).

56. 93 F. Supp. 2d 414 (S.D. New York, 2000).

57. Ibid., 420.

58. 840 F. Supp. 414, 417 (E.D. Virginia, 1994).

59. Ibid., 418.

60. For an interesting commentary on state governments and specialized license plates, see Leslie Gielow Jacobs, "Free Speech and the Limits of Legislative Discretion: The Example of Specialty License Places," 53 *Florida Law Review* 419 (July 2001). Jacobs discusses the controversies in Florida and Louisiana concerning the constitutionality of license plates representing Pro-Life (Anti-Abortion) groups that receive monies from the sale of the special plates by the government. Jacobs also notes the Arkansas legislature refused to allow the Knights of Columbus to have a special plate because the KKK might request one as well.

61. C. K. Rowland and Robert A. Carp, *Politics and Judgment in Federal District Courts* (Lawrence: University Press of Kansas, 1996), 13.
62. Ibid., 40–41.
63. Ibid., 46.
64. Ibid., 56.
65. Ibid., 40.

CHAPTER 5

1. Robert Alley, *Without a Prayer: Religious Expression in Public Schools* (Amherst, N.Y.: Prometheus Books, 1996), 116.
2. *Berger v. Rensselaer Central School District*, 766 F. Supp. 686 (1991); quoted in Alley, ibid., 120.
3. Douglas Laycock, "Freedom of Speech That Is Both Religious and Political," *U.C. Davis Law Review* 29, no. 3 (Spring 1999): 797.
4. *Lamb's Chapel v. Center Moriches Union Free School District*, 508 U.S. 384; 395–96 (1993).
5. 515 U.S. 753, 760 (1995).
6. 515 U.S. 819 (1995). The activities that cannot be funded are "religious activities, philanthropic contributions and activities, political activities, activities that would jeopardize the University's tax exempt status, those which involve payment of honoraria or similar fees, or social entertainment or related expenses." Ibid., at 825.
7. Justice Kennedy states that viewpoint discrimination, in the context of *Rosenberger*, is "discrimination against one set of views or ideas." Ibid., 830. Virginia justified its ban on funds because the "contents of *Wide Awake* reveal an avowed religious perspective," and therefore discriminated against the evangelical group's religious views and message. Ibid., 832.
8. 533 U.S. 98, 110 (2001).

9. Calvin Massey, "Public Fora, Neutral Governments, and the Prism of Property," *Hastings Law Journal* 50 (January 1999): 309.

10. *Grayned v. City of Rockford*, 408 U.S. 104, 116 (1972), per Justice Marshall, majority opinion.

11. *Perry Educ. Ass'n v. Perry Local Educators' Ass'n*, 460 U.S. 37, 44 (1983), per Justice White, majority opinion.

12. *Society for Krishna Consciousness v. Lee*, 505 U.S. 672, 682 (1992).

13. 319 U.S. 105, 109 (1943).

14. See especially Ruth Murray Brown's history of the religious right, *For a Christian America* (Amherst, N.Y.: Prometheus Books, 2002).

15. Steven Gey, "When Is Religious Speech Not Free Speech?" *University of Illinois Law Review* (2000): 381.

16. Ibid., 433.

17. See, e.g., *Schools and Religion: Executive Summary and Transcript of Proceedings Held in Washington, D.C., New York City, and Seattle, Wash., Spring/Summer 1998* (December 1999), passim.

18. See, e.g., *Peloza v. Capistrano Unified School District*, 782 F. Supp. 1412 (C.D. California, 1992), in which a teacher claimed a free speech right to teach creationism to his biology class.

19. 674 F. Supp. 172, 176 (E.D. Pennsylvania, 1987).

20. Ibid., 178.

21. *Gregoire et al. v. Centennial School District*, 701 F. Supp. 103, 107 (E.D. Pennsylvania, 1988).

22. Ibid.

23. Mark Chaves and William Tsitsos, "Are Congregations Constrained by Government? Empirical Results from the National Congregations Study," *Journal of Church and State* 42 (2000): 342.

24. See generally *Tinker v. Des Moines Independent Community School District*, 393 U.S. 503 (1969); *Hazelwood School District v. Kuhlmeier*, 484 U.S. 260 (1988); and *Bethel School District v. Fraser*, 478 U.S. 675 (1986).

25. 721 F. Supp. 1189, 1194 (D. Colorado, 1989).

26. See *Harless by Harless v. Darr*, 937 F. Supp. 1339 (S.D. Indiana,

1996), and *Nelson et al. v. Moline School District*, 725 F. Supp. 965 (C.D. Illinois, 1989).

27. Rosemary C. Salomone, "Public Forum Doctrine and the Perils of Categorical Thinking: Lessons from Lamb's Chapel," *New Mexico Law Review* 24 (1994): 18.

28. 707 F. Supp. 1005 (C.D. Illinois, 1989).

29. *Peck v. Upshur County Board of Education*, 941 F. Supp. 1465 (N.D. West Virginia, 1996).

30. The discussions by liberal and conservative interest groups in the U.S. Civil Rights Commission hearings on schools and religious speech seem to indicate a consensus that schools usually cooperate with students who request access to hold religious meetings either before or after school hours. See supra note 16.

31. *U.S. v. Boesewetter et al.*, 463 F. Supp. 370, 372 (D. District of Columbia, 1978).

32. Ibid., 372–73.

33. *Bynum v. U.S. Capitol Police Board*, 93 F. Supp. 2d 50 (D. District of Columbia, 2000).

34. Ibid., 60.

35. *Shea v. Brister*, 26 F. Supp. 2d 943, 944 (S.D. Texas, 1998).

36. Judge Brister ran as a Republican candidate for a spot on the Texas Court of Appeals for the Eleventh District, and was elected in 2000. Texas Governor Rick Perry appointed Brister in 2001 to be the chief justice of the Fourteenth District Court of Appeal. Brister will have to run for reelection to the Fourteenth District in four years. See Bill Murphy, "Brister Named Chief of Appeals Court," *Houston Chronicle*, July 11, 2001, A-19.

37. See *Lynch v. Donnelly*, 465 U.S. 668 (1984).

38. *Lubavitch of Iowa v. Walters*, 684 F. Supp. 610 (S.D. Iowa, 1988).

39. *Mehdi and Khankan v. USPS*, 988 F. Supp. 721, 725 (S.D. New York, 1997).

40. *Gonzales v. Lake County*, 800 F. Supp. 676 (N.D. Indiana, 1992).

41. See, e.g., *Warren v. Fairfax County* 988 F. Supp. 957 (E.D. Vir-

ginia, 1997), in which a non-Fairfax county resident sought to place an unattended crèche on public property near the county government building. Fairfax's policy only allows attended displays by country residents, and the district court concluded that the policy was applied in a viewpoint-neutral manner.

42. See, e.g., *Chabad-Lubavitch of Vermont v. City of Burlington*, 754 F. Supp. 372 (D. Vermont, 1990).

43. *Warner et al. v. City of Boca Raton*, 64 F. Supp. 2d 1272 (S.D. Florida, 1999).

44. *Heffron v. International Society for Krishna Consciousness*, 452 U.S. 640 (1981).

45. See *U.S. v. Kalb, Beck, and Sedlacko*, 86 F. Supp. 2d 509 (W.D. Pennsylvania, 2000), and *Black v. Arthur*, 18 F. Supp. 2d 1127 (D. Oregon, 1998). Whether the "Rainbow Family" is a religious group may be a point of contention, but to a large degree their message—difficult as it is to pin down—does contain elements of religious speech found in other, more mainstream, religious traditions.

46. See, e.g., for state license plates *Pruitt v. Wilder*, 840 F. Supp. 414 (E.D. Virginia, 1994), and public radio airways *Fordham University v. Brown*, 856 F. Supp. 684 (D. District of Columbia, 1994).

47. As Justice Kennedy notes the Court's majority opinion in *Rosenberger*, the funding system for student publications is a "forum more in a metaphysical than in a spatial or geographic sense, but the same [forum] principles are applicable." *Rosenberger v. Rectors and Visitors of the University of Virginia*, 515 U.S. 819, 830 (1995).

48. C. K. Rowland and Robert A. Carp, *Politics and Judgment in Federal District Courts* (Lawrence: University Press of Kansas, 1996), 40.

49. *Good News Club v. Milford Central School*, 533 U.S. 98, 119 (2001).

50. Ibid., 121.

51. Ibid.

52. Ibid., 129.

53. Ibid., 144–45.

54. Ibid.

CHAPTER 6

1. *Good News Club v. Milford Central School*, 533 U.S. 98, 140 (2001).
2. Ibid.
3. *Good News Club v. Milford Central School*, 21 F. Supp. 2d 147 (1998).
4. C. K. Rowland and Robert A. Carp, *Politics and Judgment in Federal District Courts* (Lawrence: University Press of Kansas, 1996), 4.
5. Richard John Neuhaus, *The Naked Public Square* (Grand Rapids, Mich.: Eerdmans Publishing, 1984), vii.
6. Richard John Neuhaus, "A New Order of Religious Freedom," in Stephen M. Feldman, ed., *Law and Religion: A Critical Anthology* (New York: New York University Press, 2000), 89.
7. 505 672, 696 (1992).
8. David Yamane, "Naked Public Square or Crumbling Wall of Separation? Evidence from Legislative Hearings in Wisconsin," *Review of Religious Research* 42, no. 2 (2000): 176.
9. 515 U.S. 753, 761 (1995).
10. Ibid., 760.
11. Ted G. Jelen, *To Serve God and Mammon: Church-State Relations in American Politics* (Boulder, Colo.: Westview Press, 2000), 62–64.
12. In other areas of the law, such as desegregation and remedial policymaking, scholars have fruitfully explored the relationship between federal district courts and local government. See Jack W. Peltason, *58 Lonely Men: Southern Federal Judges and School Desegregation* (Urbana: University of Illinois Press, 1971), and Phillip J. Cooper, *Hard Judicial Choices* (Oxford: Oxford University Press, 1988).

13. See, for example, Ruth Murray Brown, *For a "Christian America:"* *A History of the Religious Right* (Amherst, N.Y.: Prometheus Books, 2002), and Clyde Wilcox, *Onward Christian Soldiers: The Religious Right in American Politics*, 2nd ed. (Boulder, Colo.: Westview Press, 2002).

14. Quoted in Frank Guliuzza III, *Over the Wall: Protecting Religious Expression in the Public Square* (Albany: SUNY Press, 2000), 140.

15. Ibid., 143.

16. Steven P. Brown, *Trumping Religion: The New Christian Right, the Free Speech Clause, and the First Amendment* (Tuscaloosa: University of Alabama Press, 2002), 134.

17. Diana L. Eck, "The Multireligious Public Square," in Marjorie Garber and Rebecca L. Walkowitz, eds., *One Nation Under God? Religion and American Culture* (New York: Routledge, 1999), 17.

18. Richard N. Ostling, "America's Changing Religious Landscape," in E. J. Dionne Jr., and John J. DiIulio Jr., *What's God Got to Do with the American Experiment?* (Washington, D.C.: Brookings Institution Press, 2000), 20.

19. Mark Chaves et al., "The National Congregations Study: Background, Methods, and Selected Results," *Journal for the Scientific Study of Religion* 38, no. 4 (1999): 466.

20. For example, see *Widmar v. Vincent* (1981), *Rosenberger v. Virginia* (1995), *Lamb's Chapel v. Center Moriches Union Free School District* (1992), *Good News Club v. Milford Central School* (2002), and others, all of which protect evangelical, Christian speech. The two exceptions are: *ISKCON v. Lee* (1992) and *Heffron v. ISKCON* (1981), both of which concerned Krishna speech in airports and other travel terminals.

21. Ted Jelen, *To Serve God and Mammon: Church-State Relations in America* (Boulder, Co.: Westview Press, 2001), 66.

22. Frank Way and Barbara Burt, "Religious Marginality and the Free Exercise Clause," *American Political Science Review* 77, no. 3 (1983): 652.

23. Ibid., 657.
24. Louis Fisher, *Religious Liberty in America: Political Safeguards* (Lawrence: University Press of Kansas, 2002), 1.
25. Ibid., 5.
26. Ibid., 31. Fisher quotes Alexander Bickel's classic essay on the Supreme Court, *The Least Dangerous Branch* (New York: Bobbs-Merrill, 1962).
27. *Engel v. Vitale*, 370 U.S. 421 (1962); and *School District of Abington Township v. Schempp*, 374 U.S. 203 (1963).
28. Fisher, supra note 24, 141.
29. See letter from Secretary of Education Richard W. Riley to public school districts, May 1998. Http://www.ed.gov/Speeches/08-1995/religion.html. The letter is also reprinted in the summary of the U.S. Commission on Civil Rights proceedings on schools and religion. See *Schools and Religion: Executive Summary and Transcript of Proceedings Held in Washington, D.C., New York City, and Seattle Wash., Spring/Summer 1998* (December 1999), app. A.
30. Secretary of Education Rod Paige, "Secretary's Letter on Constitutionally Protected Prayer in Public Elementary and Secondary Schools," February 7, 2003. Http://www.ed.gov/inits/religionandschools/letter_030207.html. For the guidelines, see Guidance on Constitutionally Protected Prayer in Public Elementary and Secondary Schools, *Federal Register* 68, no. 40, Friday, February 28, 2003, 9645.
31. For an example of one SEA's certification process, see the instructions from the Wisconsin Department of Public Instruction guidelines and request to LEAs for written certification. School District Administrators are asked to sign the following statement, to be forwarded to the state: "I hereby acknowledge I have received and read this letter and the United States Department of Education's school prayer guidance. I certify that no policy of the school district prevents, or otherwise denies participation in, constitutionally protected prayer in public elementary and sec-

ondary schools, as detailed in the USED's school prayer guidance." Forms available on the Wisconsin DPI's website: www.dpi.state.wi.us.

32. See the First Amendment Center's news story, "Most schools complying with prayer guidelines," May 15, 2003, at www.firstamendmentcenter.org/news.

33. Quoted in the First Amendment Center's new story on school compliance, ibid.

34. See "An Analysis of the "Guidance on Constitutionally Protected Prayer in Public Elementary and Secondary Schools Issued by the U.S. Department of Education on February 7, 2003," at http://www.au.org/legal/publicschoolguidance.htm.

35. "Loudon Schools Sued Over Removal of Crosses," *Washington Post*, Wednesday, March 26, 2003, p. B06.

36. For an artists' rendition of the Shepard memorial, see Phelps's website: http://www.godhatesfags.com/main/shepard_monument.html. For a discussion of the dispute, see Emily Bazelon, "Monument from Hell: Make Room for a Matthew Shepard Hate Monument in a Town Square Near You," Tuesday, November 11, 2003. At http://slate.msn.com/id/2091054/. See also the "Plaza Chosen as Ten Commandments Monument Solution," *Casper Star-Tribune*, October 28, 2003.

37. Quoted in *Casper Star-Tribune*, ibid.

38. Emily Bazelon, supra note 36.

39. *Capitol Square Review & Advisory Bd. v. Pinette*, 515 U.S. 753, 760 (1995).

40. Ibid., 761, emphasis added.

41. *R. A. V. v. City of St. Paul*, 505. U.S. 377, 390 (1992). Note, though, the Court's recent (2003) decision in *Virginia v. Black*, 537 U.S. 808 (2003) in which the Court validates Virginia's criminal prohibition against cross-burning with the intent to intimidate. The Court notes that the First Amendment does allow states to ban speech that is a particularly virulent form of intimidation.

Selected Bibliography

CASES

Bacon v. Bradley-Bourbonnais High School District No. 307, 707 F. Supp. 1005 (C.D. Illinois, 1989).

Board of Education of Westside Community Schools v. Mergens By and Through Mergens, 496 U.S. 226 (1990).

C. H. v. Oliva et al., Medford Township Board of Education; New Jersey Department of Education, 990 F. Supp. 341 (1997).

Capitol Square Review & Advisory Bd. v. Pinette, 515 U.S. 753 (1995).

Chabad-Lubavitch of Georgia v. Harris, Governor of Georgia, 752 F. Supp. 1063 (N.D. Georgia, 1990).

Douglas v. City of Jeanette, 319 U.S. 157, 181 (1943).

Fernandes v. Limmer, 465 F. Supp. 493 (1979).

Good News Club v. Milford Central School, 21 F. Supp. 2d 147 (N.D. New York, 1998).

Good News Club v. Milford Central School, 533 U.S. 98, 140 (2001).

Gregoire v. Centennial School District, 674 F. Supp. 172 (E.D. Pennsylvania, 1987).

Hague v. CIO, 307 U.S. 496 (1939).

Heffron v. ISKCON, 452 U.S. 640 (1981).

ISKCON v. Bowen, 456 F. Supp. 437 (1978).

ISKCON v. Evans, 440 F. Supp. 414 (1977).

ISKCON v. Lee, 505 U.S. 672 (1992).

ISKCON v. Wolke, 453 F. Supp. 869 (1978).

Jones v. Opelika, 316 U.S. 584 (1942).

Lamb's Chapel v. Center Moriches Union Free School District, 770 F. Supp. 91 (E.D. New York, 1991).

Lubavitch of Iowa v. Walters, 684 F. Supp. 610 (S.D. Iowa, 1988).

Lubavitch v. Public Building Commission of Chicago, 700 F. Supp. 1497 (N.D. Illinois, 1988).

Mehdi and Khnakan v. USPS, 988 F. Supp. 721 (S.D. New York, 1997).

Niemotko v. Maryland, 340 U.S. 263, 282–83 (1951).

Perry Education Association v. Perry Local Educators' Association, 460 U.S. 37 (1983).

Sister Mary Reilly et al. v. Noel, 384 F. Supp. 741 (1974).

Tenafly Eruv Association et al. v. The Borough of Tenafly et al., 155 F. Supp. 2d. 142 (D. New Jersey, 2001).

Travis v. Owego-Apalachin School, 1990 U.S. Dist. LEXIS 8492 (N.D. New York, 1990).

Trinity United Methodist Parish et al. v. Board of Education of the City School District of the City of Newburgh, 907 F. Supp. 707, 711 (S.D. New York, 1995).

U.S. v. Silberman, 464 F. Supp. 866 (1979).

Wallace and Northgate Community Church v. Washoe County School District, 701 F. Supp. 187 (D. Nevada, 1988).

Youth Opportunities Unlimited, Inc., v. Board of Public Education of Pittsburgh, 769 F. Supp. 1346 (W.D. Pennsylvania, 1991).

ARTICLES

Blakeman, John C. "Federal District Courts, Religious Speech, and the Public Forum: An Analysis of Litigation Patterns and Outcomes." *Journal of Church and State* 44 (Winter 2002): 93–113.

Grossman, Joel B., Herbert M. Kritzer, Kristin Bumiller, Austin Sarat, and Stephen McDougal. "Dimensions of Institutional Participation: Who Uses the Courts, and How?" *The Journal of Politics* 44 (February 1982): 86–114.

Holmes, Gilbert A. "Student Religious Expression in School: Is It Religion or Speech, and Does It Matter?" *University of Miami Law Review* 49 (Winter 1994): 337–429.

Hunter, Howard O., and Polly J. Price. "Regulation of Religious Proselytism in the United States." *B.Y.U. Law Review* (2000): 537–74.

Ivers, Gregg. "Organized Religion and the Supreme Court." *Journal of Church and State* 32 (Autumn 1990): 775–94.

Kenneson, Philip. "Sixteen Contentious Words." *Reviews in Religion and Theology* 7, no. 3 (June 2000): 340–45.

Laycock, Douglas. "Freedom of Speech That Is Both Religious and Political." *U.C. Davis Law Review* 29, no. 3 (Spring 1999): 793–813.

Layman, Geoffrey C., and Edward G. Carmines. "Cultural Conflict in American Politics: Religious Traditionalism, Postmaterialism, and U.S. Political Behavior." *The Journal of Politics* 59 (August 1997): 751–77.

Massey, Calvin. "Public Fora, Neutral Governments, and the Prism of Property." *Hastings Law Journal* 50 (January 1999): 309–53.

McCarthy, Martha M. "People of Faith as Political Activists in Public Schools." *Education and Urban Society* 28, no. 3 (May 1996): 308–27.

———"Religion and Education: Whither the Establishment Clause?" *Indiana Law Journal* (Winter, 2000): 123–66.

Redman, Barbara J. "Strange Bedfellows: Lubavitcher Hasidim and Conservative Christians." *Journal of Church and State* 34, no. 3 (Summer 1992): 521–46.

Rochford, E. Burke, Jr. "Demons, Karmies, and Non-Devotees: Culture, Group Boundaries, and the Development of Hare Krishna in North America and Europe." *Social Compass* 47, no. 2 (2000): 169–86.

———."Factionalism, Group Defection, and Schism in the Hare Krishna Movement." *Journal for the Scientific Study of Religion* 28, no. 2 (1989): 162–79.

Way, Frank, and Barbara Burt. "Religious Marginality and the Free Exercise Clause." *American Political Science Review* 77, no. 3 (September 1983): 652–65.

Wybraniec, John, and Roger Finke. "Religious Regulation and the Courts: The Judiciary's Changing Role in Protecting Minority Religions from Majoritarian Rule." *Journal for the Scientific Study of Religion* 40, no. 3 (September 2001): 427–45.

Yamane, David. "Naked Public Square or Crumbling Wall of Separation? Evidence from Legislative Hearings in Wisconsin." *Review of Religious Research* 42, no. 2 (2000): 175–92.

Yarnold, Barbara. "Did Circuit Court of Appeals Judges Overcome Their Own Religions in Cases Involving Religious Liberties? 1970–1990." *Review of Religious Research* 42 (2000): 79–86.

———"Factors Related to Outcomes in Religious Freedom Cases, Federal District Courts: 1970–1990." *The Justice System Journal* 19 (1997): 181–91.

Zemans, Frank. "Legal Mobilization: The Neglected Role of the Law in the Political System." *American Political Science Review* 77, no. 3 (September 1983): 690–703.

BOOKS

Alley, Robert S. *Without a Prayer: Religious Expression in Public Schools*. Amherst, N.Y.: Prometheus Books, 1996.

Audi, Robert, and Nicholas Wolterstorff. *Religion in the Public Square: the Place of Religious Convictions in Political Debate*. New York: Rowman and Littlefield, 1997.

Brown, Ruth Murray. *For a "Christian America": A History of the Religious Right*. Amherst, N.Y.: Prometheus Books, 2002.

Brown, Steven P. *Trumping Religion: The New Christian Right, the Free Speech Clause, and the Courts*. Tuscaloosa: University of Alabama Press, 2002.

Canon, Bradley C., and Charles A. Johnson. *Judicial Policies: Implementation and Impact*. 2nd ed. Washington, D.C.: Congressional Quarterly Press, 1999.

Carp, Robert A., and C. K. Rowland. *Policymaking and Politics in the*

Federal District Courts. Knoxville: University of Tennessee Press, 1983.

Carter, Stephen L. *The Culture of Disbelief: How American Law and Politics Trivialize Religion.* New York: Anchor Books, 1994.

Cooper, Phillip J. *Hard Judicial Choices.* Oxford: Oxford University Press, 1988.

Corbett, Julia Mitchell. *Religion in America.* 4th ed. Upper Saddle River, N.J.: Prentice Hall, 2000.

Dionne, E. J., Jr., and John J. DiIulio Jr., eds. *What's God Got to Do with the American Experiment?* Washington, D.C.: Brookings Institution Press, 2000.

Epstein, Lee, ed. *Contemplating Courts.* Washington, D.C.: Congressional Quarterly Press, 1995.

Feldman, Stephen M., ed. *Law and Religion: A Critical Anthology.* New York: New York University Press, 2000.

Finke, Roger, and Rodney Stark. *The Churching of America, 1776–1990: Winners and Losers in Our Religious Economy.* New Brunswick, N.J.: Rutgers University Press, 1992.

Fisher, Louis. *Religious Liberty in America: Political Safeguards.* Lawrence: University Press of Kansas, 2002.

Fowler, Robert Booth, Allen D. Hetzke, and Laura R. Olson. *Religion and Politics in America: Faith, Culture, and Strategic Choices.* Boulder, Colo.: Westview Press, 2000.

Garber, Marjorie, and Rebecca L. Walkowitz, eds. *One Nation under God? Religion and American Culture.* New York: Routledge, 1999.

Glendon, Mary Ann. *Rights Talk: The Impoverishment of Political Discourse.* New York: Free Press, 1991.

Hertzke, Allen. *Representing God in Washington: The Role of Religious Lobbies in the American Polity.* Knoxville: University of Tennessee Press, 1988.

Ivers, Gregg. *To Build a Wall: American Jews and the Separation of Church and State.* Charlottesville: University Press of Virginia, 1995.

Jelen, Ted G. *To Serve God and Mammon: Church-State Relations in American Politics.* Boulder, Colo.: Westview Press, 2000.

Kobylka, Joseph F. *The Politics of Obscenity: Group Litigation in a Time of Legal Change.* Westport, Conn.: Greenwood Press, 1991.

Kohut, Andrew, John C. Green, Scott Keeter, and Robert C. Toth. *The Diminishing Divide: Religion's Changing Role in American Politics.* Washington, D.C.: Brookings Institution Press, 2000.

Kosmin, Barry A., and Seymour P. Lachman. *One Nation Under God: Religion in Contemporary American Society.* New York: Harmony Books, 1993.

Leege, David C., and Lyman A. Kellstedt, eds. *Rediscovering the Religious Factor in American Politics.* Armonk, N.Y.: M. E. Sharpe, 1993.

Lyles, Kevin L. *The Gatekeepers: Federal District Courts in the Political Process.* Westport, Conn.: Praeger, 1997.

Manwaring, David R., Donald R. Reich, and Steven L. Wasby. *The Supreme Court as Policymaker: Three Studies on the Impact of Judicial Decisions.* Carbondale, Ill.: Public Affairs Research Bureau, 1972.

Moore, Kathleen M. *Al Mughtaribum: American Law and the Transformation of Muslim Life in the United States.* Albany: State University of New York Press, 1995.

Morgan, Richard E. *The Politics of Religious Conflict: Church and State in America.* New York: Pegasus, 1968.

Neuhaus, Richard John. *The Naked Public Square.* Grand Rapids, Mich.: Eerdmans Publishing, 1984.

Newton, Merlin Owen. *Armed with the Constitution: Jehovah's Witnesses in Alabama and the U.S. Supreme Court.* Tuscaloosa: University of Alabama Press, 1995.

Noonan, John T., Jr., and Edward McGlynn Gaffney Jr., eds. *Religious Freedom: History, Cases, and Other Materials on the Interaction of Religion and Government.* New York: Foundation Press, 2001.

Peltason, Jack W. *58 Lonely Men: Southern Federal Judges and School Desegregation.* Urbana: University of Illinois Press, 1971.

Rowland, C. K., and Robert A. Carp. *Politics and Judgment in Federal District Courts*. Lawrence: University Press of Kansas, 1996.

Segers, Mary C., ed. *Piety, Politics, and Pluralism: Religion, the Courts, and the 2000 Election*. Lanham, Md.: Rowman and Littlefield, 2002.

Spinner-Halev, Jeff. *Surviving Diversity: Religion and Democratic Citizenship*. Baltimore: The Johns Hopkins University Press, 2000.

Wilcox, Clyde. *Onward Christian Soldiers: The Religious Right in American Politics*. 2nd ed. Boulder, Colo.: Westview Press, 2002.

Witte, John, Jr., and Richard C. Martin, eds. *Sharing the Book: Religious Perspectives on the Rights and Wrongs of Proselytism*. Maryknoll, N.Y.: Orbis Books, 1999.

DATABASES

Jones, Dale E., Sherry Doty, James E. Horsch, Richard Houseal, Mac Lynn, John P. Marcum, Kenneth M. Sanchagrin, and Richard Taylor. *Religious Congregations and Membership in the United States 2000: An Enumeration by Region, State, and County Based on Data Reported by 149 Religious Bodies*. Nashville, Tenn.: Glenmary Research Center, 2002.

Index

Lyles, Kevin, 31
Lynch v. Donnelly, 121–22

Marshall, Justice Thurgood,
  58–60
  concurrence in *Board of
    Education v. Mergens*,
    59–60
Mather, Lynn, 33
Matsch, Judge Richard, 193–94
*May v. Evansville–Vanderburg
  School Corporation*,
  143–44
McAvoy, Judge Thomas J.,
  130–31, 221–22
McCarthy, Martha, 14
*McCreary v. Village of
  Scarsdale*, 123, 125
*Medi and Kahnhan v. United
  States Postal Service*,
  90–92
Menorahs
  public displays of, 72–73,
    102–103, 148, 155, 199
Million Man March, 105–106
Morgan, Richard, xv, 84, 86–87
Murdock v. Pennsylvania,
  182–83

Naked Public Square argument,
  xvi, 15–16
National Congregations Study,
  232
National Education Association,
  235

National Labor Relations Act,
  37
National of Islam, 105
National Park Service, 83
National School Boards
  Association, study of
  religious expression in
  public schools, 147
Nativity displays, 155–56
Neuhaus, Richard John, xvi,
  15–18, 67, 125, 224–25
New York State
  state law on public schools as
  public forums, 130
Niemotko v. Maryland, 23, 48,
  54, 129
No Child Left Behind Act, and
  religious speech of
  students, 237–41, 268n. 29
Noel, Philip, Governor of
  Rhode Island, 9

O'Connor, Justice Sandra Day,
  57–58
  in *Board of Education v.
    Mergens*, 58
  in *Cornelius v. NAACP*, 152
Ohio Statehouse, 155, 172
*One World Family Now v. City
  of Miami Beach*, 94
Ostling, Richard, 232

Paige, Rod, Secretary of
  Education, 237

Partisanship, and federal district
judge decision making,
160–61, 204–09
Pauley, Judge William H., 158
Peltason, Jack, 29
*Perry Education Association v.
Perry Local Educators'
Association,* 23, 28, 36,
38, 40, 43, 111, 131, 152
Phelps, Reverend Fred,
245–247
sponsorship of Matthew
Shepard monument in
Casper, Wyoming, 245–46
*Police Department of City of
Chicago v. Mosely,* 27
Port Authority of New York and
New Jersey, 40–41, 149
Powell, Justice Lewis, 55
in *Widmar v. Vincent,* 55–56
Praschak, Henry, 2
Henry Praschak Fund, 2–4
Praschak Wayside Park, 2
Prince v. Massachusetts, 47
Promise Keepers, 71
Pruitt v. Wilder, 159
Public Forum law, x, xi, 7, 10,
23–28, summary of,
131–33, 134–38
Public parks
as public forums, 153–57
religious speech in, 201–03
Public Schools
as public forums, 138,
141–45

religious speech in, 186–96
religious speech in secondary
and primary schools,
144–45

R.A.V. v. City of St. Paul, 247
Redman, Barbara, 102
Reed, Justice Stanley, 38, 44,
50–51
dissent in *Murdock v.
Pennsylvania,* 50–51
Rehnquist, Chief Justice
William H., 40–41, 74
in *International Society for
Krishna Consciousness v.
Lee,* 149
Reilly, Sister Mary, 9–11, 14,
17
Reinders, Clarence, 2–5
Religious displays. *See*
Christianity, Crescent and
Star, Menorahs
Rhode Island
Noel, Governor Philip, 9
State Capitol Rotunda, 9–10,
17, 134, 151
Riley, Richard, Secretary of
Education, 146, 236, 268n.
29
memorandum on religious
speech in public schools,
236
*Rivera v. East Otero School
District,* 192–93